★ WOMEN HEROES OF WORLD WAR II ★

Women Heroes of World War II

32 Stories of Espionage, Sabotage, Resistance, and Rescue

SECOND EDITION

Kathryn J. Atwood

CHICAGO
REVIEW
PRESS

Second edition
First hardcover edition published in 2019
First paperback edition published in 2025
Published by Chicago Review Press Incorporated
814 North Franklin Street
Chicago, Illinois 60610
ISBN 978-0-89733-551-5

The Library of Congress has cataloged the first edition as follows:

Atwood, Kathryn J.
  Women heroes of World War II : 26 stories of espionage, sabotage, resistance,
and rescue / Kathryn J. Atwood. — 1st ed.
      p. cm.
  Includes bibliographical references and index.
  ISBN 978-1-55652-961-0 (hardcover)
  1. World War, 1939–1945—Women—Biography—Juvenile literature. 2. World
War, 1939–1945—Participation, Female—Juvenile literature. 3. World War,
1939–1945—Underground movements—Juvenile literature. I. Title.
  D810.W7A85 2011
  940.54'850922—dc22

                              2010041830

Cover and interior design: Sarah Olson
Cover photos: (top) Muriel Engelman (platoon leader in front, saluting) and other
American nurses marching in parade in Chester, England, 1944, courtesy Muriel
P. Engelman; (bottom, left to right) Andrée de Jongh, courtesy Sherri Greene
Ottis; Irene Gut, courtesy United States Holocaust Memorial Museum; Hazel
Ying Lee, courtesy of the WASP Archive, Texas Women's University, Denton,
Texas; Nancy Wake, Australian War Memorial

Printed in the United States of America

To my cheering section,
John, Muriel, Helen, Gary, and Carol

And my inspirations,
Aaron, Jeremy, and Abby

I don't consider I did anything extraordinary. . . . I did it because I wanted to, because it was useful, because it had to be done.
—PEARL WITHERINGTON

The righteous are as bold as a lion.
—PROVERBS 28:1

Contents

Foreword

IN HER *WOMEN HEROES* titles, Kathryn Atwood has performed a commendable service by bringing to light the heroic exploits of many women during the wars of the past century. Often, once a war is over and the initial euphoria of loved ones returning home has passed, people strive to simply get on with their lives, and the memories remain bottled up. The personal sacrifices and dangers veterans encountered are all in the past—until someone interested enough in war history, such as Kathryn, delves in and uncovers heretofore unknown or unpublicized acts of bravery.

As a World War II army nurse returnee, I spent my first three weeks at home closeted in my bedroom, mounting hundreds of black-and-white photos of "my war" into an album and adding captions to each one. I didn't want to forget, nor have I, the bombed-out homes bordering our tent hospital or our partially destroyed

tents hit by buzz bombs or the ambulances unloading wounded
soldiers. There were photos of good times, too, and I didn't want to
forget those either. I just hoped that someday when I had a family
of my own, they would be interested in my album of memories.
And yet when that day arrived, Elvis and the Beatles were much
more interesting to my kids than a walk through Mom's past.

I and my fellow nursing classmates were in our third and final
year of nurses' training in 1941 when we heard the news that Pearl
Harbor had been bombed. I was reaching into the crib of one of
my young patients on Pediatrics when an upper classmate rushed
by, calling out, "Pearl Harbor was bombed!" Pearl Harbor? We
didn't even know where or what it was.

We learned soon enough, huddled around the radio the following day in the Doctor's Room on Pediatrics, as we solemnly
listened to President Roosevelt's famous Date of Infamy speech,
spelling out how the Japanese had bombed the U.S. Navy base in
Hawaii. That speech appealed to the sense of unity and patriotism
that immediately swept the country. Men rushed to enlist in some
branch of the military. Most of my classmates and I determined
that as soon as we graduated we would also enlist, for surely nurses
would be needed. And they were.

This second edition of *Women Heroes of World War II* contains
six new profiles of women who were all in some way connected
to the military. In the United States alone, nearly 350,000 women
served in the military during World War II, at home and abroad.
Some of us in the Army Nurse Corps went overseas. My own story,
contained in this book, brought me and my fellow army nurses to
Belgium, where we worked in a tent hospital nursing the wounded
of the Battle of the Bulge and other battles.

Some American women, like fly girl Hazel Ying Lee, whose
story is included in this new edition, trained as Women Airforce
Service Pilots and flew military aircraft across the country. Others volunteered for the Women's Army Corps, the Navy Women's

Reserve, the Coast Guard, the Army Nurse Corps, and the Navy Nurse Corps. Women drove trucks, repaired airplanes, worked as laboratory technicians, rigged parachutes, and served as radio operators.

The Soviet Union, whose women were allowed to participate in combat, is also represented in this new edition by way of a young partisan woman named Zoya Kosmodemyanskaya and a pilot named Anna Yegorova.

As all these stories demonstrate, women have proven their love for their country and their capability to function as well as men in military service; in his 1962 address to the West Point corps of cadets, General MacArthur summed up the requirements as "Duty, Honor, and Country."

I and my fellow nurses never forgot the thrill and pride as we watched the American flag fluttering in the breeze at reveille while we were overseas. And when our return ship, carrying thousands of male and female troops, sailed silently through the early morning fog of the Hudson River past the Statue of Liberty, there was not a dry eye aboard that vessel.

Muriel Phillips Engelman, the lead nurse pictured in the large photo on the cover of this book, was the author of the memoir *Mission Accomplished: Stop the Clock*. She was commissioned a second lieutenant in the Army Nurse Corps in April 1943 during World War II. She was later promoted to first lieutenant. Two of her three years in the Army Nurse Corps were spent overseas in England, France, and Belgium, where she helped maintain a 1,000-bed tent hospital during the Battle of the Bulge and lived under the constant bombardment of buzz bombs. In 2018, she was appointed a Chevalier of the National Order of the Legion of Honor by the French government for her wartime work. She regularly spoke to students, civic organizations, and veteran groups about her experiences and work during the war. Muriel died in 2022 at the age of 101.

Introduction

WHO WERE THE heroes of World War II? Winston Churchill, the British prime minister, who refused to surrender while the mighty German air force tried to bomb Great Britain into submission? Jean Moulin, a man who worked tirelessly to unify the French Resistance and died under torture rather than betray his fellow resisters? Or were the heroes of World War II the thousands of Allied troops who stormed the beaches of Normandy, France, on June 6, 1944, and helped put an end to the Nazi occupation of Europe? All these men were heroes. Without their courageous acts, Nazi Germany certainly would not have been defeated.

But there were other heroes in World War II, many whose names are not as familiar as those of U.S. generals Patton and Eisenhower but whose courageous actions helped win the war. These are the women heroes of World War II. A few of them were already quite famous before the war, and some of them became so afterward, but many more were simply ordinary. They were hairdressers and watchmakers, social workers and university students, teenagers and housewives, all of them very different women who had one thing in common: they were outraged at Hitler's actions.

Hitler's troops invaded Poland on September 1, 1939, which officially began World War II. Shortly after Hitler invaded Poland, France and Great Britain—technically allies of Poland—declared war on Germany, and Hitler in turn declared war on both of them. But France and Great Britain did not come to Poland's aid, and for eight months after the Polish invasion nothing happened between Great Britain, France, and Germany during this peaceful but tense period called the Drôle de Guerre (French for "strange" or "funny" war).

Then, on April 9, 1940, German troops invaded Denmark and Norway, claiming to be protecting them from a possible Allied invasion (but in fact using them as buffers against a possible British attack on Germany). On May 10, 1940, German troops simultaneously invaded the Netherlands, Luxembourg, Belgium, and then France.

Although there was some initial defensive fighting from each of these countries, by the end of June 1940 the Germans had conquered most of Western Europe. Hitler could now attempt to implement the ideas he had written about years earlier in his rambling memoir, *Mein kampf* (My Struggle). In the book he described his desire to make Germany the dominant culture in Europe. Hitler planned to eventually "Germanize" those he had conquered from "Aryan" countries (whose populations had Germanic features; very generally, blue-eyed blonds), forcing them to forsake their own culture for that of Germany. As for the Slavic peoples (whom he considered to be inferior to the Aryans) such as the Soviets and the Poles, he planned to destroy or enslave them and then take their lands and goods for Germans and Germanized Aryans.

Hitler seized the occupied countries' farmlands, oil fields, mines, and factories. Then, depending on their owners' race, he either murdered them, shipped them off to forced labor camps, or left them behind to keep the country running and survive on what they could manage through strict ration cards.

Hitler then turned his attention to his central obsession: his hatred for Jews. He believed that before the Aryans could emerge as the dominant race of Europe, the Jews—supposedly the racial enemies of the Aryans—had to be destroyed. As the Nazis in every occupied country tried to implement Hitler's anti-Semitism, stripping Jews of their citizenship, property, and money and forcing them to live in unhealthy, overcrowded areas called ghettos, eventually a monstrous plan came into place: the Final Solution. Ghetto after ghetto was emptied by malnutrition, disease, and, finally, by cattle car trains that shipped the ghetto survivors into concentration camps or death camps in Poland and Germany.

Many people in occupied countries thought the Nazis were there to stay, so they cooperated with them, some enthusiastically, and some just so that they could survive. But there were others who were outraged and determined to do something—anything —to fight the Nazis. This was called the Resistance. While some worked alone, most people in the Resistance formed groups. Organizations such as the British Special Operations Executive (SOE) and the American Office of Strategic Services (OSS), kept some of these groups supplied and organized so that they could fight their secret but deadly battles against the German occupiers. Other militant Resistance groups received money from their own governments, some of which had escaped to London and were operating out of exile.

The Germans took control of the newspapers in all of the occupied countries, printing only German propaganda. They also ordered everyone in those countries to turn in their radios so that they would have no access to outside news. Some Resistance

---

FORCED LABOR CAMPS, CONCENTRATION
★★★ CAMPS, AND DEATH CAMPS ★★★

The Nazis ran three basic types of camps during World War II. Forced labor camps were usually set up next to agricultural areas or munitions factories. Hundreds of thousands of people from occupied countries—first the Poles and later those from Western Europe—filled these German camps and factories. While conditions in labor camps were bad and the promised pay nonexistent, the workers were kept just healthy enough to be productive. The hundreds of concentration camps (located mostly in Germany and Poland), however, were created to punish and kill. Prisoners arriving at concentration camps were either killed immediately, used for medical experiments, or worked and starved to death through the Nazi "annihilation through work" policy. There were also death camps that existed exclusively to kill Jews upon their arrival: Treblinka, Sobibor, Belzec, and Chelmno.

---

workers sought to fight German propaganda by printing underground (illegal) newspapers that reported Allied news obtained from hidden radios. These newspapers were encouraging to many residents of occupied countries, not only because they printed the truth, but because their existence was proof that there were others who were trying to resist the occupation.

Some resisters did their best to help Allied servicemen trapped in Nazi-occupied territory through escape lines—a series of safe houses (hiding places) that led to freedom. Others worked to hide Jews and those on the run from the Nazis. Still others created false identification papers or stole ration cards—which were necessary to buy groceries—so that the "hiders" could survive while concealed or traveling to freedom.

Women were involved in all aspects and all levels of Resistance work, although the most common job for a female in the Resistance was that of a courier, someone who carried messages and documents from place to place. Courier work was crucial during the occupation because phone lines were tapped and mail was censored to root out Resistance activities. And since most men in occupied countries were supposed to be working in German munitions factories, it was dangerous for them to be seen in public. Women, less in demand for factory work, could move about in public more freely. Plus, the Germans did not—at first—imagine that women could possibly be involved in Resistance activities.

Yet if these female couriers were caught carrying materials related to Resistance work, they would be immediately arrested. All Resistance activities were dangerously illegal in Nazi-occupied Europe, and anyone who was caught, whether male or female, usually received either an immediate death sentence or a one-way ticket to a concentration camp. But this would occur only after the unfortunate Resistance worker had undergone severe interrogation and torture so that the Nazis might obtain the names and addresses of other connected resisters.

In spite of the serious dangers involved, most Resistance workers felt they had no choice but to resist occupation. The arrogant and cruel Nazi regime was completely contrary to everything they believed in; their consciences demanded action. And on the horizon, there was always the hope that the United States would eventually enter the war and use its large population and military potential to help wipe Hitler off the European map.

However, during the summer of 1940, when the Nazi darkness had spread across mainland Europe, and the Battle of Britain—fought between the British Royal Air Force and the German Luftwaffe air force—raged in the skies above England, U.S. involvement in the war didn't seem likely. Although Winston Churchill, Great Britain's new prime minister, had repeatedly urged U.S. president Franklin Roosevelt to help him fight Hitler, at least half of all Americans were strongly opposed to sending American troops overseas to fight in a European war.

That all changed on December 7, 1941, when Japan, Germany's ally, destroyed the U.S. naval fleet stationed at Pearl Harbor, Hawaii. The United States declared war on Japan and then Germany declared war on the United States. Hundreds of thousands of young American men and women quickly enlisted in the armed services so that they could fight Japan and Japan's allies, the Axis powers (which included Italy, Japan, and Germany).

Hitler made a fatal mistake when he invaded the Soviet Union in June 1941. The Soviets immediately joined the Allied powers, and by 1943 Hitler had lost several million fighting men on the Russian front. When Allied troops—composed largely of U.S., Canadian, and British soldiers—finally landed on the coast of Normandy on June 6, 1944, they were met by determined but depleted German forces. The Allied troops pushed the Germans east while the Soviet troops pushed them west. Yet, the Nazis fought on for another year, energetically continuing their destructive racial policies and severely punishing anyone remotely involved with Resistance work, until Germany formally surrendered to the Allies on May 7, 1945. May 8 was declared V-E (Victory in Europe) Day.

Although most Allied women in the armed forces had worked in supportive roles and had not been directly involved in combat, many Soviet women had been. Without the successful combat missions of these Soviet women, the crucial support work of other Allied women in the armed services, the daring missions of female SOE and OSS agents, and the varied work of the female Resistance workers who had lived every moment of the occupation in danger, the war probably would not have ended the way it did, or at least as soon as it did. Allied governments recognized the contributions of many of these women after the war by granting them top awards. And the Jewish organization Yad Vashem granted its Righteous Among the Nations award to both men and women who, to their great peril, had hidden Jewish people from certain death.

The women whose stories are featured in this book are not the only female heroes of World War II. There were hundreds of thousands of women who fought against the Nazi regime in many different ways. Some of them are remembered only by a short chapter in a book, others by a paragraph on a website. The stories of thousands more might never be known.

But most of these women—the famous and the obscure—had one thing in common: they did not think of themselves as heroes. They followed their consciences, saw something that needed to be done, and they did it. And all of them helped win a war, even though many of them paid the ultimate price for their contribution. But their sacrifice was not in vain, especially if their courage continues to inspire others to fight injustice and evil wherever they find it.

★★★ YAD VASHEM ★★★

The name Yad Vashem (literally "a hand and a name") is taken from Isaiah 56:5, a verse that speaks of eternal remembrance. Yad Vashem was established in Jerusalem, Israel, in 1953 as the world center to commemorate the Holocaust including each victim who was lost. Another important goal of the organization is to seek out Gentiles (non-Jews) who risked their lives to help Jews during the war and to award them with the title of Righteous Among the Nations. Those who are given this award receive a medal and a certificate of honor, and their names are commemorated on the Mount of Remembrance in Jerusalem.

PART I

Germany

HOW COULD THE Holocaust have happened in 20th-century Germany, a society that valued art and philosophy, where university professors were highly esteemed, and where Jews were leaders in every realm of society? There are three main reasons: the Treaty of Versailles, the Great Depression, and Adolf Hitler.

German military aggression had been a major cause of World War I (1914–1918), a conflict that had taken the lives of millions of soldiers and destroyed the economies of many European countries. After Germany surrendered, Great Britain, and especially France—Germany's major combatants at the war's end who had suffered the most casualties—wanted to make Germany pay for the damage. They did so by way of the Treaty of Versailles, signed by German leaders the summer following the armistice (the end of the fighting). The treaty placed tight restrictions on the German military, forced Germany to give up portions of its territory, and, most crushing of all, forced Germany to pay war reparations.

The terms of the Treaty of Versailles caused humiliation and resentment among the German people, and the war reparations eventually led to severe inflation of the German economy. Wealthy Germans spent their life savings just to buy food, while the poor starved. The economy's collapse brought political instability as people lost faith in their current leaders, and an array of political parties vied for the attention of the German people.

No political leader caught quite as much attention as Adolf Hitler, the head of the new Nationalsozialistische Deutsche Arbeiterpartei (National Socialist German Workers' Party), or Nazi for short. When Hitler was arrested for treason in 1923, he spent his nine-month jail sentence writing his autobiography *Mein kampf,* which eventually became a German bestseller. In the book, Hitler railed against those he blamed for Germany's current problems: Germany's former military leaders, Communists, and especially German Jews.

The book was obsessed with the issue of race: Hitler believed that Germans, as a nation composed largely of blue-eyed blonds, were part of the Aryan race, superior to all others. As such, Germany had a duty to destroy the Jews and to kill or enslave Slavic people such as Poles and Soviets.

Many thoughtful Germans found Hitler absurd and didn't think he would ever be taken seriously as a national leader. But they didn't take into consideration Germany's desperate problems, which were only made worse by the Great Depression of the 1930s (which began in the United States but severely affected the economies of Europe). In the midst of Germany's political turmoil and collapsed economy, Hitler and the Nazi party gained prominence in Germany. In 1933 Hitler was appointed the chancellor (prime minister) of Germany.

★★★ THE THIRD REICH ★★★

Nazi Germany is often referred to as the Third Reich (Third Empire). In using that name, Hitler was attempting to portray Nazi Germany as a descendant of the 1,000-year Holy Roman Empire (the first Reich), a large territory in central Europe during the Middle Ages, and the German empire (the second Reich), which had unified many small German states into one country between 1871 and 1918. Hitler also referred to Nazi Germany as the Thousand Year Reich, believing that it would last as long as the Holy Roman Empire.

Within six months, Hitler bestowed on himself the grand title of Führer (a German word meaning "leader" or "guide"), dissolved the Reichstag (the democratic German governing institution), outlawed all other political parties, and built concentration camps for his political opponents. He established the Gestapo, an organization of plain-clothed secret police ordered to weed out any and all political opposition, which often arrested people simply for uttering a single negative comment about the Nazi party.

He instituted the Hitler Jugend (Hitler Youth), a state-run program for all children ages 10–18. The Hitler Youth program was geared to make Germany's children proud, militant Nazis. They engaged in warlike games, killed small animals (to become insensitive to suffering and death), sang songs about German streets running with Jewish blood, and were encouraged toward fanatical, personal devotion to Hitler, a devotion that was to take precedence over their relationships with their parents. (Children were encouraged to turn in their own parents to the Gestapo if they heard them say anything against the Führer.)

Schools also became places of indoctrination, where history classes taught that Hitler was descended from great German heroes, math classes discussed how much money the state lost while supporting mentally challenged individuals, and biology classes taught the superiority of the Aryan race and the inferiority of the Jewish race.

Many Germans were blinded to the cruelty and darkness of the Nazi regime. Hitler's policies created jobs, and, in defiance of the Treaty of Versailles, Hitler was rebuilding the armed forces, something that had long been a source of pride to many Germans. If personal freedom of expression was the cost, so be it, many thought. At least Germany was becoming strong again. This nationalistic pride grew during the summer of 1940 when Germany had conquered nearly all of mainland Europe. It seemed that Hitler's promise of a 1,000-year German Reich was coming true.

But there were some Germans who strongly objected to the loss of personal freedoms in Nazi Germany and to Hitler's treatment of the Jews. Jews had been harassed by the Nazis for years before the Nazi party came to power. But when Nazism became the law of the land, Jews lost their citizenship, and there was no one in the government they could turn to for protection. One November night in 1938, anti-Semitic Germans were given a green light from Hitler to destroy Jewish synagogues, homes, and businesses all over Germany and Austria in what became known as Kristallnacht (Crystal Night, usually referred to as the Night of Broken Glass). Afterward, Jews fled the countries by the hundreds of thousands.

The German Jews who remained eventually began to be shipped out of Germany to be "resettled" in the east, but it soon became clear that they were being shipped to cruel concentration camps. Many Jews were saved by German resisters who risked everything to conceal them. When Joseph Goebbels, Hitler's propaganda minister, officially declared Germany's capital city of

Berlin to be *Judenfrei* (Jew-free) in the middle of 1943, there were thousands of Jews still hiding there.

Rote Kapelle (Red Orchestra) was the name the Gestapo gave to several Resistance organizations in different countries. The Red Orchestra in Berlin was composed of a small group of people with Nazi affiliations who worked to overthrow the Nazi government from the inside by passing top-secret and high-level information to the Soviets. They also recruited Resistance members and helped hide Jews.

One of the women involved in the Berlin-based Red Orchestra was an American named Mildred Fish Harnack, a scholar, translator, and professor of the German language. After she was caught and tried, she received a prison sentence. But Hitler specifically ordered a new trial for her, which resulted in the death sentence. Just before she was beheaded, she was reported to have said, "And I have loved Germany so much."

Hitler's decision to invade the Soviet Union in 1941 proved disastrous for Germany. When the Allies landed on the beaches of Normandy in June 1944, they met German forces who fought furiously but whose numbers had been depleted from the long and fruitless battle against the Soviets. Finally convinced that his regime would be defeated, Hitler committed suicide on April 30, 1945. The German armed forces formally surrendered to the Allies on May 7, 1945.

Mildred Harnack in 1938.
German Resistance Memorial Center

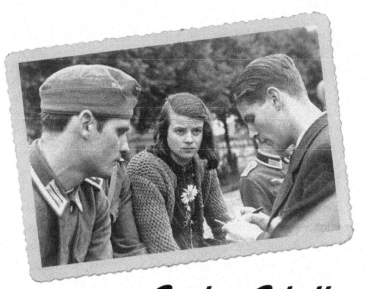

Sophie Scholl

THE WHITE ROSE

ON FEBRUARY 22, 1943, a German university student named Sophie Scholl, her brother Hans, and one of their friends, Christoph Probst, were all awaiting trial in the Nazi-run "People's Court" in the Munich Palace of Justice. The judge who was to preside over their case, Roland Freisler, suddenly swaggered into the courtroom, dramatically dressed in flowing red robes. Judge Freisler was known as the hanging judge because he passed death sentences on nearly everyone tried in his court. This trial, its audience filled with those loyal to Hitler's Third Reich, looked like it would be no exception. Judge Freisler opened the proceedings with a furious and demented tirade, making great billowing gestures with

Hans Scholl, Sophie Scholl, and Christoph Probst, July 23, 1942.
United States Holocaust Memorial Museum, photo © George J. Wittenstein

14

his robes and screaming that the defendants were guilty of treason, conspiracy, rendering the armed forces unfit to protect the
German Reich, giving aid to the enemy, and crippling and weak-
ening the will of the German people.

The defendants were not given a chance to speak on their own
behalf, but in the midst of the judge's tirades, Sophie Scholl suddenly cried out, "Somebody had to make a start! What we said and
wrote are what many people are thinking. They just don't dare say
it out loud!"

What exactly had Sophie said—and written—that had caused
her to be on trial for her life? That can be answered in three words:
the White Rose.

The White Rose. That was the name on the leaflet Sophie Scholl
had just found under a desk. It was June 6, 1942, and Sophie had
begun her studies at the University of Munich six weeks earlier. As
she read through the pamphlet, Sophie was almost trembling with
excitement; there were ideas in it that had often crossed her mind
but that she hadn't been able to fully articulate. Although she loved
Germany and had even, for a while, been an enthusiastic participant in the Union of German Girls (the female branch of the Hitler
Youth organization), she had since come to understand that there
was something very wrong with Nazi Germany.

When she was only 12 years old, she had wondered aloud
why her Jewish friend, who had blue eyes and blonde hair, wasn't
allowed to be a member of the Hitler Youth, while she, with her
dark hair and eyes, was. Her father, a staunch opponent of Hitler
and the Nazi party, always argued with his son, Hans, about Hans's
enthusiastic leadership role in the Hitler Youth program. Sophie listened to these arguments in silence and later observed Hans carefully as he became completely disillusioned with the Nazis.

Sophie almost didn't pass her qualifying high school exam—
the Abitur—because she stopped participating in her high school
classes when they became more about Nazi indoctrination than
about real learning. She did the work and passed, however, and
although she was eager to go straight to a university, she was first
forced by the state, as all girls her age were, to serve six months of
manual labor for the National Labor Service, enduring not only
exhausting work but also more Nazi indoctrination administered
by fanatical and cruel female Nazis.

She finally had been allowed to enroll at the University of
Munich, the same university where her brother Hans was study-
ing, and now, six weeks later, she was holding this White Rose pamphlet in her hand. The third sentence was particularly gripping:

> Who among us has any conception of the dimensions of shame
> that will befall us and our children when one day the veil has
> fallen from our eyes and the most horrible of crimes—crimes
> that infinitely outdistance every human measure—reach the
> light of day?

The "most horrible of crimes" referred to in the pamphlet was
the Nazi practice of euthanasia (mercy killing) of Germans with
mental disabilities and others who were considered "unproduc-
tive" because of certain physical defects. The bishop of Münster,
Clemens August Graf von Galen, had delivered an impassioned
sermon against this practice one year earlier, on August 31, 1941.
The sermon was reprinted and then secretly but widely duplicated
and distributed.

It is not certain whether Sophie had ever seen a Bishop von
Galen sermon leaflet, but it is certain that her brother Hans had,
and she wanted to speak to him immediately. Sophie rushed to his
rented room. He wasn't there, so she waited for his return, occupying herself by flipping through some of his books. She noticed

that he had underlined a phrase in one of his philosophy books: "If a state prevents the development of the capacities which reside in man, if it hinders the progress of the spirit, then it is reprehensible and corrosive." She quickly looked at the White Rose pamphlet again. That phrase, word for word, was in the pamphlet. She knew at once that Hans was involved with the White Rose.

When Hans returned to his room, Sophie confronted him by showing him the pamphlet in her hand. Did he have anything to do with it? He had, in fact, written it, but at first he wouldn't admit this, telling Sophie instead that "these days it is better not to know some things in case you endanger other people." But Sophie was persistent, and before their conversation was over, Hans had not only told her everything regarding his own involvement, he had also given her permission to join the White Rose.

With Sophie helping them, the six central members of the White Rose created and distributed three more leaflets during the summer of 1942. The leaflets, intellectual in tone and filled with quotes from the Bible and famous philosophers, called upon Germans to resist the Nazi government. The leaflets were targeted toward university professors and students in hopes that the most intelligent thinkers in Germany could not possibly fail to see the evil of the Nazi government. And if the brightest minds could be convinced to resist, surely the rest of Germany would follow.

One associate of the White Rose said later that Hans Scholl and Alexander

"Why are the German people so apathetic in the face of all these abominable crimes, crimes so unworthy of the human race? . . . The German people slumber on in their dull, stupid sleep and thereby encourage these fascist criminals."

—from the second White Rose leaflet

Schmorell were the minds of the White Rose (because they were the principal authors) but that Sophie was its heart. She helped to copy, distribute, and mail the leaflets and was also in charge of the group's finances, which included buying paper and stamps from many different post offices so as not to create suspicion.

For suspicion there certainly was. The Gestapo (the Nazi secret police) was desperate but unable to discover the pamphlets' authors. They called on anyone who received a leaflet to turn it in or face immediate arrest. The Gestapo thought the perpetrators must be a large group. Little did they know that the most active members of the White Rose totaled a mere six people!

In July 1942, Hans Scholl, Willi Graf, Alex Schmorell, Jürgen Wittenstein, and others—all medical students—received orders to spend their semester break working as medics at the Russian front,

WHO WERE THE MEMBERS OF
★★★ THE WHITE ROSE? ★★★

The White Rose was not a membership club in the usual sense. It began casually with a group of university friends who often met to discuss art, music, literature, and philosophy. Soon they realized that they had the same political opinions. They were all decidedly anti-Nazi and, inspired by the successful duplication of Bishop van Galen's sermon, decided to write their own "sermons" of protest. The core group, the ones most responsible for the creation and distribution of the leaflets, were Hans Scholl, Sophie Scholl, Christoph Probst, Alexander Schmorell, Willi Graf, and Traute Lafrenz. But numerous others were involved, such as fellow student and friend Jürgen Wittenstein, who edited several of the leaflets, and Kurt Huber, a university professor, who wrote the sixth leaflet.

the battle zone between Germany and Russia. This meant that the work of the White Rose had to stop temporarily, and the duplicating machines were dismantled and hidden.

When the young medics returned in November 1942, they had a new perspective on the war. Despite the German propaganda that had been declaring glorious victories in Russia, the young medics had seen the truth, that the German army was exhausted and being beaten by the Soviets. And en route to the Russian front, they had seen the horrendous conditions in the Warsaw ghetto, the place where many of Poland's Jews were being slowly starved.

★★★

"We must bring this monster of a state to an end soon. A victory for fascist Germany in this war would have inconceivable and terrible consequences."
—from the third White Rose leaflet

★★★

★★★

"We will not be silent. We are your bad conscience. The White Rose will not leave you in peace!"
—from the fourth White Rose leaflet

★★★

Now more determined than ever to overthrow the Nazi government, the members of the White Rose quickly wrote the fifth leaflet. They wanted to give an impression that the White Rose was part of a much larger network, so they got on trains and mailed the leaflets—20 percent more than any of their previous mailings—to and from many different German cities.

On February 3, 1943, after the Nazi government admitted defeat by the Soviets at Stalingrad, Hans Scholl, Alex Schmorell, and Willi Graf went out that night (as well as two subsequent nights, February 8 and 15) and painted slogans such as "Freedom," "Down with Hitler," and "Hitler mass murderer" in public places all over Munich, including city hall and the university.

Then they decided to do something even bolder. On February 18, 1943, Hans and Sophie carried a large suitcase filled with copies of the sixth White Rose pamphlet into a lecture hall at the University of Munich. They placed piles of the leaflets outside the classrooms, on windowsills, and on the large stairway that led down to the main floor.

They had just left the building when Sophie suddenly realized that there were perhaps 100 more leaflets left in the suitcase. They went back inside, climbed the stairs to the top landing of the university's inner court, and tossed the remaining leaflets into the air, just as students were exiting their lecture halls. It would be the

Sophie and some members of the White Rose at the Munich East train station before the medical students left for the Russian front, July 23, 1942.
United States Holocaust Memorial Museum, photo © George J. Wittenstein

last thing that they would do as free Germans. A custodian named Jakob Schmid, a Nazi, saw them on the top landing, just as the leaflets hit the floor. He followed Sophie and Hans as they tried to blend in with the crowd of exiting students and made sure that they were both arrested.

On February 22, 1943, Sophie Scholl, her brother Hans, and Christoph Probst were executed just hours following their trial. There would be more arrests, imprisonments, and executions of those who had been involved, but as of that sad day the work of the White Rose, as it had been, was no more. As Sophie and Hans faced their executions, they were surprisingly optimistic. Although their tracts had reached many Germans, the news of their executions would certainly reach many more; surely other students would rise up, take their place, and continue their work.

Sadly, this didn't happen. There were a few isolated incidents at the university that involved graffiti and the words "Scholl lives! You can break the body, but never the spirit," but by and large, the University of Munich students did not agree with the work of the

"Germans! Do you and your children want to suffer the same fate that befell the Jews? . . . Are we to be forever the nation which is hated and rejected by all mankind? No. Disassociate yourselves from National Socialist gangsterism. Prove by your deeds that you think otherwise."

—from the fifth White Rose leaflet

White Rose. A rally held at the university shortly after the first executions was attended by hundreds of students, who gave custodian Jakob Schmid a thunderous ovation for helping to capture the Scholls.

However, the work of the White Rose leaflets did not end with the executions of their creators. When the story of the White Rose was discovered months later by the Allies, thousands of the leaflets were duplicated and dropped all over Germany by airplane. Many more Germans now had a chance to read them. For those who were still trying to resist Hitler, the words in the leaflets and the story of the young people who had paid the ultimate price for those words gave them courage and hope.

"We grew up in a state where all free expression of opinion has been suppressed. The Hitler Youth, the SA [Sturmabteilung], and the SS [Schutzstaffel] have tried to drug us, to revolutionize us, and to regiment us in the most promising years of our lives."
—from the sixth White Rose leaflet

"Our people stand ready to rebel against the National Socialist enslavement of Europe in an impassioned uprising of freedom and honor."
—the last words of the sixth White Rose leaflet

★★★ LEARN MORE ★★★

Hans and Sophie Scholl: German Resisters of the White Rose by Toby Axelrod (The Rosen Publishing Group, Inc., 2001).

"Memories of the White Rose" by George J. (Jürgen) Wittenstein, M.D. (a friend of the Scholls and associate of the White Rose) The History Place: Points of View www.historyplace.com/pointsofview/white-rose1.htm.

Sophie Scholl and the White Rose by Annette Dumbach and Jud Newborn (Oneworld, 2007).

"The White Rose Leaflets and Their English Translations" The Holocaust Education & Archive Research Team (HEART) www.holocaustresearchproject.org/revolt/wrleaflets.html.

Maria von Maltzan

THE COUNTESS WHO HID JEWS

IT BEGAN WITH strange phone calls. Hans Hirschel, the Jewish boyfriend of Maria von Maltzan, was hiding from the Nazis in Maria's Berlin apartment. He noticed that during some evenings, the phone would ring twice, then stop. Even if she was right next to the phone, Maria wouldn't pick it up. Instead, she would look at her watch. One minute would pass. Then the phone would again ring twice and stop. Another minute would pass. Then, when the phone rang again, Maria would finally pick it up. The conversations were always extremely short, and Hans couldn't hear what was being said.

Maria von Maltzan.
German Resistance Memorial Center

These phone calls were always followed by Maria abruptly going out into the night. Maria ignored Hans's questions and continued to respond to the short, strange phone calls by heading out, night after night.

One night, Maria came home from one of these outings and calmly began to apply some antiseptic to a wound on her neck. Hans was shocked. "For God's sake, Marushka," he said to Maria, "that's a bullet wound! What's going on?"

"Hans," Maria said calmly, "never ask me about where I've been and what I've done. It's better that you don't know."

What Hans did know was that Maria Helene Francois Izabel von Maltzan, the girlfriend whom he affectionately referred to as Marushka, the daughter of a German count who had been raised on a beautiful 18,000-acre estate, had not been surprised by the roundup of Jews in Berlin. In fact, she wasn't surprised by any of Hitler's actions against the German Jews. After all, she had carefully read Hitler's autobiography, *Mein kampf*, while a university student in Munich. Most Germans were so thrilled with Hitler's promises to transform economically depressed and politically divided Germany into a glorious Third Reich that they ignored his ravings against the Jews. Maria, however, clearly understood and detested those ravings. She knew that Hitler would try to destroy the Jews of Europe if he ever got the chance.

When the Nazis first took control of Germany's government in 1933—the same year Maria finished her doctoral studies in the natural sciences—she said to a friend, "I love this country so much, and I'm just beside myself with what's happening." She joined various Resistance groups and did what she could to fight the Nazis. Because she was a count's daughter and closely related to several Nazi officers she was at first considered above reproach and was able to obtain useful information from elite Nazi social gatherings. But eventually she came under suspicion of assisting the enemies of the Third Reich. When called in for questioning, however, her cool demeanor, her Nazi connections, and her excellent acting skills always led to her release.

In 1942, despite several massive Jewish roundups the previous year, thousands of Jews were still living in the German capital of Berlin, where Maria lived and had studied veterinary medicine. German Wehrmacht (regular armed forces) officials wanted the roundups stopped since many of Berlin's Jews kept the city's bustling munitions factories running. But Joseph Goebbels, Hitler's propaganda minister and the gauleiter (high-ranking Nazi official) in charge of Berlin, was particularly embarrassed that so many Jews remained in the capital city.

His wishes soon trumped those of the Wehrmacht officials, and in February 1943, massive Jewish roundups resumed in Berlin. When Goebbels announced several months later that Berlin was *Judenfrei*, there were still thousands of Jews living in Berlin. But they were in hiding, and many of them had been so for months.

Maria's apartment, a converted store near the railroad, had always been open to anyone who was on the run from the Nazis. Many of them stayed only temporarily, often during their last nights in Berlin before they escaped by train. But Hans Hirschel, Maria's boyfriend, a scholar and a writer, remained in Maria's apartment. Maria obtained writing assignments for him, changed the wording a bit to disguise the real author, and then sold them, using the money to supplement the income she obtained by working various odd jobs.

When Hans had moved in with her, Maria noticed that his large couch with space inside might be a good hiding place during an emergency search. She drilled some air holes into the bottom of it, then covered the bottom with a thin material that would mask the holes but still let in air. Then she fixed the couch so that once someone was hidden inside, it could not be opened from the outside.

The Nazis knew that they had not found all of Berlin's Jews, so they stepped up their searches. Maria had long come under suspicion for hiding Jews. One day a Nazi official searching for Jews came into Maria's apartment, looked at the couch where Hans was hiding, and said, "How do we know nobody is hiding in there?"

Maria calmly answered, "If you're sure someone is in there, go ahead and shoot. But before you do that, I want a written, signed paper from you that you will pay for new material and the work to have the couch re-covered after you put holes in it."

The official did not shoot and soon left the apartment.

Maria was also involved with a Jewish rescue operation that was working out of the Church of Sweden in Berlin. Maria worked with a young man named Eric Wesslen who was "buying" people back from one particular Nazi official. Eric would give this official certain items in exchange for prisoners, both Jewish and political. Once these people were delivered to him, he would rely on Maria, who had developed a network of safe houses, to find them a temporary shelter. Maria also provided these refugees with false ID papers so that they could more easily get around without fear of being rearrested.

Maria and Wesslen also smuggled people out of Germany and into Sweden in a system that was called *schwedenmöbel* (Sweden furniture). Sometimes she would use a vegetable cart to transport refugees out of Berlin and into the woods. Other times, she would meet the people in the woods after they had been brought there by someone else. She used her real identity card during the day and a false one—identifying her as a woman named Maria Mueller—at night.

One morning, following an evening when Maria had received one of the many phone calls that Hans had found so mysterious, Maria told Hans that she would be home late because of some business. By now, Hans knew better than to ask her what the business was. That afternoon, Maria took a train out of Berlin, got off, walked into the woods, and found a group of 20 people waiting for her. Maria led the group for about a mile. They came to a clearing where they could see a small shack next to some railroad tracks.

"You're to hide in the woods on the other side, 50 meters from that shack," Maria told them. "When the train comes, stay hidden until someone fetches you. You'll be told what to do. Now move out, one at a time, and God be with you."

Maria wanted very much to stay and ensure that the people she had led there would be safe, but her work was only half finished. She had to retrace her steps to make certain that no one had followed them. She knew that the train was scheduled to arrive at any moment. When it did, a group of men, hidden in a different part of the woods, would rush to the train and open one of the boxcars. (The conductor and train workers had been previously bribed with food and money.) Inside the boxcar would be crates of furniture. The men would remove the furniture and replace it with the refugees, seal the box back up, and eventually destroy the furniture. The crates of people would then be loaded onto a freighter and later unloaded in Sweden, where it would finally be safe for the refugees to come out of hiding.

Although Maria sensed that the refugees were on their way to safety, as she retraced her steps she had a bad feeling that something was about to go wrong. If she were stopped by a German patrol, she would have a very hard time explaining what she was doing in the woods in the middle of the night.

When Maria was nearly out of the woods, she heard dogs barking. Just 100 yards ahead of her, she saw a beam of light. Then another beam of light appeared behind her. She was trapped! The dogs were barking because they had picked up her scent. What could she do?

There was a brook nearby. If she could get there before the dogs found her, they would lose her scent. It was her only chance of escape. She jumped in the brook and swam with the current until she had reached a pond surrounded by low-hanging trees. She swam across the pond and waited until the dogs' barking became more and more distant.

She waited there for hours, exhausted and freezing. She knew that the patrollers with the dogs were probably still looking for her, waiting just outside of the woods. Her only hope was an Allied bombing, a frequent occurrence in Germany at this time. During the confusion following a bombing, there was a good chance that her pursuers would stop looking for her.

When she finally thought it might be safe to come out of hiding, she heard the sweetest of sounds: the sirens sounding an air raid warning! Just as she got to the edge of the woods, an Allied bomb hit a factory right in front of her. Maria helped extinguish the fire caused by the bomb, then asked an official for a note stating that she had helped so that she would have paperwork to present to officials at checkpoints explaining why she was so far from home and in such a bedraggled state.

When Maria finally arrived at the Swedish church in Berlin, Wesslen asked her if she was going to faint. She said no and asked him if the refugees had made it to safety. He told her they had. She was handed a glass of champagne, took one sip, and promptly fainted.

Maria von Maltzan personally rescued more than 60 Jews and political enemies of the Nazis and assisted in the rescue of many others. After the war, she and Hans were married. Maria practiced veterinary medicine and often treated animals for free.

A film based on the relationship between Maria and Hans, called *Versteckt* (Hidden), was filmed in Berlin in 1984. In 1986, Maria published her autobiography, *Schlage die trommel und fürchte dich nicht* (Beat the Drums and Be Without Fright). She died in Berlin in 1997.

★★★ LEARN MORE ★★★

The Last Jews in Berlin by Leonard Gross (Carroll & Graf Publishers, Inc., 1992).

Rescuers: Portraits of Moral Courage in the Holocaust by Gay Block and Malka Drucker (Holmes & Meier, 1992) contains a chapter interview of Maria.

Melitta von Stauffenberg

THE PLOT TO KILL HITLER

JULY 20, 1944, was a hot day in Berlin, the capital of Germany. A pilot named Melitta von Stauffenberg, who was doing research for the German Luftwaffe, was rushing from her workshop to the airfield, in spite of the temperature, as she did most days, testing her detailed research with actual flight.

Hundreds of miles away, Claus von Stauffenberg, Melitta's brother-in-law, a decorated colonel of the German Wehrmacht (regular armed forces), was also suffering from the heat. At a little past noon, Claus entered the Wolf's Lair, the name of Adolf Hitler's Eastern Front headquarters, hidden in the woods of Eastern Prussia. Claus told the guard that he wanted to change out of his

Melitta von Stauffenberg, 1943.
Melitta Gräfin Stauffenberg: Das Leben einer Fliegerein, © Gerhard Bracke

sweaty shirt before meeting the führer. When he emerged from a private room and joined the crowded meeting of military leaders, Hitler motioned for the colonel to sit next to him. Claus did so, placing his briefcase on the floor. He then excused himself to take a phone call, leaving the briefcase.

There was no phone call. Colonel von Stauffenberg left the building and entered a waiting car. The car hadn't even reached the first gate when he heard the sound of an enormous explosion. The führer, he thought, the man who was destroying Germany, must surely be dead, killed from the bomb Claus had left in the Wolf's Lair.

Hitler wasn't dead. But 12 hours later, Colonel von Stauffenberg was. Arrested and stripped of his medals, he was executed by firing squad. Then, over national radio, Adolf Hitler screamed a promise of vengeance on the "tiny clique of ambitious, wicked, and stupidly criminal officers" who had been involved in the failed assassination plot.

One person in this "tiny clique," someone Colonel von Stauffenberg had trusted "without reservation," was honorary flight captain Melitta von Stauffenberg.

Melitta had been 11 years old when the First World War began. The use of airplanes in warfare was still relatively new, but it developed at lightning speed during the four years of the war. German combat pilots—including Melitta's own uncle—seemed dashing and heroic, especially when compared to the weary soldiers being maimed and killed in the trenches.

Germany was defeated in 1918 and forced to sign the Treaty of Versailles the following year. One of the terms of the treaty, designed to prevent Germany from again waging war, was that all German military aircraft were to be destroyed, and the manufacture of any engine-powered aircraft banned. Gliders—aircraft that didn't need a motor to remain airborne—became popular for recreational flight; teenage Melitta participated with enthusiasm.

She was a serious student as well. After graduating from the Technical University of Munich, Melitta began working at the German Research Institute for Aeronautics, known as DVL, as a flight mechanic and mathematician, researching the science of flight. Her work was so excellent that Melitta was often consulted by much older and more experienced colleagues. She also enrolled in flight school and became, she admitted later, "thoroughly addicted to the enchantment of flying, in theory and practice."

In 1931, Melitta was introduced to Alexander von Stauffenberg, a young poet and historian from an aristocratic German family. Melitta and Alex discovered a range of common interests, including a deep love for their nation and its culture. They were soon romantically involved, and as Melitta spent her free time with Alex at his family homes, she became close friends with all the Stauffenberg brothers: Berthold, Alexander's twin, an attorney; and Claus, their younger brother, who was enjoying a rising career in the German military.

These young people, busy with their professions and friendships, were not immediately affected by the economic and political turmoil swirling around them, or even Adolf Hitler's rise to power. But on November 15, 1935, the Reichstag—the German

Melitta at an airfield, 1934.
Melitta Gräfin Stauffenberg:
Das Leben einer Fliegerin,
© Gerhard Bracke

Parliament—enacted laws that would directly affect Melitta. These were the Nuremburg Laws, which forbade Jews from marrying or having intimate relationships with non-Jews and prevented any Jews from being citizens of Nazi Germany.

Melitta's paternal grandfather (her father's father) had been Jewish.

Although having only one Jewish grandparent did not make her technically Jewish according to the new Nazi law, neither did it allow her to be considered Aryan. Melitta was worried, and rightly so. Certificates proving one's Aryan ancestry were soon required for certain jobs, university studies, and even marriages.

In 1936 Melitta left the DVL, most likely after being pressured to leave, despite her excellent work. The DVL was a government-run organization, and her lack of an Aryan certificate was becoming an embarrassment to her employers. Melitta's sister was forced to quit her doctoral studies and her brother lost the opportunity to work at a foreign embassy, all of them for the same reason—no Aryan certificate.

Melitta now made a clear distinction in her mind between her beloved Germany and the Third Reich. Everything she did from this point on would be for her country, her family, and her friends. Not for the Nazi regime.

She found work at Askania, a private aeronautics company, doing test flights and research. Although her new employer was not technically a military-focused company, Melitta knew that her work for Askania was being used by the German military to prepare for war. She told a fellow test pilot, "It will come to a terrible end."

As the government of Nazi Germany geared up for war, it also forced certain social norms on its people. The government began to officially pressure single men to marry, not only to squash any possible rumors of homosexuality—which was dangerously illegal—but also to populate the country with what the government deemed racially superior Aryan children. To accomplish this, the state encouraged men to "marry someone desirable for the Third Reich."

When Alex von Stauffenberg wedded Melitta on August 11, 1937, he was conforming to only one aspect of state policy—he was getting married. But Melitta was hardly what the Third Reich considered an ideal German wife. She still didn't have her Aryan certificate. Alex didn't care; he loved Melitta, and part of him enjoyed thumbing his nose at the Nazi regime. He had often criticized the state in his university lectures and papers.

The marriage helped Melitta tremendously. She was now a countess, Melitta Schenk Gräfin von Stauffenberg, and belonged to a highly respected aristocratic German family. She returned to her grueling work schedule: research that included hundreds of near-vertical nose dives in a variety of planes. This work was gaining her increasing fame and an honorary title of flight captain, honors that stood in stark contrast to the dangerous rumors

Some of Melitta's technical drawings.
Melitta Gräfin Stauffenberg: Das Leben einer Fliegerin, © Gerhard Bracke

circulating about what another female pilot snidely referred to as Melitta's "racial burden."

Melitta tried to ignore the rumors and the personal threat they posed. She hoped her excellent work would save her. It eventually did. Hermann Göring—the World War I flying ace who was head of the Luftwaffe and second-in-command to Hitler—was so impressed with Melitta that he soon awarded her with an Iron Cross. And on June 25, 1941, Melitta received something even better: an "equal to Aryan" certificate.

She immediately applied for the same status for her family members, risking her reputation to do so. Ten thousand German descendants of Jews applied for this status. Fewer than 300 received it. Melitta and her family were among the 300.

Most able-bodied men in Germany were required by the state to serve in the military, and Alex was drafted in February 1942. That summer, he was sent to the Eastern Front, where the Germans were involved in a disastrous attempt to defeat the Soviet Union. Alex was wounded and sent back to Berlin to recuperate.

Hitler had seemed invincible while invading western Europe, and even during the initial success of Operation Barbarossa, the invasion of the Soviet Union. But now, with the Wehrmacht mired in a clearly unwinnable battle on the Eastern Front, many German officers began to realize that Germany might actually lose the war.

Claus was one of these officers. Sickened by the mass murders of civilians on the Eastern Front and the enormous loss of German fighting men there, he applied for a transfer and was posted to North Africa. In November 1942, Claus's commander, Field Marshal Erwin Rommel, asked for permission to retreat from an impossible position. His request was refused, and he was ordered to fight to the last man. In the fighting, Claus was severely wounded and sent back to Germany.

While recuperating in a Berlin hospital, Claus said to his wife, Nina, "It is time I saved the German Reich." Nina didn't think he could possibly be serious. He had just lost his left eye, his right hand, and two fingers from his left hand. But he meant what he said. A military coup, he believed, was the only way Germany could be saved from a humiliating defeat and an unconditional surrender to the Allies. If the Nazis were out of power, he reasoned, he and other German leaders might discuss more favorable terms of surrender.

Meanwhile, Alex had recovered and was back at the Eastern Front. Melitta was exhausted and depressed, not only from her constant work and worries for Alex, but also because the Allied bombing raids of Berlin were becoming increasingly destructive. By March 1944, these raids had left 1.5 million Berliners homeless.

On May 21, 1944, Melitta wrote in her diary: "Early call, Claus, Berthold, Haeften, finally came to an agreement." Melitta, the two Stauffenberg brothers, and their close friend, Werner von Haeften, spent a long day together, swimming and sailing, activities that insured their conversations could not be overheard. On that day, most likely, Claus related to Melitta his plan to assassinate Hitler and overthrow the Nazi government. He asked if she would be willing to fly him to Hitler's military headquarters in the forests of East Prussia in order to do the deed, then fly him

Melitta, 1943.
Melitta Gräfin Stauffenberg:
Das Leben einer Fliegerin,
© Gerhard Bracke

directly back to Berlin to announce the führer's death and complete the coup.

Melitta agreed immediately.

She was now involved in aerodynamic tests designed to intercept Allied bombers. Her work, she felt, would save the lives of
German Luftwaffe pilots and the German civilians being killed in
the Allied raids. She was in no way trying to support Hitler. Quite
the opposite—she blamed him for all these deaths, telling her
trusted friends that he "needed to disappear as soon as possible."

Melitta had several more meetings with the conspirators in
which they discussed the details of the proposed coup. But sometime in July, Claus—now commander in chief of the Reserve
Army—decided to use a different pilot. Although Melitta was perfect for the job in most ways, the type of plane she would normally
use for personal reasons (one that wouldn't arouse suspicions)
wouldn't do because they would have to stop to refuel, and then
might have to answer unwanted questions.

On July 20, 1944, Claus brought a briefcase containing a bomb
to Hitler's military headquarters in Eastern Prussia and placed it
next to Hitler. After he left the room, another officer at the meeting, trying to move closer to the führer to see the map on the table
more clearly, moved the briefcase slightly, farther under the thick
oak table. When the bomb detonated, the table took most of the
blast, protecting Hitler. Although four people in the room would
later die of their wounds, the injured Hitler would remain alive.
And he was furious.

Claus's role was quickly discovered. He was shot that night
along with three other conspirators, including Werner von
Haeften.

When Melitta heard that the assassination attempt had failed,
she warned her family members to keep their distance from her
for their own safety. Her office and apartment were ransacked one
day while she was out. Then she was arrested and imprisoned by

the Gestapo. Approximately 7,000 people were arrested because of the attempted coup, some simply because they were overheard saying "what a pity" that it had failed. Some were eventually released, others killed.

Would Melitta be among the latter group? Her colleagues were determined that she wouldn't be. Convinced she hadn't been part of the plot and wanting her back at work, they urged Göring to release her.

Melitta was told she could be freed if she fulfilled two conditions: (1) she must give up her married name—she would now be "Countess Schenk"—and (2) she must immediately return to work. She agreed to those terms but boldly made her own demand: she would be free to visit any imprisoned Stauffenbergs, including her husband. Her work was considered so vital to the desperate, frenzied war effort that she was released on September 2, her terms intact.

Melitta spent her free time bringing the Stauffenbergs food and supplies while trying to lift their spirits. She spent Christmas with the Stauffenberg children who were being held under guard together but who were not otherwise being treated harshly. Then she visited pregnant Nina, Claus's widow, who was being held in solitary confinement in an annex of the Ravensbrück concentration camp. Melitta gave Nina news of her husband's death and her children's current safety.

She also visited Alex—now dangerously thin and being moved from one camp to another—on eight separate occasions, doing what she could to supplement his meager diet. When she attempted to see him a ninth time, she was told that he had been moved to the Buchenwald concentration camp. Frantic but determined to find him, Melitta flew from place to place, once missing him by mere hours.

On April 7, 1945, as she continued her search, Melitta was attacked by an American plane that mistook hers for a German bomber. Her skull was fractured in the attack, but she still managed a successful emergency landing.

Though medics attempted to save her life, Melitta died a few hours later and was buried in a local cemetery.

Alex—along with Nina and all the Stauffenberg children—survived the war. As soon as possible, Alex located his wife's body and had it reburied in the Stauffenberg family vault.

When Alex died in 1964, a collection of his poems was published, most of which praised his heroic brothers. But one of them, titled "Litta," gave tribute to his courageous, brilliant wife, who had died trying to keep him alive.

★★★ LEARN MORE ★★★

Countdown to Valkyrie: The July Plot to Assassinate Hitler by Nigel Jones (Frontline Books, 2009).

The Women Who Flew for Hitler: A True Story of Soaring Ambition and Searing Rivalry by Clare Mulley (St. Martin's, 2017).

PART II
Poland

WORLD WAR II officially began on September 1, 1939, when German tanks and planes stormed into Poland with a new type of warfare called blitzkrieg, or "lightning war," in which an enemy was quickly overwhelmed by the simultaneous use of aircraft, tanks, and armed soldiers. Poland's military leaders had known that a German invasion was likely, but they didn't prepare their military defenses sufficiently. Poland's military allies, France and Great Britain, who had promised to come to Poland's aid in the case of an invasion, had urged Polish leaders not to aggravate Germany by openly preparing for a defensive war. When Germany did invade, France and Great Britain did nothing to help. After one month of fighting Germany alone and waiting in vain for assistance, Poland's armies officially surrendered to Germany.

The Polish army surrendered to the Soviet Union too. Several weeks after the German invasion of Poland's western border began, the Soviets invaded Poland's eastern border. Joseph Stalin, the Soviet leader, believed the eastern section of Poland should be part of the Soviet Union since it had belonged to the Russian Empire before World War I. Hitler had agreed to his request before the invasion. Poland no longer existed; it was now divided between the Soviet Union and Germany.

The Soviets and the Germans both slaughtered or deported Poles by the hundreds of thousands, beginning with the leaders of the following groups: the church, the military, the government, business, and education. They believed that once these Poles were gone, the rest would be easy to control. Eventually, several million Poles were either sent to slave labor camps built especially for them or killed immediately.

The Germans were surprised to discover that many Polish children had Germanic features. These children were forcibly separated from their families and subjected to a series of racial tests to determine how Aryan they were. If they passed the tests, they were assumed to be of Germanic descent and sent to special homes to be "Germanized" so that they could be adopted by German couples. Children who didn't pass the tests were sent to concentration camps.

Poles who were allowed to remain in Poland in the German section were segregated from the new German population—Germans who had moved into homes previously owned by Poles—and were treated with cruelty and disdain.

As badly as these non-Jewish Poles were treated, Poland's Jews were treated even worse. They were squeezed into tiny ghettos where living conditions were horrible and where many died quickly from disease, exposure, and starvation. But the worst was yet to come. Toward the end of 1941, the Nazi occupiers began to build camps that could kill large numbers of Jews very quickly. Jews from Poland, and later, Jews from all over occupied Europe, were shoved onto cattle cars destined for these camps, where they were starved and worked to death, or immediately killed.

Although some Christian Poles were either too anti-Semitic or too focused on their own survival to help the Jews around them, many groups and individual Christian Poles did try to help. Two women—Zofia Kossak and Wanda Krahelska-Filipowicz—were the first to try to merge these groups into one. The eventual result was Zegota. A secret organization based in Warsaw that was solely devoted to helping Poland's Jews, Zegota was the largest organization of its kind in all of Nazi-occupied Europe. Of the 40,000 to

★★★ ZOFIA KOSSAK ★★★

Zofia Kossak was a prominent conservative Catholic writer living in Warsaw who was openly anti-Semitic in her views. But after witnessing the horrors of the Warsaw ghetto, she wrote and distributed an angry leaflet called *Protest*, in which she graphically described conditions in the ghetto and then demanded that Catholic Poles do their Christian duty by helping the Jews. Heavily involved with Jewish rescue and the Polish underground press, Kossak was eventually captured and sent to the Auschwitz concentration camp, and later released. But when the Allies gave the Soviets control of Poland after the war, Kossak was one of the first people to be labeled an enemy of the state. She escaped after a person whose family she had rescued gave her a secret exit visa to Great Britain.

Zofia Kossak.
Yad Vashem

50,000 Polish Jews who survived the war, almost half were helped in some way by Zegota.

Catholic nuns, often working with Zegota, also did a great deal to rescue Jews in Poland, especially children. The German and Soviet slaughter of Poles had created many orphans, and Polish orphanages run by orders of nuns were generally safe places to hide Jewish children. Polish nuns were known to travel great distances to rescue Jewish children, so much so that many Poles assumed any children traveling with nuns must be Jewish.

Before the Polish military surrendered to Germany and the Soviet Union, many Polish servicemen escaped to serve side by side with Allied troops in most major battles of the war. (Nearly 20 percent of the British Royal Air Force were Polish, and they were renowned for their daring courage.) And while the official Polish army had surrendered, the Armia Krajowia (the Home Army), or the AK, had not. The AK was the largest rebel army in all of Nazi-occupied Europe and participated in acts of sabotage (explosive destruction) and assassination against the Germans and Soviets. It also worked hand in hand with Zegota, sometimes by assassinating *szmalcowniks*, whom Zegota had named the Great Plague. *Szmalcowniks* were Poles who were responsible for the betrayal and death of many hidden Jews and the people who sheltered them. Zegota often hired AK members to assassinate *szmalcowniks* so that their traitorous work could be stopped.

Toward the end of the war, the AK also made valiant efforts to take back Poland from the retreating Germans before the Soviets could. Nonetheless, after the war, the Allied powers handed over control of Poland to the Soviet Union because Stalin, the Soviet leader, insisted on it. The new Communist Polish government, carefully supervised by the Soviet Union, declared members of the AK, Zegota, and other Resistance workers to be enemies of the state. Thousands were executed, as were many Jews. Poland would have to wait another 40 years before it would be free.

Irene Gut

"ONLY A YOUNG GIRL"

IRENE GUT, a 19-year-old Polish girl, took a seat in the church, her mind filled with worries about food and heat, worries that would have been inconceivable to her just a few years before. The German blitzkrieg that had rained fire from the sky two years earlier, when she had been a 17-year-old student nurse, had turned her beloved Poland into smoke, rubble, and ash. Irene had fled from the hospital with the other doctors and nurses as they had followed the retreating Polish army amid the screeching chaos of the blitzkrieg. They had traveled east for miles and miles with no particular destination; just as far away as possible from the unstoppable German onslaught.

Irene Gut when she was a student nurse.
United States Holocaust Memorial Museum

After learning that their country no longer existed—that Hitler and Stalin had divided Poland between themselves—they ended up near the Soviet border in the forests of Lithuania and the Polish Ukraine in a desperate struggle to survive. And try as she might, Irene could never forget the worst experience of all: being discovered, beaten, and raped by Soviet soldiers.

Now she was finally back in her hometown of Radom, Poland. But it was not the same town she remembered. Swastikas were everywhere. Jews were beaten and mocked in the streets. Nazi soldiers regularly shot anyone suspected of overt rebellion as well as anyone who accidentally broke one of the numerous new laws. All the Poles were near starvation, eating what little they could get with the strict ration cards distributed by the Germans while the occupiers ate to their fill.

Irene was suddenly stirred from her worries. She could hear German soldiers outside the church, shouting orders loudly. They forced the worshippers outside and pulled the children and elderly people to one side. Then they piled everyone else, including Irene, into a truck. The captives were all driven to another part of Radom to work in a German munitions factory. There was no pay, little food, and the working conditions were grueling. Irene soon became very weak. One day she fainted on the job, right in front of an officer of the German Wehrmacht (regular German armed forces). When she awoke, she was in his office. His name was Major Eduard Rügemer. When he discovered that Irene spoke fluent German, he gave her a new job serving meals to German officers and their secretaries in the dining room of a large hotel near the munitions factory.

The hotel was right next to Radom's Jewish ghetto, and one day Irene witnessed a horrible sight. Jews in the ghetto—including pregnant women and children—were screaming, trying to run from SS officers who were chasing them down, trying to kill them. Then Irene saw one officer catch a mother holding an infant.

With one movement of his hand, he pulled the baby away from its mother and threw it to the ground on its head.

Irene was horrified. She had been raised in a very sheltered, religious home and couldn't understand how God could allow such terrible things to occur. She wanted to turn her back on God, to leave her faith. But then she realized something: God gives everyone a free will, to choose either good or evil. The Nazis had obviously chosen evil. What would her choice be?

Irene already knew the punishment for helping Jews. She had seen and heard the warning many times, on posters and loud-speakers broadcasting in the street: "Whoever helps a Jew shall be punished by death." Irene made a decision. She told God that if she had an opportunity to help the Jews, she would, although it meant risking her own life. She began to sneak leftover food into the ghetto.

The German army was moving east, toward the Russian front, where the Germans were now battling the Soviets. The officers, the munitions factory, and Irene followed them to a large complex in Ternopol, Ukraine. Now, in addition to her dining room duties, Irene was to also oversee the laundry facility, which was staffed— as was the munitions factory—by Jews from the local *arbeitslager*, or work camp. The men and women who worked there soon came to trust Irene, and they told her all that they had suffered at the hands of a very cruel SS officer called Sturmbannfürer (the equivalent of an army major) Rokita, who was in charge of the *arbeitslager*. Irene was determined to help them in any way she could. One of them shrugged, "What can you do? You're only a young girl." Irene knew he was right, but she was determined to try anyway.

Since Sturmbannfürer Rokita ate his meals regularly in the dining room where Irene worked, she deliberately lingered over his table and was able to overhear discussions regarding raids on factories where Jewish workers would be killed. Irene would then convey this information to the Jews in the laundry room, who

---

★★★ THE WEHRMACHT AND THE SS ★★★

The Wehrmacht was the name of the regular German armed forces, while Schutzstaffel, or SS, was a separate, fanatical, extremely elite Nazi organization. Any German could be part of the Wehrmacht, either by enlistment or the draft, but to join the SS one had to undergo rigorous racial tests to prove Aryan credentials, sign an oath of personal loyalty to Hitler, and be a member of the Nazi party. Younger members of the SS had graduated from the Hitler Youth program, which indoctrinated German children with Nazi ideology at a young age. The SS had its own armed forces branch, called the Waffen SS, and an intelligence branch, called the Sicherheitsdienst, or SD. The primary responsibility of the SS was carrying out Hitler's racial policies, which meant hunting down, imprisoning, and killing Jews. The SS also ran the concentration camps and was the organization most directly responsible for Nazi crimes against humanity committed during the war. Hitler distrusted the Wehrmacht leaders, but he needed them to run the war.

---

would in turn warn their friends in the factory. Many of them were able to escape into the woods and avoid being killed.

Major Rügemer and Sturmbannführer Rokita were always arguing at the dinner table. Rügemer's job was to keep the munitions factory running smoothly while Rokita's job was to get rid of the Jews, the very workers from Rügemer's factory. One day when she was waiting on the tables in the dining room, Irene overheard Rokita tell Rügemer that Ternopol was scheduled to be *Judenrein* (Jew-pure) by the end of July, less than a month away.

Irene knew that her friends were doomed—it would take a miracle to save them. About three days later, she got one. Rügemer called Irene into his office and told her that he was going to take a large house in town and wanted her to be his housekeeper there while maintaining her duties in the dining room and laundry facility. When she went to inspect Major Rügemer's new villa, she discovered that the enormous basement had obviously been built as a servants' quarters. And there was a large chute that ran from the basement to the outside for sliding in coal—or people. Irene concocted a desperate plan.

On the evening before Ternopol was to be made *Judenrein*, the German officers and their secretaries went to a party in town while specially trained SS teams searched every corner of the city for hidden Jews. Irene had hidden her friends in the laundry room. When the SS searchers had gone and before the others returned from the party, Irene sneaked her friends into the air duct inside Rügemer's bathroom, where they remained all that night and the next day.

The following night, Rügemer, suffering from a hangover, asked Irene for a sleeping pill, which she gladly gave him. Then she led her friends out of the major's bathroom and out the front door of the complex, with the address of the villa in their hands.

The next morning, Irene was relieved to find her friends hiding in the villa's basement. They devised a warning system that involved Irene keeping the front door locked at all times so that when Major Rügemer came home, he couldn't get in without Irene opening the door.

The 12 Jews hidden in Major Rügemer's house were very comfortable, and Irene might have been amused at the irony of hiding Jews in the home of a German officer if it hadn't been such a deadly game. She was reminded of that danger one day as she passed through the town square. A Jewish couple with a young child and a Polish couple with two small children were being pushed up the stairs to a gallows in the middle of the square. Everyone who was nearby was forced by German soldiers to watch the scene. Nooses were put around the necks of each person, children included, and all of them were hung. The Jewish family had been killed simply for being born Jewish. The Polish family had been killed for trying to hide them.

When Irene returned to the villa, still in shock from the grisly scene, she walked into the kitchen and was greeted by three of the Jewish women, who asked her what was wrong. Irene couldn't speak. Her shock not only made her speechless, it also made her forget to lock the door behind her. Minutes later, Major Rügemer was standing in the kitchen, staring at Irene and the Jewish women. His face was trembling with rage. Then he strode into the library and slammed the door.

Irene followed him. "I trusted you!" he shouted. "How could you do this behind my back, in my own house? How? Why?"

Irene fell to the floor, sobbing at Rügemer's feet and begging him not to turn in her friends.

Rügemer refused to listen. "No!" he shouted. "I am an old man. I have to go now. I'll give you my decision when I return."

Later that evening, Rügemer returned to the villa. He was drunk. He told Irene that he would keep her secret and that the three women (the only ones he knew about) could remain hidden in his house. But his silence would come with a price: Irene was to become his mistress and willingly share his bed.

Irene was shocked and humiliated. Not only was she extremely religious, and Rügemer an old man, but her only experience with men so far had been the horrendous rape by Soviet soldiers. However, she wouldn't let innocent people die. Without telling her friends what their safety was costing her, Irene agreed to Major Rügemer's demand.

This situation lasted for several months until the Soviet army pushed the Germans westward, back toward Germany, and everyone in Ternopol fled to avoid the approaching Soviet armies.

After parting from Rügemer and her Jewish friends, Irene found work as a courier for the Polish Home Army (the AK), which was fighting the enemies of Poland—the Germans and the Soviets—in any way it could. When the war was nearly over, Irene began to search for her family. She got as far as the Polish city of Kraków, where she was reunited with the Jews she had hidden. Then she was arrested by Soviet police, who accused Irene of being an AK leader; they interrogated her daily. She told them nothing about the Partisans. She escaped from the Soviet prison and, with the help of her Jewish friends, made it safely out of Poland. She eventually moved to the United States.

Irene didn't talk about her wartime experiences for many years. Then, in 1975, she heard a neo-Nazi claim that the Holocaust was a hoax; that it had never happened. Irene realized she now had a responsibility: she began to travel widely in order to speak about what she had seen, eventually writing her story (with author Jennifer Armstrong), called *In My Hands: Memoirs of a Holocaust Rescuer.*

In 1982 the Jewish organization Yad Vashem recognized Irene as one of the Righteous Among the Nations. She was also given a papal blessing by Pope John Paul II in 1995. Irene died in 2003. In 2006 she was posthumously granted the Order of Merit of the Republic of Poland.

★★★ LEARN MORE ★★★

In My Hands: Memoirs of a Holocaust Rescuer by Irene Gut Opdyke with Jennifer Armstrong (Knopf, 1999).

"Irene Gut Opdyke"
www.achuka.co.uk/special/opdyke.htm
This website contains an interview with Irene.

Rescuers: Portraits of Moral Courage in the Holocaust by Gay Block and Malka Drucker (Holmes & Meier, 1992) contains a transcription of an interview with Irene.

Irena Sendler

LIFE IN A JAR

A PETITE POLISH woman approached the nine-foot wall of the Warsaw ghetto. The entrance was blocked with barbed wire and armed guards. The woman told the guards that she was a social worker and was there to assist the sick. That statement was true, but she was there for an additional reason, one that she dared not share with the guards. In her pocket she had the addresses of several homes. The people who lived there weren't necessarily sick, but they all had children. She was going to get these children out if she could.

The woman was Irena Sendler, a Polish Christian who had many ties to the Jewish community. Her father had been a doctor

Irena Sendler.
Yad Vashem

53

who often cared for patients who couldn't pay him back, including many Jews. When he died, representatives of the city's Jewish community approached Irena's mother and offered to pay for Irena's education in gratitude for her father's kindness.

Irena had grown up playing with Jewish children and had even learned to speak Yiddish, a language spoken by European Jews. One of her good friends was a Jewish woman named Ewa. They were both social workers for the Department of Social Welfare in Warsaw, providing whatever was necessary to the poorest people in the city, especially any children living in poverty.

When the Jewish ghetto was formed in Warsaw, Ewa and Irena suddenly found themselves on opposite sides of a nine-foot brick wall, a wall guarded diligently by the Germans, day and night. It wasn't easy for Poles to get in, and it was nearly impossible for Jews to get out.

Irena and Ewa began working together to provide help for the neediest Jews in the ghetto, the children. Children were the most vulnerable to the two biggest threats associated with ghetto life: disease and hunger. The most effective way to save them was to get them out.

The first children Irena secretly removed were those who had been orphaned and left homeless on the ghetto streets.

Children in the
Warsaw ghetto.
Yad Vashem

But even the children who still had parents were at great risk for disease and undernourishment. And there was always the growing threat of deportation to camps, a dark and unknown destiny. Children, Irena knew, would be the easiest to save. The Nazi and Soviet occupation had created many orphans; the Jewish children could pretend to be Polish orphans.

Ewa had provided Irena with names and addresses of certain families. Irena carried this list in her hand as she approached the guard at the ghetto's entrance. Once she was inside the gates, she knocked on the doors at the addresses Ewa had given her. The doors would open cautiously as Irena introduced herself and explained why she was there. Many of the parents were shocked. A complete stranger was asking them to hand over their children because she *might* be able to remove them from the dangers and hardships of the ghetto and *might* be able to place them in a convent or a private home? Some parents refused outright, some agreed quickly, while others were willing to be convinced that this was best for their children. But the one question Irena heard over and over from almost every parent was "Can you guarantee that my child will survive?" Irena was not even certain that she would make it past the guards safely. But she would do her best. That was the only promise, the only hope she could give to the desperate parents.

Irena used several routes to take the children out of the ghetto, but the one she used most often led through the courthouse building located inside the ghetto. She would take the child inside the building. Then, they would walk down a flight of stairs to the basement. One particular spot in the basement ceiling contained an opening that led to the street above, where an ambulance waited to take the child out of the ghetto and to a hiding place.

One reason many Jewish parents were hesitant to hand over their children to a Polish Christian woman was that even if Irena could actually guarantee their child's safety, the child might be coerced into forgetting his or her Jewish identity and embrace Christianity instead. These fears were not groundless. Rescued children were each given a new Polish name to replace their Jewish one, to protect them from the Nazis. "Your name isn't Rachel, but Roma," Irena would say to one, and to another, "Your name isn't Isaac, but Yacek. Repeat it 10 times, 100 times, 1,000 times." Irena also taught them Christian prayers, so that they would appear to be Christian if tested.

But even as she was imploring children to memorize their new Christian identities so that their lives could be saved, Irena was also preserving each child's true identity. She made up a list on small strips of tissue paper that contained each child's false Polish name, true Jewish name, and location where he or she was currently living. She placed two identical lists into two separate bottles and buried them under an apple tree in a friend's yard. She had to be extremely careful in hiding the lists; if the Nazis found them, they would be able to track down every single child Irena had saved.

On October 20, 1943, Irena was having a party to celebrate her name day (the date she had been baptized in the Catholic Church). She set aside the identification lists that she had been updating. Her friend, an associate in the work to hide Jewish children, stayed overnight.

Suddenly, in the early morning hours, there was a horrendous pounding at the door. It was the Gestapo!

Irena ran straight to the lists and threw them to her friend, who caught them and promptly placed them inside her bra. The Gestapo spent two destructive hours in Irena's apartment, looking for information that would enable them to arrest other members of Zegota, the large Polish Resistance organization dedicated to helping Jews that Irena had been working with since 1942. Irena didn't dare look at her friend, for fear the Nazis would search her as well and find the hidden lists.

When they couldn't find anything related to Resistance work, the Nazis ordered Irena to come with them. She dressed in a hurry, forgetting to put on her shoes. The sooner they all left the apartment, the less likely the Gestapo would be to find the lists of children's names.

The Gestapo interrogated Irena in two locations, the second time at the infamous Pawiak Prison, doing whatever they could to get her to talk. They showed her a list of informers who had betrayed her, and they advised her to do the same. They tortured her repeatedly, beating her feet and legs until they broke her bones. She refused to say anything, so the Nazis finally decided to execute her.

Just before she was to be executed, Irena was suddenly released instead. Zegota Resistance workers had bribed a Nazi official to free her. Irena actually saw posters that publicly announced her death.

★★★ THE IRENA SENDLER PROJECT ★★★

In 1999 three female high school students from Kansas were given a yearlong extracurricular project for National History Day: find information on an obscure Polish woman named Irena Sendler who was said to have rescued 2,500 Jewish children from the Warsaw ghetto. The end result was a play written and performed by these students called *Life in a Jar*, which, by November 2009, had more than 280 performances in the United States and Poland and brought Irena's story to the world stage. When the girls discovered that Irena was still alive, they were able to fly to Poland and meet her in person on five separate occasions before she died in 2008. They now run the Irena Sendler Project website (www.irenasendler.org).

When the war was over and it was time to reunite the children with their parents, it was discovered that most of the parents had died in the Treblinka death camp. Many of these orphans were relocated to Israel, where they were able to grow up with a strong Jewish identity. Irena had directly saved or helped to save 2,500 of them.

Irena received the Yad Vashem Righteous Among the Nations award in 1965 and the 2003 Jan Karski Award for Valor and Courage. She was also nominated for the Nobel Peace Prize in 2007. She died in Warsaw in 2008.

★★★ LEARN MORE ★★★

The Courageous Heart of Irena Sendler (CBS, 2009) is a TV movie starring Anna Paquin in the title role.

Life in a Jar: The Irena Sendler Project
www.irenasendler.org
This website was created and is maintained by the high school students who discovered Irena's story and who conducted hours of personal interviews with her.

Life in a Jar: The Irena Sendler Project by Jack Mayer (Long Trail Press, 2010) is available from the Irena Sendler Project website.

Life in the Warsaw Ghetto by Gail B. Stewart (Lucent Books, 1995).

Stefania Podgorska

THE TEEN WHO HID THIRTEEN

IF STEFANIA PODGORSKA hadn't hated farm life so much, she might never have become a rescuer of Jews. After visiting some of her older sisters who lived in Przemysl, a bustling Polish city near the Russian border, Stefania was determined to stay there instead of returning to the family farm with her mother.

Her mother didn't want to leave her 14-year-old daughter in the city, but she finally relented. Within a week Stefania found a job in a grocery store owned by a Jewish woman named Lea Adler Diamant. Stefania became such good friends with Mrs. Diamant and her sons that she eventually moved into their apartment above the store, helping Mrs. Diamant with the household chores.

Stefania and her younger sister Helena.
United States Memorial Holocaust Museum

★★★ GERMAN-SOVIET RELATIONS ★★★

Before Hitler's troops invaded Poland in September 1939, Germany and the Soviet Union signed the Nazi-Soviet Non-Aggression Pact, which contained a secret clause in which they agreed to divide Poland. Germany began its assault on Poland from the west on September 1, and on September 17 the Soviet Union invaded from the east. But in June 1941, less than two years later, Germany attacked the Soviet Union and pushed the Soviets out of Poland.

The 1939 German invasion of Poland caused few initial changes for Stefania and the Diamants. German soldiers were stationed there. Then they were gone. Then Russian soldiers replaced them. Then they also left.

But when the Germans returned to Przemysl in 1941, strict anti-Jewish laws were enacted, and a Jewish ghetto was created in the city, right behind the Diamant's grocery store and apartment. The 20,000 Jews of Przemysl were forced to leave their homes and possessions and squeeze into the tiny area.

The Diamants were also forced into the ghetto. They begged Stefania to keep their apartment. She agreed and lived on the first floor while another girl lived on the second.

One night Stefania was woken by piercing screams. When she asked the ghetto guard about it the next day, he shrugged and told her that there had been an *aktion* in the ghetto.

A few nights later Stefania was again woken by screams from another *aktion*. This time, she could clearly hear Mrs. Diamant's voice screaming above the rest. "I can't leave my children!" she cried. "What will happen to my children?" The next morning Stefania learned that Mrs. Diamant had been shipped to the Auschwitz concentration camp.

One night a short while later, Stefania heard a knock at the door. She answered it to find a young man wearing torn clothes stained with dirt and blood.

"It's Joseph," he said, as Stefania stared at him.

"Joseph who?" Stefania asked. It was Mrs. Diamant's son. He was so dirty and bloody that Stefania hadn't recognized him. As she dressed his wounds he told her how he had jumped off a train that was headed for a concentration camp and come back to the city. None of his former Polish friends in Przemysl would hide him, so he finally came back to the apartment that had once been his home.

Joseph was very ill, but when he recovered he fetched his brother's fiancée, Danuta, who was still trapped in the ghetto, and brought her to the apartment. The ghetto would be closed soon, and all the Jews would be either killed or sent to a concentration camp. Joseph and Danuta had many friends left in the ghetto, more than could be hidden in the Diamant apartment. Stefania wondered how she could help. Stefania's six-year-old sister, Helena, had also come to live with her because their mother had been forced to leave Poland to work in a German munitions factory. Stefania needed to find a place that would be large enough for herself, her younger sister, Joseph, Danuta, and as many of their friends as possible. But where was that house?

Stefania had never been particularly religious, although she had attended church with her family while growing up. But now

---

★★★ AKTION ★★★

Aktion is the German word for "action." In the context of the Jewish ghettos of World War II, it came to mean either an outright killing of Jews in a ghetto or a mass deportation to a concentration or death camp.

she felt a tremendous urge to pray. She went outside and wandered through an empty section of town that had once been bustling with Jewish people. She began to pray that God would show her a new place to live. Then, as she recounted years later, she suddenly heard a voice. It told her that when she turned the next corner, there would be two women standing in the street with brooms. They would tell her where to find an apartment.

When Stefania turned the corner, there were the two women with their brooms. When she asked them about a house, they pointed to one that had front and rear entrances and, best of all, a very large attic. It was perfect! Joseph and Danuta quickly took their friends out of the ghetto and brought them to Stefania's new home. She and Joseph built a hidden room in the attic.

Among Stefania's new "tenants" were two Jewish children who had escaped from the ghetto. Their fathers, wanting to join their children in Stefania's new home, made a plan: they would bribe the local postman to hide them in his mail cart and take them from the ghetto to Stefania's new house.

Stefania and Joseph waited at the window of the house at the appointed time, but the postman didn't come. Then after about 10 minutes, four men began to walk back and forth directly in front of the house: two Polish policemen and two German soldiers.

After about three hours of extremely tense waiting, Stefania finally went outside and casually asked one of the Polish police officers what was going on. Had someone been killed?

"Maybe someone *will* be," the Polish officer replied.

"So you're protecting us?" Stefania asked, probing for answers. "Maybe Hitler and Stalin are coming to this very street to fight it out between themselves, and you're going to protect me and my little sister?"

The policeman laughed, but he finally told Stefania why they were there. Two Jews were supposedly going to sneak out of the ghetto that day, and they were headed to her street. The Polish officer didn't believe the story, but orders were orders, and they had to stay and keep watch.

Stefania's heart sank, but she smiled at the policeman and said that she couldn't imagine that any Jew would be foolish enough to risk death to escape the ghetto. Then she headed straight for a nearby church, where she prayed very hard that the Germans and Polish policemen would leave before the postman came with the Jews so that the children would not have to grow up as orphans.

When she got home, the policemen and soldiers had gone, and the fathers had just arrived in the postman's cart. The postman had gotten lost on the way to Stefania's house and had driven the fathers all over town before finally finding the correct address.

Stefania had a job in a factory, and there she met a handsome Polish boy who would often visit her. Stefania liked the boy very much, but she was afraid. How could she possibly know ahead of time how he would respond to her secret? Would he help her hide the 13 Jews who were now living with her? Or would he turn them all in, Stefania included? Stefania had no way of knowing, so although she really liked him, she made a desperate plan to end his visits.

She obtained a photograph of a handsome German officer in a distinctive SS uniform and hung it over her bed. The next time the boy from the factory came to call, he saw the photo and asked Stefania who it was.

"That is my new boyfriend," she said. "I am dating him, and I will stay with him."

The boy was shocked. "You and an SS man?" he asked.

Stefania nodded. The boy stood there for several minutes without saying anything. Then he walked slowly out of the house. As Stefania watched him from the window, she wanted desperately to run after him, to tell him everything, but she didn't. Her heart was broken.

During the final months of the war, an empty building directly across from Stefania's house was converted into a German hospital, and soon the formerly quiet street was swarming with German soldiers, doctors, and nurses. One day, two German soldiers knocked on Stefania's door and read to her from an official-looking document. They said she had been commanded to vacate her home within two hours, as the house was required by the Third Reich. If she didn't comply, she would be killed.

Two hours! How could Stefania possibly find a new home for them all in two hours? There was nothing available anymore, and even if there was, how could 13 Jews possibly leave the house in daylight without anyone noticing?

The Jews pleaded with Stefania to save herself and her sister and leave them to their fate. Stefania refused. She did the only thing she could think of. She prayed. She asked everyone to join her. Each of them followed Stefania's example and knelt down in silent prayer.

Suddenly, Stefania heard the voice again. The voice told her not to leave, that everything would be all right if she stayed. She was told to send the Jews to the hidden room in the attic and then to open the door and the windows and clean her apartment. And she was to sing. Stefania relayed what she had heard to the Jews. They thought she had lost her mind. But since there was no alternative, they did as she asked. Stefania opened the door and the windows and cleaned the house while singing loudly. Neighbors came by, urging her to leave, telling her that "she was too nice, too young, to be dead," but she ignored their warnings.

Right on schedule, an SS man came to the house and found Stefania singing and cleaning. He smiled and told her that she could stay since the Germans only needed part of her house anyway. For the next eight months, two nurses from the hospital and their German boyfriends lived in Stefania's house directly underneath the 13 Jews. The Germans became suspicious once, but the secret room was solidly built, and the Jews remained undetected. Soon, the hospital closed down, and the nurses followed the German army, which was being pushed out of Poland and back into Germany by the Russians.

One day, two Russian soldiers knocked on Stefania's door and asked her if she had any vodka to exchange for chocolate. They told her that the war was nearly over, that the Russians had pushed the Germans back into Germany.

The Jews overheard the conversation and burst into the room, weeping with joy. They were finally free.

After the war, Mrs. Diamant's son Joseph asked Stefania to marry him, and the couple eventually moved to the United States. Stefania received a Righteous Among the Nations medal from Yad Vashem. She died in 2018 at the age of 97.

Stefania (front row, center), Helena (front row, left), and some of the Jews they hid, including Stefania's future husband, Joseph (back row, left). *United States Holocaust Memorial Museum*

★★★ LEARN MORE ★★★

Conscience and Courage by Eva Fogelman (Random House, 1994) contains a lengthy section on Stefania's story.

Hidden in Silence (Lifetime Television, 1996) is a made-for-TV movie about Stefania's rescuing activities.

Rescuers: Portraits of Moral Courage in the Holocaust by Gay Block and Malka Drucker (Holmes & Meier, 1992) contains an interview chapter on Stefania.

PART III
France

NAZI GERMANY INITIATED the invasion of France on May 10, 1940. Six weeks later, on June 22, 1940, France shocked the world by surrendering. The Battle of France was over quickly, even though France's army was larger than Germany's. France had also built a powerful defense fortress called the Maginot Line on its German border after World War I, which French leaders believed would successfully prevent another German invasion.

However, the German blitzkrieg was a powerful and superior way of warfare, never before seen, even by the larger but less prepared French army. And although German forces attacked the Maginot Line in several operations, most of the German army moved around it by invading Belgium and the Netherlands before attacking France along its undefended border. Too many French soldiers were stuck manning the now-useless Maginot Line.

But the main reason for the quick surrender was that the French government and its people did not have the heart for another long war like World War I, which cost over one million French lives. Marshal Petain, a greatly respected general who had become a national hero during World War I, was a central voice calling for the French army to lay down its arms.

The formal surrender of France to Germany occurred, at Hitler's insistence, in the same train car that had been used for the surrender of Germany during World War I. Afterward, Petain quickly established a collaborationist government with the Germans; that is, he openly cooperated with them and did not treat them as the enemy. The Germans officially occupied northern and western France, and Petain had more or less control of the south, which came to be known as Vichy France because the central headquarters were located in the southern town of Vichy. Petain's Vichy government was very anti-Semitic, enacting and enforcing anti-Jewish laws even before the Germans ordered them to. Some French people had no problem with the Vichy government. Others speculated that Petain must be secretly working against the Nazis even as he pretended to collaborate with them.

But many French people were outraged at Petain's attitude. They looked for leadership elsewhere, to French general Charles de Gaulle, one of the few officers who had led his troops to victory several times during the Battle of France. De Gaulle's vocal protests against surrender caused him to fall out of favor with the French military leadership, and he fled to London where he established the Forces Françaises Libres (Free French Forces), or FFL. The FFL trained in Great Britain and fought the Germans in North Africa throughout the war. They were also part of the Allied invasion on D-day. French women who were able to escape to Great Britain joined the women's section of the FFL and generally were assigned supportive roles such as secretarial work or nursing.

De Gaulle broadcast stirring radio messages of Resistance from London directed to any French people who might be listening on their now-illegal radios. At first, the French Resistance was a handful of disconnected people in the northern, occupied section of France doing whatever they could think of: transcribing and distributing de Gaulle's radio speeches, wearing the colors of the French flag, attaching stickers with anti-German slogans in public places, or demonstrating against food shortages caused by the enforced rationing.

But as corruption of the Vichy government became more and more apparent, Resistance activities sprang up all over France and became more organized. A large part of this organization was due to the persuasive efforts of a man named Jean Moulin, a notable hero of the French Resistance. He and his sister, Laure, would often stay up all night decoding secret messages sent to Jean from Resistance groups all over France. Jean was eventually betrayed and died under torture while refusing to give out any information about the many Resistance groups he knew so well.

One type of Resistance group Jean Moulin had worked hard to unite was known as the maquis. The maquis were bands of French resisters who had avoided the forced conscription (draft) into German munitions factories by hiding in rural areas. They were ready and willing to fight the Germans but often lacked supplies. The British and American organizations, the SOE and the OSS, often supported maquis groups by providing them with funds, organization, and ammunition (see chapters on Nancy Wake, page 197; Pearl Witherington, page 204, and Virginia Hall, page 227). Local French women often served as couriers for the maquis and occasionally were allowed to fight alongside them. And many French farming families took great risks (and many were killed) by giving aid, shelter, and food to maquis and SOE and OSS agents.

Another major Resistance activity was espionage (spying). French espionage organizations obtained information regarding

German activities and secreted it to Allied leaders. Others shared their information with the many illegal underground presses that sprang up all over France to educate and inspire Resistance workers. Although few French women had been leaders in France's publishing industry before the war, many of them became heavily involved with the underground French press, not only in distribution but also in the writing and editing of many papers.

Despite rampant French anti-Semitism, there were many Jewish rescue operations in France. During the war, relief organizations such as the Quaker-run American Friends Service Committee were run almost entirely by women. At first, these women worked to relieve the suffering of Jews in Vichy-run concentration camps. Later, they organized rescue operations from those camps. Alice Resch Synnestvedt, one such volunteer, personally escorted at least 300 Jewish children to safety during the war.

Before the war began, French women could not vote. But partly due to their obvious and significant contributions to the French Resistance, they were finally granted suffrage by the French provisional government in 1944.

On August 25, 1944, Paris was liberated by the Allied troops, which included the Free French Forces. All of France was free by September 20, 1944. General Eisenhower, the U.S. leader of the Allied invasion, publicly acknowledged the contributions of the French Resistance when he said, "Throughout France the Resistance had been of inestimable value in the campaign. Without their great assistance the liberation of France would have consumed a much longer time and meant greater losses to ourselves."

Marie-Madeleine Fourcade

"ONLY A WOMAN"

"YOU WILL ORGANIZE the underground side."

Marie-Madeleine couldn't believe her ears. Commandant Georges Loustaunau-Lacau, who was affectionately known to his friends and coworkers as Navarre, had just told her to organize a massive French spy network. Marie-Madeleine knew how important Navarre thought espionage was; she had worked as his main assistant in the publication of a magazine that was devoted to spying. Navarre was convinced that it was the most effective way to win the war he was certain was overshadowing Europe. When Hitler took control of Austria and part of Czechoslovakia—the Sudetenland—in 1938, Navarre's magazine, *L'ordre national*,

Marie-Madeleine Fourcade.
Noah's Ark by Marie-Madeleine Fourcade

reported on all of Hitler's actions and also predicted, quite accurately, what he would do next.

Running *L'ordre national* almost single-handedly for Navarre was one thing; organizing a huge network of spies, mostly men, was an overwhelming thought. "But Navarre," Marie-Madeleine cried, "I'm only a woman!"

"That's another good reason," he replied. "Who will ever suspect a woman?"

Marie-Madeleine continued to protest: "I'm very afraid I won't be able to live up to what you expect of me, Navarre. This job is terrifying. I'm hardly 30, and you're asking me to command hardened old campaigners like yourself. I'd rather serve in the ranks [than be in charge]."

There was a long silence. Navarre stopped walking about the room, sat down at his desk, and began to write something on a piece of paper. Marie-Madeleine looked at the back of his neck. It showed a wound from his recent involvement in the Battle of France. The injury was still unhealed. She thought of the other battles he had fought, some during the previous World War and some that he had not fought with guns but with truth and integrity, battles that had cost him dearly. If she didn't accept this work, would she be giving him another wound?

"You don't think that someone else . . . ?" she began hesitantly.

Without turning around, he replied, "No. I can't trust anyone but you."

Marie-Madeleine took a deep breath. "I'll try not to let you down. I accept."

Navarre turned around and handed her the paper he had been writing on. It contained her orders, and she was to memorize them. They would be used to fight Hitler's occupation of France.

Her first mission was to divide the unoccupied zone of France (the southern region known as Vichy) into sections and to recruit and send agents into these sections. These agents would then watch German troop movements, both on land and sea, and send the information back to headquarters. Navarre would decide which information was important enough to forward to the French Resistance headquarters in London. This network of spies, headed by Navarre and organized by Marie-Madeleine, was called Alliance. (Later, it was called Noah's Ark.)

Marie-Madeleine was starting to feel fairly confident in her work for Alliance when she suddenly discovered that her job title had changed drastically. Navarre had been arrested! He was sentenced to two years in prison by the Vichy government, headed by Marshal Petain. Up until this moment many in France, and even some in Alliance, had believed that Petain might have been secretly working with General de Gaulle, the head of the French Resistance in London, even as he pretended to oppose him. But when Navarre was sentenced to two years in prison, all hope was gone. Some members of Alliance were now confused. Who was the man to be trusted, Petain or Navarre?

★★★ NOAH'S ARK ★★★

The spies in Alliance had code names composed of letters and numbers (such as ASO 43 and PLU 122) that would hide their true identities. One day some of Marie-Madeleine's files, which included some of these code names, fell into enemy hands. While pondering this catastrophe on a train ride, Marie-Madeleine dozed off and dreamily pictured each agent as a particular animal. The very tall agent sitting across from her suddenly became Giraffe. Another agent, who had huge ears, became Elephant. The airmen would all be named after birds; the agents watching the ports would be fish. She named herself Hedgehog. From that time on, Alliance was often referred to as Noah's Ark.

Marie-Madeleine hadn't the slightest doubt about the answer to this question. Petain had condemned General de Gaulle to death and had made a bargain with the Germans. Navarre, on the other hand, she would trust with her life. And now he was putting his trust in her, only in a greater way. She knew exactly what Navarre's trial and sentence meant to her: the work and safety of the Alliance members—3,000 spies—would be on her shoulders for the duration of the war. She would also have sole responsibility for deciding which pieces of information were important enough to send to the French Resistance offices in London. There was no question of stepping down. She was determined to continue the work of Alliance.

The Alliance spies were so numerous and so successful that they eventually came to the attention of the Germans. Many Alliance agents were captured and interrogated, and unfortunately, some of them surrendered information. Names were given out. The Germans were on the lookout for those in high positions in the network; if they could find them and get them to talk, Alliance might be destroyed.

One day a fellow agent, nicknamed Grand Duke ("Night Owl"), visited Marie-Madeleine and warned her that the Nazis were going to make a thorough search of the town for members of the French Resistance on the following day. He asked her where she was hiding all of her communications. When she showed him, he realized that she was holding more than enough evidence to prove she was high in the chain of Alliance command. If this information were found, Marie-Madeleine would certainly be arrested, interrogated, and eventually killed. He urged her to leave with him immediately.

Marie-Madeleine almost thought he was joking. She told him that they had plenty of time, since the raid was not until the following day, and that he should pick her up at eight o'clock the next morning.

Grand Duke agreed to that plan and left. Shortly afterward, Marie-Madeleine heard a commotion in the main entrance of the apartment building; her door was still open. It was the Gestapo, and they were headed right for her apartment! She tried desperately to shut and bolt the door, thinking that it would give her a few minutes to jump out the window and escape into the courtyard. But it was too late. Soon, there were two dozen Gestapo agents in her room, demanding to know where Grand Duke was.

Marie-Madeleine pretended to be angry at this intrusion, and when they asked her why she had tried to shut them out, she answered that if she'd known they were the Gestapo, she would have opened the door right away. She was such a good actress that they nearly believed her. Some of them left to search elsewhere in the building. Marie-Madeleine was hoping that those who remained would not notice her gathering up crucial Alliance messages from the table and throwing them quickly under the couch.

While the Gestapo agents searched her apartment, Marie-Madeleine tried to stay calm, asking them casually what they were hoping to find.

The leader spoke up and described Grand Duke to her. He said Grand Duke was a very important spy in a certain spy organization that they hadn't yet been able to destroy. The name of the spy organization was Alliance.

Marie-Madeleine inwardly froze. She tried very hard to stay calm. The search was almost over, and the Germans were about to leave. Just then, one of them noticed something under the couch. He went down on all fours and pulled out the communications Marie-Madeleine had shoved under there. Marie-Madeleine was immediately arrested.

As she packed her bag for the prison, Marie-Madeleine desperately tried to think of a way to prevent Grand Duke from coming to her apartment the next morning and falling into the trap the Gestapo would surely set for him. There was only one way she could warn him, she thought, as she was driven to the prison. She must escape that night and reach his house before he came to pick her up at the apartment the next morning.

The Germans left her alone in her cell. She looked at the bars that guarded her window. She tried to push her head through gaps. She noticed that her head fit through one gap in the bars but not the rest. She undressed, held her dress in her teeth, and began to push herself out between the widest gap in the bars. First her head went through. Then, one shoulder squeezed through. Squeezing her hips through was extremely painful, but soon she was free and dropped to the ground outside.

"Wer da?" ("Who's there?"), she heard a guard say. She lay flat and still as he flashed his light over the area. When his light flashed off, she crawled away on all fours, put on her dress, and ran. By dawn, she came into the center of the town, where she could hear dogs barking in the distance. Her escape had surely been discovered! All the roads would soon be closed. There was a bridge she needed to cross, but it would now be carefully guarded. How would she be able to warn Grand Duke in time?

She wandered about desperately until she came to a field where some old peasant women were gleaning (gathering grain) just below the bridge she needed to cross. Marie-Madeleine joined them. Out of the corner of her eye, she could see the soldiers on the bridge, pacing back and forth and stopping every woman who tried to cross, demanding identification papers. The soldiers ignored the women in the field below, Marie-Madeleine included. She managed to regain the road farther down, gleaning her way past the bridge and the soldiers.

She arrived at Grand Duke's home just minutes before he left for hers. She had saved him from certain arrest.

Shortly after her escape, Marie-Madeleine met a French man from the area who explained to her the thing that had most puzzled her about her escape from the prison. He told her that when he and his friends built the local prison and the cement that held the bars was still fresh, they would push one of the bars just a little. They called it the bar of freedom.

Marie-Madeleine managed to keep Alliance going strong until the end of the war, providing the Allies with not only invaluable information regarding German troop movements, the location of weapons arsenals, and the nature of the new German *Vergeltungswaffen* ("vengeance weapons")—the V-1 buzz bombs and the V-2 rockets—but also a detailed map showing the locations of German defenses on part of the Normandy coast that the Allies used when they invaded Nazi-occupied France on D-day, June 6, 1944.

After the war, Marie-Madeleine was given numerous awards, including being made a member of the Légion d'honneur by the French government and a member of the Order of the British Empire. She also became a member of the European Parliament. In 1968, she wrote a memoir called *L'Arche de Noé* (Noah's Ark) detailing her work in Alliance.

★★★ LEARN MORE ★★★

Noah's Ark by Marie-Madeleine Fourcade (E. P. Dutton & Co., 1974 English translation).

Women in the Resistance by Margaret L. Rossiter (Praeger Publishers, 1986) contains a section on Marie-Madeleine Fourcade.

Andrée Virot

AGENT ROSE

THE GERMANS WERE coming. Everyone in Brest, a French coastal town in the far northwest province of Brittany, had shut themselves inside their homes. Andrée Virot was inside her beauty salon, filled with a deep sadness. The street outside was absolutely quiet.

Suddenly, loud running footsteps shattered the silence. Andrée ran to the window. French soldiers were trying to escape from the fast-approaching Germans. In their military uniforms, they would certainly be taken prisoner by the Germans. Andrée quickly invited them to hide in her beauty salon. Then she ran from house to house, asking neighbors for men's clothing. Everyone was

Andrée Virot in the early 1940s.
Andrée Virot Peel and Loebertas Publishing

willing to help, and the soldiers were able to go on their way disguised as civilians.

A short time later, a huge number of German troops appeared on the street, making a loud noise with their motorbikes, roughly pushing the people of Brest against the walls so they could parade through. As Andrée watched, a German officer approached her, sneering, and said, in very good French, "This upsets you, does it not? We are the conquerors!"

Andrée didn't realize how precious her freedom or her country had been to her until that day, when she lost both to the Germans. When it became clear that Germans were now going to control everything printed in the newspapers that reached Brest, Andrée realized that the freedom to know the truth was something she especially wanted to fight for. So when she and her friends heard Charles de Gaulle's radio message from London, they decided to copy it down and distribute it in as many places as possible. She then began to help distribute Brest's underground newspaper.

Brest had been the headquarters of the French navy. When the Germans gained control of the town, they used France's ships and submarines for their own plans, so Brest's dockyards were always busy with German military activity. Frenchmen whom the Germans forced to work in the dockyards were able to observe activities and overhear conversations that were important to those trying to fight the Germans.

One day, one of the French dockyard workers passed some important information to Andrée, which included a stolen document. Andrée passed it on to an agent she knew who was working in the French Resistance. One thing led to another, and soon Andrée was working for an agent in London. Her code name was to be Rose, and she was put in charge of one section of the Brittany Bureau of Information, locating and passing on vital information regarding German activities on the coast of Brittany. She, and those working under her, reported on the movements of German troops and sailors, exactly where the Germans were building fortifications on the coast, and how much military equipment was being transported and where.

Allied planes—British and, later, American—began conducting bombing raids against the German navy in Brittany. The bombing

THE SPEECHES OF GENERAL
★★★ CHARLES DE GAULLE ★★★

It is unclear exactly which Charles de Gaulle speech Andrée and her friends copied and distributed. De Gaulle's first speech broadcast from London, *L'Appel du 18 Juin* (the Appeal of June 18), was not widely heard, but his speech of June 22 was. It is possible that Andrée copied either one or both. The following are translated excerpts of both speeches followed by an excerpt from *L'Affiche de Londres* (the Poster of London), which famously summarized de Gaulle's views on the Resistance.

> But has the last word been said? Must hope disappear? Is defeat final? No! . . . Whatever happens, the flame of the French resistance must not be extinguished and will not be extinguished.   —from "The Appeal of June 18"

> I invite all French land, sea and air forces, I invite the engineers and armament workers who find themselves in British territory to unite around me . . . I invite all Frenchmen who wish to remain free to listen to me and follow me.
> Long live free France, with honour and independence!
> —from "The Speech of June 22"

> France has lost a battle! But she has not lost the war!
> —from the Poster of London

was fierce, frequent, and destructive, but the Germans always fought back by attacking these planes with antiaircraft guns, and they were often successful. The downed airmen, if they survived the crash, would then be captured by the Germans and sent to prison camps. That is, if the French people did not find them and hide them first.

Andrée and her team were in charge of rescuing these downed airmen. After hiding or destroying their parachutes, the team would find civilian clothes for the airmen and then locate safe houses where they could hide while escape plans were made. A rescue submarine was sent to the coast one night per month, when the moon was new. It was difficult to avoid being seen by the German guards who were stationed all along the coast, but Andrée, or one of her fellow Resistance workers, would take the airmen to the coast by bicycle. Sometimes they would have to find a hiding place to wait in until dark. Then, the airmen would walk out to the shore, get into the rowboats that had been launched onto the water by the rescue submarine, and row to the submarine.

Andrée and her team also worked in the French province of Normandy. Here they traded important information via planes, which would land in a rectangle of farmland, directed by the team's flashlights. On one of these information exchanges, Andrée received a personal letter of thanks from Winston Churchill that read, "This last mission is the equivalent of a victory on the battlefield!" Andrée was profoundly moved by this note and knew that the Allied invasion of France was near. So she was very disappointed when she was told she must, for security reasons, destroy the note immediately.

A Resistance worker in Brest was captured by the Gestapo and, after being forced to watch members of his family tortured, gave the Gestapo the names of several Resistance workers, including Andrée's. The family of this captured man warned those involved, but Andrée had only hours in which to act. She was told to escape to Paris and join the Resistance there, which she did, disguised as a blonde.

Another agent was captured and, under torture, gave away Andrée's name and address in Paris. On May 10, 1944, Andrée was finally arrested. She was interrogated, brutally tortured, and then put into a cell with other prisoners, where she stayed for several weeks. Just before her second interrogation, she received news that the Allies had landed on the beaches of Normandy several days before. This news gave Andrée so much courage that she managed to fool her interrogators into believing she was no one of importance. And when she got back to her cell, Andrée decided to write the news of the Allied invasion backward on the window of her cell, so that anyone passing by might see it. They did, but, unfortunately, the passersby were German guards. They threw Andrée into a darkened cell and kept her there, alone, for an entire week.

A few days after she was allowed to rejoin the other prisoners, Andrée and the others were packed onto a cattle car. They tried to keep their spirits up by loudly singing the "Marseillaise," the French national anthem. As the trip went on, they noticed that when the train made its occasional stops, French was no longer being spoken, only German. They were on their way to Ravensbruck, the infamous women's concentration camp.

There Andrée and the other prisoners each had a number tattooed on her arm. They were subjected to roll calls in the middle of the night, offered only thin clothing in spite of freezing temperatures, and given little to eat. Often, during the roll calls, which took hours, cartloads of corpses would be carried past them on their way to the crematorium, where the bodies would be burned. Andrée was appalled at the Nazi guards' cruel and inhuman acts, which she witnessed on a daily basis at Ravensbruck. She was amazed that so many Germans were willing, and apparently eager, to treat their fellow humans beings in such unfeeling and cruel ways.

Andrée had made friends with some Polish prisoners who, although they had not been Resistance fighters, had been arrested and brought to Ravensbruck simply because they were Polish. They had been taught perfect French, were very friendly, and enjoyed many conversations with Andrée. Then one day, they saved her life.

During a roll call, a Nazi official was moving slowly through the rows of prisoners, looking at each prisoner intently. He stopped and looked at Andrée for a long moment.

"Take that woman's number," he shouted, lashing at Andrée with his whip, "for the gas chamber!"

A guard came up to Andrée and violently twisted her arm so that he could see the number tattooed on it. He wrote her number on a piece of paper, then walked away and placed the paper on a table containing a pile of similar papers with the numbers of other doomed prisoners. Andrée was filled with a deep sadness. She would never see her family again. She would not live to see France freed from Nazi tyranny.

Suddenly, one of her Polish friends started to crawl on the ground through the rows of prisoners until she reached the table with the papers. She snatched the paper with Andrée's number on it, returned to her place in line, and then ate the paper. Amazingly, none of the guards saw her. Andrée's life was saved.

After being moved to a different camp called Buchenwald, Andrée learned that the Allied armies were now in Germany. She could hear the noises of battle, the sounds of bombarding planes, coming closer and closer. A group of leaflets appeared in the camp with the following message: "Take courage, we are on our way!"

Then one day, an order for a roll call came in the afternoon, which was very unusual. Also unusual was the order to "line up." Andrée realized what it meant: they were going to be shot. The Nazis would attempt to hide from the world what they had done. This was indeed what the guards were planning. They had exchanged their distinctive armbands for those of the Red Cross, hoping to trick the Allies and evade arrest. The firing squad was approaching the prisoners.

Then, suddenly, they turned and ran in the opposite direction. The prisoners soon discovered the reason: one of the prisoners, who understood German, had been hiding under the telephone table and had overheard a call in which a woman said to the commandant of the firing squad, "The Americans are at the gates of the town. We saw you enter the camp to kill the prisoners. If you want to stay alive, spare the lives of these prisoners." The soldiers evidently believed the phone call.

For her work in the French Resistance, which included saving the lives of over 100 Allied servicemen, Andrée received numerous awards from the governments of France, England, and the United States. In 1999 Andrée wrote her memoir, *Miracles Do Happen!*, and in 2008, a British film about her life was released called *Rose: Portrait of a Resistance Fighter*. She died in March 2010 at the age of 104 in the village of Long Ashton, North Somerset, England, where she had made her home for many years.

★★★ LEARN MORE ★★★

Miracles Do Happen! by Andrée Virot Peel (Loebertas, 1999).

"Andrée Marthe Virot Peel" by Marilyn Turkovich
Voices Education Project
http://voiceseducation.org/content/andree-marthe-virot-peel.

"WWII Resistance Fighter Celebrates Her 104th Birthday by Breaking Silence on Wartime Heroics"
British Mail Online
www.dailymail.co.uk/news/article-1134967/WWII-Resistance-fighter-marks-104th-birthday-breaking-silence-wartime-heroics.html.

Josephine Baker

SPY SINGER

A BEAUTIFUL, GLAMOROUS woman at the Italian embassy party was making quite a stir. No one who noticed Josephine Baker laughing, talking, and flirting with the party guests would have suspected for a moment that she was there on a mission as an Allied spy. After a while, she walked casually toward the ladies' room. She had overheard something that might prove to be valuable information. When she was safely in the ladies' room, she quickly wrote down what she had heard and pinned the note to her underwear. Then she went back to the party to once again play the part of a vivacious entertainer. Who would dare even think of searching for evidence of espionage in the undergarments of Josephine

Josephine Baker in the 1940s.
Getty Images

Baker, the famous African American turned Frenchwoman who had taken Paris by storm by dancing skillfully in scanty outfits? Apparently no one.

Josephine Baker was born in St. Louis on June 3, 1906, into extreme poverty. She had very few bright spots in her bleak childhood, but one of them was dancing. She loved to watch the dancers at the Booker T. Washington Theater and tried to mimic all the new dance steps she saw performed there. When she was 10 years old, she won a dance competition put on by a traveling salesman. The prize, and the audience's reaction to her dancing, gave her a purpose: she was going to be a dancer.

In 1917, Josephine lived through an experience that was to shape the rest of her life. Increasing racial tensions in East St. Louis, just across the Mississippi River from St. Louis, caused by the rising black population during World War I, whites' anxiety over losing jobs, irresponsible newspaper stories, and, above all, racism, combined to create violent and destructive race riots. Black homes were destroyed, and white mobs attacked and killed black people while the police watched and did nothing. Some black people tried to fight back, but most of them—about 1,500 in total—fled to St. Louis. Josephine stood by the foot of the bridge, watching them come. She would never forget their panicked and terrified expressions as they rushed desperately across the bridge away from the violent racism that had chased them out.

Josephine eventually found steady work as a dancer. Her dancing was unusual and interesting, an energetic mixture of many different styles that she combined to make her own. She attracted the interest of some touring show producers who were able to offer her more money. She was then noticed by producers for a show that was leaving for Paris. They needed a comedienne and a dancer, and Josephine excelled at both. She was at first a little hesitant about going across an ocean to a strange land, but many things made her want to take the risk. One reason was the racism she experienced in the United States. Another was that she was always ready for an adventure.

When she arrived in Paris, she was shocked to find that the producers wanted her to dance in skimpy outfits, some of which didn't even cover her breasts. She had set her heart on being clothed in long, elegant gowns, not in costumes that only partially covered her body.

But she was eventually convinced. Things were quite different in Paris than they were in the United States. In 1920s Paris, Josephine's dancing and skimpy outfits weren't considered immoral but, rather, artistic and representative of the new Jazz Age. The 1920s were referred to by that name partly because jazz music, which had been created by African Americans, was very popular at the time. Parisians were also interested in the Harlem Renaissance, a cultural movement in New York City that was admired worldwide and that embraced black artists, writers, and music. Because Josephine seemed to embody everything that was beautiful about African Americans, she was an absolute fascination to Parisians. She was the most photographed woman of 1926 and became a symbol of the decade. She inspired writers such as Ernest Hemingway and artists such as Pablo Picasso. She starred in a film called *Zou-Zou*, making her the first black woman to have a leading role in a film. She also developed her singing voice to the extent that she was able to successfully star in an Offenbach operetta called *La Creole*. Because she was highly paid for her dancing and singing, she became extremely wealthy; some believed her to be the richest black woman in the world at the time.

But not everyone approved of Josephine's dancing—or her race. When she went on a European tour in 1928, she performed for many enthusiastic audiences in 25 different countries, and she began to realize how racist some European countries were becoming. In countries that were beginning to embrace Nazi ideology, such as Austria and Germany, many of Josephine's audiences were

openly hostile, sometimes hurling insults and ammonia bombs
onto the stage when she tried to perform. This was partly because
of her skimpy dancing outfits but largely because of her race. Nazi-
run newspapers condemned Josephine not only for her costumes
and wild dancing but also for daring to appear onstage with white
"Aryan" performers.

After her European tour, Josephine always equated Nazism
with racism. One decade later, on November 9, 1938, when the
Nazis destroyed Jewish homes, businesses, and synagogues all over
Germany on the day that would be forever remembered as Kristallnacht (Night of Broken Glass), Josephine decided that she must do
something to fight the Nazis. She joined an organization called the
International League Against Racism and Anti-Semitism.

She was also noticed by the Deuxième Bureau, an organization
of French military intelligence that was part of General de Gaulle's
Free French Forces. The bureau was looking for undercover agents
who could afford to work without pay, especially those who could
travel from place to place easily, obtaining visas without excessive
questioning or arousing suspicions. Josephine was perfect for the
job since, as an entertainer, she always had a reason for traveling.

Jacques Abtey, head of the bureau's military intelligence in
Paris, thought that it was a foolish idea to entrust Josephine Baker
with something as serious as espionage. Not only was she a female
entertainer, but she also seemed to change her relationships with
men almost as frequently as she changed her dancing outfits; she
didn't seem trustworthy to him. But when Abtey interviewed
her she told him, "France has made me what I am. . . . They have
given me everything, especially their hearts. Now, I will give them
mine. Captain, I am ready to give my life for France. You can make
use of me as you will."

Abtey was quickly convinced of her patriotism as well as her
ability to be an excellent agent. He gave her the title of honorable correspondent, and after she had received several weeks of

training in weapons, languages, self-defense, and memory tests, he sent her on her first mission.

Josephine was already a welcome guest at parties given at the Italian embassy. The war hadn't officially started yet, but everyone knew it was coming, and the Allies needed information regarding the possibility of Italy entering the war. Josephine went to several parties at the embassy. No one suspected that the sparkling Josephine Baker was actually listening intently for political information, which she would then relay to Abtey.

Before the Germans invaded Paris, Joseph Goebbels had denounced Josephine as a decadent artist. After the invasion, the Germans passed a law that expressly forbade the performance of black or Jewish entertainers. However, none of this mattered to Josephine. As soon as the Germans set foot in France, she vowed that she would never perform in her beloved adopted country as long as even one Nazi remained.

She left Paris for her chateau, a large rural home in southern France that she had named Les Milandes. The chateau was far from the northern, occupied section of France, which made it useful to the Resistance. It was a stop-off for Resistance workers, a safe house for refugees needing a place to hide, and was also used for storing weapons. One day, five German officers arrived at Les Milandes, demanding to search the house. One of them said, "We are informed, madame, that you are hiding weapons in your chateau. What do you have to say to that?"

Josephine replied, "I think that monsieur l'officier cannot be serious. It is true that I had Red Indian grandparents, but they hung up their tomahawks quite a while ago now, and the only dance I've never taken part in is the war dance." The Germans believed her story and left.

However, it was obvious that Les Milandes was being watched and that Josephine needed to leave. Her superiors at the Deuxième Bureau decided that she and Abtey should travel together to gather information and make contact with the Resistance in places such as Spain, Portugal, and North Africa. Josephine would give performances, and Abtey would pose as her secretary under a false name. Josephine attended many parties, always keeping her ears open, and Abtey took note of German military activity. They used invisible ink to record everything in the margins of Josephine's sheet music.

In June 1941, while in North Africa, Josephine became dangerously sick with a consecutive series of illnesses and was forced to stay in a clinic in Casablanca until December 1942. When she finally felt strong enough to perform again, she began to entertain the Allied troops—which now included soldiers from the United States—who were stationed in North Africa, often traveling to two or three locations per day without pay and in extremely difficult and dangerous conditions. Sandstorms were frequent, water was scarce, wild animals were plentiful, and German gunfire was constant; Josephine had to duck airplane bullets during a show more than once.

Because Josephine was part of the Resistance, she knew more than most other wartime entertainers about immediate war plans. "Often I knew the men would be sent into battle before they knew," she said later of her experiences entertaining Allied troops in North Africa. "To see them in front of me so full of life and enthusiasm, and knowing that many of them wouldn't come back alive, was the hardest part of the tour."

It was in North Africa that Josephine was reminded of the racism that was still rampant in the United States. Before her shows began, she noticed that the white soldiers were always seated in the front and the black soldiers in the back. She refused to perform until the seating was desegregated. It usually was.

For her efforts during the war, Josephine became the first American-born woman to receive the Croix de Guerre (Cross of War). She also received the Légion d'honneur (Legion of Honor) and the Rosette of the Resistance, and was made a member of the Forces Françaises Libres. She was wearing the FFL uniform when she spoke at the March on Washington for Jobs and Freedom, August 28, 1963, just before Dr. Martin Luther King Jr. delivered his stirring "I Have a Dream" speech.

Josephine Baker died in 1975, at the age of 68, four days after having performed in a highly acclaimed musical revue in Paris that celebrated her 50 years in entertainment. At her funeral, she received full military honors from the French government.

★★★ LEARN MORE ★★★

Haney, Lynn, *Naked at the Feast: The Biography of Josephine Baker* (Robson Books: London, 1995).

Wood, Ean. *The Josephine Baker Story* (Sanctuary Press: United Kingdom, 2000).

Magda Trocmé

WIFE, MOTHER, TEACHER, RESCUER

MAGDA TROCMÉ, the wife of the Protestant pastor André Trocmé, lived with her family in the small French village of Le Chambon-sur-Lignon. She was cooking dinner one evening when she heard a knock at the door. Who could it be at that time of day? When she opened the door, she saw a woman covered with snow, shivering with fear and cold. The woman asked if she could come in. Magda guessed that the woman must be a Jew. She also knew that it was illegal to hide or help Jews.

It was the winter of 1940. Just months before, German troops had victoriously entered France, occupying the northern and western section and allowing the southern section, known as Vichy

André and Magda Trocmé with their children in the late 1930s.
Trocmé family collection

France, to govern itself under German authority. Vichy France was very anti-Semitic, and the swift laws enacted against the Jews proved that point painfully. French Vichy officials aggressively began to round up all Jews in France, beginning with Jews of other nationalities and then moving on to Jewish French citizens, placing them all in internment camps (temporary camps) before eventually transferring them permanently to concentration camps where they were sure to die.

This horrible news quickly spread, reaching all 12 villages of the Vivarais-Lignon Plateau in southern France, including the little village of Le Chambon-sur-Lignon. The two Protestant pastors of that village, André Trocmé and Edouard Theis, began a series of sermons, preaching from the Bible stories of the Good Samaritan and the Sermon on the Mount. They strongly encouraged their congregation to make Le Chambon-sur-Lignon a "city of refuge" (based on the biblical Israelite cities of refuge) for any Jews. The Resistance work of the village was to be civil disobedience only, distinctly non-violent, in keeping with the pacifism (a philosophy of opposition to any type of violent action) embraced by both Trocmé and Theis.

Most of the villagers living on the Vivarais-Lignon Plateau, including those in Le Chambon-sur-Lignon, were naturally empathetic to the endangered Jews. Most of them were descended from the Huguenots, the first Protestants in Catholic France who had been cruelly persecuted for their faith. Pastor Trocmé's congregation listened to his sermons and heartily believed that they could make Le Chambon a haven for the Jews.

And so, when a freezing, frightened woman appeared at Magda Trocmé's door, Magda's response was quick and firm: "Well, come in!" She didn't need her husband's sermons to convince her to help this woman, but because she supported his work in every way, it gave her even more of a reason to help. Her own religious convictions were quite different from André's. Her beliefs focused not so much on devotion to God as much as a dedication to assist anyone in need. She'd always had a passion for helping people, a passion that had led her to attend the New York School of Social Work as a young woman.

When André first met Magda while he was attending Union Theological Seminary in New York, he was struck not so much by her beauty or intelligence, both of which she had in abundance, but by her simple concern for others. When a group of students was leaving for an outing in Washington, DC, André heard Magda tell one of the young men to take his sweater so he wouldn't get sick from the cold weather.

Whether it was protecting a college friend from the cold or attending to this German Jew who was shivering and fleeing for her life, Magda wanted to help people. She sat the woman down by the fire, gave her some food, dried her wet shoes in the oven, and then went out to try to get the woman some help.

But when she asked the town's mayor for assistance, he strongly discouraged Magda from protecting the woman. Magda was too

THE RESCUE OPERATIONS OF THE
★★★ VIVARAIS-LIGNON PLATEAU ★★★

Le Chambon-sur-Lignon was not the only village on the Vivarais-Lignon Plateau to hide Jews, and André Trocmé was not the only pastor in the area who strongly encouraged his congregation to do so. There were 11 other pastors and thousands of individuals living on the plateau who were involved with Jewish rescue and who made the area one of the most successful rescue operations of Word War II. But André Trocmé was certainly a leader of the movement and the catalyst who initiated much of the rescue operation for the entire plateau.

concerned about doing right to be worried about her own danger, and she also knew that many of the other villagers were probably hiding Jews. But she realized that by telling the unsympathetic mayor about the woman, she had just jeopardized the woman's life. The woman must, unfortunately, leave for her own safety.

Magda returned to the parsonage, horrified to see that the woman's shoes were now burnt. After scouring the village for another pair, she gave the woman directions to another refuge outside of Le Chambon-sur-Lignon where she was sure there was shelter. Then Magda sent her on her way.

Although she did all she could do for the woman, the destiny of that first refugee who had knocked on her doorstep haunted Magda for the rest of her life. How could she possibly know if the woman had made it to safety?

Magda quickly learned whom she could and could not trust, and slowly but surely the parsonage—and the entire village—was buzzing with refugee work. A number of refugees lived at the parsonage, some longer than others, and Magda was also part of the busy network that continually sought hiding places for the steady stream of refugees pouring into Le Chambon-sur-Lignon. She had four of her own children to care for, plus four student boarders who were attending the school that her husband and Edouard Theis had founded in 1938. She was also a full-time teacher of Italian at the school, which was providing an education for the many refugee children now in the village.

Magda was often so exhausted that she was unable to sit down and eat. Her daughter Nelly recalls that she would occasionally perforate the shell of a raw egg and suck the egg out, just to keep from fainting. But Magda's stress was self-imposed; she willingly accepted her many duties and would have done nothing different. She explained it this way: "I never close my door, never refuse to help somebody who comes to me and asks for something. This I think is my kind of religion. When things happen, not things that

I plan, but things sent by God or by chance, when people come to my door, I [feel] responsible."

If the activities of Le Chambon-sur-Lignon were becoming well known to outside rescue organizations, they couldn't possibly be hidden from the local Vichy police. One day a Vichy official demanded from André Trocmé the names of all the Jews he knew were hidden in Le Chambon-sur-Lignon. André refused, telling him that the Jews were his brothers. He said, "We don't know Jews, we only know men." The official then threatened André with imprisonment.

A few months later, in the late afternoon, there was a knock on the door of Magda and André's home, the parsonage. Visitors were far from unusual at the busy parsonage, but the two adult Jews living in the house went to hide before Magda answered the door, most likely on Magda's orders. When she opened it, she saw two gendarmes (French local police officers) standing there. They asked her if André was at home. He was not, but she invited them to sit down and wait for his return. Since it was dinnertime, she invited the gendarmes to eat dinner with the family, as was customary in the parsonage.

How could Magda bear to be so hospitable to two men who were certainly there to take her husband to prison, perhaps to his death? Her answer is this: "We always said, 'sit down' when somebody came [at mealtime]. Why not say it to the gendarmes?" In this surprising gesture, Magda was embodying the Christian ideals that André had preached the day after France signed the armistice with Germany years before: "The duty of Christians is to use the weapons of the Spirit to resist . . . violence . . . without fear, but also without pride and without hatred."

When André arrived home, the gendarmes allowed him to pack a suitcase and then led him away with Edouard Theis and Roger Darcissac, the head of the public school. Many people from the village came to bid them good-bye, singing the Protestant hymn "A Mighty Fortress Is Our God." André might have been filled with many worries as he drove off with the gendarmes that night, but he was unshakably confident of one thing: he knew that the rescue operation of Le Chambon-sur-Lignon would continue without him—that his wife and each villager would continue the work that he and Edouard had started, even if they both died in prison. The work did continue, and in the end the little village of Le Chambon-sur-Lignon and the neighboring communities on the Vivarais-Lignon Plateau managed to rescue approximately 5,000 refugees, including approximately 3,500 Jews.

André and Magda both survived the war. They became co-secretaries of the Mouvement International de la Réconciliation, the European branch of the Fellowship of Reconciliation—a pacifist organization they had both belonged to for years—lecturing and traveling extensively for the Fellowship. Later, they moved to

A postcard from a photograph taken during the war of the Vivarais-Lignon Plateau.
Trocmé family collection

Geneva, Switzerland, where Magda taught high school Italian and Italian-French translations at the School of Interpreters at the University of Geneva, and where André again became a pastor.

Decades after the war, members of Yad Vashem became aware of the rescue operation in Le Chambon-sur-Lignon and wanted to honor André Trocmé with their Righteous Among the Nations award. André didn't understand why he would be singled out when so many other people, including Magda, had been responsible for the rescue operation on the plateau. "Why me?" he asked, "and why not my wife, whose behavior was much more heroic than mine?" Yad Vashem responded several years later by granting Magda the designation too, as well as many other individual villagers from the Vivarais-Lignon Plateau. Yad Vashem also recognized all who had participated in the rescuing activities on the plateau by erecting in their honor an engraved stone in Jerusalem. Former refugees placed a bronze memorial plaque on a public building near the village church in Le Chambon-sur-Lignon.

★★★ LEARN MORE ★★★

Angels and Donkeys: Tales for Christmas and Other Times by André Trocmé, translated by Nelly Trocmé Hewitt (Good Books, 1969). André Trocmé told these stories to the children in his and Magda's home village of Le Chambon-sur-Lignon.

Hidden on the Mountain: Stories of Children Sheltered from the Nazis in Le Chambon by Karen Gray Ruelle and Deborah Durland Desaix (Holiday House, 2006).

I Will Never Be Fourteen Years Old: Le Chambon-sur-Lignon and My Second Life by Francois Lecomte, translated by Jaques P. Trocmé (Beach-Lloyd Publishers, 2009).

Marthe Hoffnung

"DO I LOOK LIKE A SPY?"

MARTHE HOFFNUNG was born in 1920 into a large, close-knit, devout Jewish family in the northeastern French city of Metz, just 30 miles from the German border. Metz, and its province Lorraine, had been part of Germany before the First World War. Its older citizens spoke German, while the younger generation, including Marthe and her siblings, were fluent in both French and German.

The family's lives changed forever when Nazi Germany invaded France. To protect the citizens of Metz, local officials ordered them to move west to Poitiers. They were still there in June 1940 when France surrendered. The Germans stationed in

Marthe's identity card, 1943.
Behind Enemy Lines: The True Story of a French Jewish Spy in Nazi Germany *by Marthe Cohn with Wendy Holden, courtesy of Marthe Cohn*

Poitiers seemed anxious to please the French civilians—except the Jews, that is. Anti-Semitic laws became increasingly intense as the occupation continued. Each evening, the Jewish homes in Poitiers were visited by SS officers, checking to see if the families were keeping the curfew.

On June 17, 1942, SS officers appeared at the Hoffnung home as the family had gathered together for dinner.

The head officer spoke. "Which one is Stephanie?" he asked.

Stephanie, one of Marthe's sisters who was very sick, stood up. "I am," she said quietly.

"You're under arrest," said the officer, as he grabbed her by the arm and took her out of the house.

The family soon discovered Stephanie's "crime": the family had been part of a rescue network for non-French Jews who were being rounded up and placed in prison camps. Stephanie had sent a ration coupon to a farm in the network, and it had been traced back to her.

Gestapo officers tried to force Stephanie to incriminate the people who had been found with the envelope. When she refused, she was transferred from the local jail to an internment camp where she was allowed one weekly visit from one person.

Marthe created an escape plan for her sister, but Stephanie wanted to remain in the camp. She was a medical student and was giving hope and medical assistance to her fellow prisoners, especially the children. Plus, she reminded Marthe, if she managed to escape, the Germans would certainly arrest the whole Hoffnung family.

Marthe knew she was right. She also knew that her family had to leave the occupied zone for the south, the so-called free zone. Yet she was torn; there were so many reasons for Marthe to stay in the north. Stephanie, for one. Jacques Delaunay, for another. He was a non-Jewish medical student to whom Marthe had become engaged the previous year.

At first, Jacques didn't want Marthe to go. "What about you and me?" he asked.

But he quickly understood that it was exactly what Marthe should do. "You have to leave," he said. "I can't stand by and see you treated this way."

He promised to write every day. Then the Hoffnungs were off.

They arrived safely in the south, where they eventually heard, via letters from Jacques, that Stephanie had been moved to different camps within France before her deportation to an unknown location. Marthe and her family were frantic with worry. But Marthe decided to do what she could to be useful: she finished the nurse training course she had started before fleeing the north.

In July 1943, Jacques and Marthe met in Paris, where Jacques gave her some chilling news. He had joined a band of resisters—five students, including his brother, Marc. They had engaged in sabotage and had killed a French collaborator.

Terrified for his safety, Marthe urged him to flee to Spain, but Jacques refused. He wanted to wait and escape with the other resisters.

After returning home, Jacques, Marc, and their three friends were arrested, tortured horribly, and executed.

Marthe's hatred for the Nazis and their French collaborators had been growing throughout the occupation, but now it reached new heights. By the time the Allies had liberated Paris in August 1944, she had one thought on her mind: to avenge Jacques's death and Stephanie's deportation by joining the French army, which was now fighting the Germany army in Alsace and Lorraine, two French provinces that Nazi Germany had annexed.

But how? She didn't have the required documents. Her identity papers were all forged.

Her answer came through Jacques's mother. When French army and resistance leaders asked Mrs. Delaunay, the mother of two resistance heroes, if there was anything they could do for her, she told them that she wanted Marthe to be accepted into the French army.

Now a registered nurse, Marthe was first given a social work position. But three weeks later, when her superior officer discovered by chance that Marthe spoke fluent German, he asked if she would be willing to do intelligence work behind enemy lines. Because the Germans were still fighting fiercely, he said, defending themselves and their country, the French army was eager to find undercover agents to assess the position, strength, and type of German troops in any given area, so that the Allies could quickly defeat them and end the war.

Marthe agreed immediately, and her training soon began. She had to memorize all the different types of German uniforms, ranks, equipment, and ammunition. She had to distinguish between Gebirgsjäger (mountain troops), Fallschirmjäger (parachute troops), the Waffen SS (SS troops), and the Panzerkorp Großdeutschland (tank troops). The French army would respond differently to these different troops, so it was very important that Marthe could identify them, even from a distance.

To explain why she would be traveling alone throughout the war-ravaged country, Marthe created a false identity, complete with a detailed background story. She would say that she was Martha Ulrich, a German nurse who was searching for her fiancé, a soldier named Hans. Martha was especially desperate to find her fiancé because she was an only child and had lost both parents in an Allied bombing raid.

Whenever she had information, Marthe was to visit her contacts: an antifascist German family who lived on a farm near the Swiss border. The oldest daughter's husband, who had been born and raised in Alsace, was a member of French military intelligence, and he would be responsible for relaying Marthe's reports to his superiors.

When she finished her training, a Swiss intelligence officer known only as "Monsieur le maire" (French for "Mr. Mayor") took Marthe to a spot near the German-Swiss border. After giving her instructions, he let her go, telling her he would wait until she crossed.

Marthe crawled through a huge field and then hid behind some bushes as she watched two heavily armed German soldiers criss-crossing each other, guarding the border. She had been told to approach the guard on the right when he turned and before he met up with the other guard on the road.

She waited for the right moment. It came. But Marthe couldn't move. She was paralyzed by fear. Le maire was certainly watching her at this very moment. What would he think if she didn't start moving? He would consider her a coward. And all her training would have been for nothing.

Then she remembered something one of her superior officers had once told her: "There will be times when you have to reach deep within you to find courage." She thought of Stephanie, who had gone to prison rather than betray anyone. She thought of Jacques, how he had died for doing what was right. Those two had chosen their moments to be heroes. Now it was Marthe's turn.

She picked up her suitcase, brushed the dirt off her clothes, and walked toward the road. She strode up to the guard, raising her arm in the Nazi salute.

"Heil Hitler!" she said.

Clearly surprised to see her, the guard returned her salute and then asked Marthe for her papers. Marthe had noticed his slight limp. He seemed old and tired and apparently didn't have the energy to be suspicious. He let her go.

Marthe knocked on the door of her first contact. It was the home of a German family named Schmidt who didn't know her real mission and who had never met her. Marthe had with her a

letter of recommendation from a doctor named Mueller who was
known and respected in the area, but who was secretly working
for the Allies.

A woman named Ilse answered the door. She was surprised
to see a stranger but, after reading the letter from Dr. Mueller,
allowed Marthe in with genuine friendliness.

In the morning, though, Ilse's manner had become oddly cold.
The Schmidts had been warned about spies being in the area, she
said, and after thinking about it, Marthe's torn stockings made her
wonder if she too was a spy. Had she crawled through some bushes
on her way across the border?

Marthe laughed. "Look at me, Frau Schmidt. Do I look like a
spy?"

Ilse looked at the petite blonde woman before her and suddenly
found the idea hilarious; from that moment on, she seemed to
believe Marthe's false story wholeheartedly.

Then Marthe got to work. She took public transportation whenever possible, and during one bus ride she couldn't help but overhear a German Wehrmacht officer describing the mass murders of
Russian and Polish Jews to a group of laughing German women.

Marthe had to get off the bus in order not to throw up at his
descriptions. But after walking for a few hours, she saw something
that almost made her heart stop beating: "Spread out like a vast toy
army, was a huge military encampment with men and trucks and
armor, all openly on display."

She made a mental note of everything she saw, including all the
landmarks in the area, then walked to the home of her contacts,
where she was greeted warmly by Greta, the married daughter.
Marthe wrote up her report, gave it to Greta's husband, and went
back to continue her work.

As Marthe cycled throughout the chaos and disintegration of
Nazi Germany, always making mental notes for her reports, one
day she noticed a large group of German ambulances on a moun-

tain road. She cycled up to the medics who were standing there. A senior medical officer asked where she was headed. She said she was on her way to visit family friends. Marthe wanted to ask him why there were so many ambulances in one spot, but she knew she couldn't do so without the possibility of raising his suspicions.

However, the bored medical officer, who was apparently enjoying Marthe's company, just started telling her. He said they were headed for Switzerland, adding, "There's a little surprise awaiting the French in the Black Forest."

"Ah," said Marthe, grinning and nodding. "A little surprise. I like surprises."

Thousands of German soldiers, he said, were hiding in the Black Forest, waiting to ambush the Allied armies. Then, without even being asked for details, he gave Marthe the exact location.

Marthe chatted with him a bit longer, then shook his hand and left, her mind spinning. She needed to get this information to French intelligence as quickly as possible. It was already midafternoon, and she would have to cycle approximately 90 miles.

After five hours of biking, she was too exhausted and hungry to continue, so she stopped at a restaurant. It was run by pro-Nazis. While Marthe devoured her soup, the owners asked her, in a suspicious manner, why she was in the area. Marthe again became Martha Ulrich and repeated her often-practiced lies. Her false tears for her lost fiancé seemed to melt their suspicions. They even helped her catch a ride with a convoy of German soldiers, who took her and her bike onto one of their wagons.

She reached the farmhouse just hours after Greta's husband had left. Marthe would have to get the message to French intelligence herself. There wasn't even enough time to code it. She would take it to the Swiss border guards, and they would have to get it to the proper authorities.

Greta tried to talk her out of doing this. The German and Swiss border posts were so close together that there was the dangerous possibility Marthe would be caught, the uncoded report in her pocket.

Marthe would not be dissuaded. She spent the night writing up the report, then left the farm first thing in the morning, eventually getting it into the hands of a Swiss border guard, who promised to deliver it. When he learned that Marthe was immediately returning to Germany, he clicked his heels together and saluted her.

Marthe didn't waste time wondering about the eventual outcome of her work. She just kept doing it. But when she heard, a short time later, that Germany had surrendered, and that the war in Europe was over, she couldn't bring herself to join the festivities. Jacques was dead, Stephanie was still missing, and the rest of her family was scattered across France.

"I dutifully joined in the celebrations with the regiment," she wrote later, "listened to the fine speeches and the congratulatory telegrams, but inside I felt dazed, as if I were a spectator to it all and not a participant."

As she continued her intelligence work after the war, trying to locate items stolen from France, Marthe began to encounter "strange groups of people . . . men and women—little more than skeletons—barefoot or in rough wooden clogs and grey striped pajamas. . . . Their bodies were wasted, unclean and unshaved, and their dark-rimmed eyes peered out of their gray faces blankly, as if they'd forgotten how to focus."

They were concentration camp survivors, and as they told Marthe their stories, her heart filled with dread for Stephanie. Until that moment, she hadn't understood the real purpose of the camps where her sister had been imprisoned.

Years later, the family finally learned that Stephanie had been sent to Auschwitz. They never found a death record but realized by then that she couldn't possibly have survived. Stephanie was the only one of Marthe's immediate family to have died, but 29 of her other relatives also perished in the Holocaust.

The French government awarded Marthe the Croix de Guerre, and she left French intelligence in January 1946. She spent time working as a military nurse in Indochina and then returned to France, where she helped her brother Fred run their family store and continued working as a nurse. Marthe then moved to Switzerland to live with her married sister Cecile and further her nursing education. While taking English lessons there, Marthe met an American medical student named Major Lloyd Cohn. They were married in 1958 in the United States.

In 1998, Marthe traveled back to France and requested to see her military records. She was then awarded the Médaille Militaire. Later she was also awarded the title of Chevalier of the Order of the Légion d'Honneur and the German Verdienstkreuz—the Cross of Merit.

Her memoir was published in 2002, and a French and English documentary about Marthe called *Chichinette—How I Accidentally Became a Spy* came out in 2019.

Marthe lives in Palos Verdes, California, but travels around the world, talking about her wartime experiences.

★★★ LEARN MORE ★★★

"The 4'11" Jewish Woman Who Entered the Lion's Den to Spy on Nazi Germany" by Alex Suskind, *Times of Israel*, September 17, 2017, www.timesofisrael.com/the-411-jewish-woman-who -entered-the-lions-den-to-spy-on-nazi-germany.

Behind Enemy Lines: The True Story of a French Jewish Spy in Nazi Germany by Marthe Cohn with Wendy Holden (Three Rivers, 2002).

PART IV
The Netherlands

ON THE EVENING of May 9, 1940, Netherlanders heard Hitler give a speech over Dutch radio saying that they had nothing to fear from the impending rumors of war. As a reward for the Netherlands' neutrality during World War I, Hitler promised that he would not invade the country.

But several hours later, in the early morning of May 10, they realized that Hitler's promise was a lie: his troops simultaneously invaded France, Belgium, Luxembourg, and the Netherlands. Dutch defenses were thrown into confusion when Germans parachuted in, disguised as Dutch soldiers. Rumors about German disguises grew wilder and wilder and distracted the Dutch troops. Dutch police stopped as many people as possible at certain checkpoints, asking them to pronounce certain words that would identify them as either Dutch or German.

But no matter how many imposters the Dutch police caught, the Germans kept coming. The Dutch army put up a strong defense for a small country that had not been well prepared for war. For five days they fought the Nazi blitzkrieg until Hitler, surprised and impatient with the delay, ordered the entire city of Rotterdam to be destroyed with massive bombing in the middle of the day. Hundreds were killed (many of them schoolchildren) and thousands left homeless. When the Germans threatened to destroy other Dutch cities in a similar manner, the Dutch army finally surrendered.

Many Dutch people initially felt betrayed when they discovered that Queen Wilhelmina had escaped to Great Britain during the invasion. But then they realized that she had taken the royal treasury with her, which the Germans had hoped to use to fund the Nazi war machine. From England, Queen Wilhelmina was able to send regular radio broadcasts to the Dutch people—at least to those who had not turned in their now-illegal radios to the Germans—telling them the truth about the war, giving them direction, and encouraging them not to give up hope.

Queen Wilhelmina
of the Netherlands.
Getty Images

Many German Jews had fled to the Netherlands during the 1930s because there was very little anti-Semitism there. But when Hitler invaded the Netherlands, many of these German Jews immediately committed suicide. Laws against Jews, stripping them of their rights, were enacted several months into the occupation.

Dutch men were promised good wages if they would work in German munitions factories. Some did, only to discover that the promise of high wages was a lie and that working conditions were horrible. Many Dutch men soon became *onderduikers* (literally "under-divers"), those who went into hiding or changed their identities. When Dutch men refused to volunteer for work in munitions factories, the Germans began conducting frequent and random roundups with help from members of the NSB.

The German occupiers made all Dutch political parties illegal except for the Nationaal-Socialistische Beweging (Dutch Nationalist Socialist party), or the NSB. The members of the NSB openly collaborated with the Nazi occupiers. Anxious to prove their loyalty to the Nazi party, they were often more cruel and violent than the Germans were.

In February 1941, NSB members began to commit acts of violence against the Jews living in Amsterdam. Street fighting broke out between Jewish defense groups and the NSB that culminated in hundreds of Jewish men being arrested and sent to concentration camps.

Angry about the treatment of the Jews in Amsterdam, Dutch workers and the Dutch Communist Party organized a general strike in Amsterdam on February 25, 1941, which became known as the February Strike. Public transportation shut down, as did factories, shops, businesses, and schools. Workers stormed into the streets shouting, "Strike! Strike! Strike!" The surprised Germans quickly stopped the February Strike, but not before it had spread to several other areas. Many of those who had participated were arrested and deported to Germany, but those who remained wanted to do more to fight the Germans.

Many Dutch Resistance workers hid Jews, *onderduikers*, and Allied airmen whose planes had gone down. Others joined espionage groups that collected information important to the Allies regarding German activity in the Netherlands. Some worked on newspapers that published lists of traitors, transcripts of the Queen's radio addresses, and photographs of the royal family, all illegal possessions in the Nazi-occupied Netherlands. Others worked with groups engaged in sabotage against the Nazi occupiers and the members of the NSB. And others stole extra ration cards for those hiding refugees and created false identification cards for anyone whose real identity was in trouble with the Germans (Hannie Schaft and Diet Eman both used different identities during the occupation, see pages 122 and 114).

The Resistance gained more workers after the Germans tried to force all Dutch university students to sign a loyalty pledge to Nazi Germany in the spring of 1943. Students who refused to sign the pledge were not allowed to continue their studies and were ordered to work in German munitions factories. Eighty percent of Dutch university students refused to sign, and many of them joined the Resistance.

During the autumn of 1944, the Germans were being pushed out of the Netherlands by the Allies, but they maintained their grip on the western section. During the occupation, the Germans had shipped much of the Netherlands' plentiful stores of food and fuel to Germany. A railroad strike had been ordered earlier by the Dutch government in England because Dutch leaders thought the Allies were going to liberate all of the Netherlands sooner than they actually did. The Germans responded to the strike by forbidding food transports to the western part of the country for many months. As a result, the winter of 1944–45—a particularly cold one—became known as *hongerwinter* (the hunger winter) in this area. Dutch people there spent most of their time in a desperate search for food and fuel. The Germans also shut off electricity and running water. Before the Allies were finally able to drop food supplies in April 1945, at least 20,000 Dutch people had starved to death.

By May 5, 1945, all of the Netherlands had been liberated, mostly by Canadian troops. May 5 is annually celebrated in the Netherlands as Bevrijdingsdag (Liberation Day) to commemorate the official end of the German occupation.

Diet Eman

COURIER FOR THE DUTCH RESISTANCE

ON MAY 10, 1940, 20-year-old Diet Eman woke to what sounded like someone beating a rug with a *mattenklopper* (rug beater). But she suddenly realized that it was the middle of the night and that the "pop-pop-pop" sound was coming much too fast to be a Dutch housewife doing her chores.

Diet ran to join her father and mother, who were already standing outside in front of their house. In the night sky they could see an airplane battle. They ran back into the house and turned on the radio. It was true: Hitler had invaded the Netherlands, only a few hours after promising over Dutch radio that he wouldn't. They were at war with Nazi Germany.

Diet Eman, 1940.
Diet Eman

In spite of the danger, the next day Diet decided to bicycle to work at the bank as usual. She was surprised when she was stopped on the street by a Dutch policeman, who ordered her to slowly speak the words *Scheveningen* and *schapenscheerder*. The Dutch police were trying to weed out Germans posing as Dutch, who most likely would not be able to pronounce those Dutch words.

But no matter how many phony Dutchmen the police were able to find, the Germans kept coming. After five days of defensive fighting, and after the city of Rotterdam was bombed to the ground, the Netherlands surrendered to Germany.

When Diet first saw the German soldiers goose-stepping (marching in an ultramilitaristic way particular to the Nazis) into her city, The Hague, she vowed not to speak a word of German as long as the Germans remained, even though she could speak it fluently. She also stopped socializing with Dutch friends whose families were eager to entertain German soldiers in their homes, homes that were now decorated with portraits of Hitler.

But Diet wanted to do more than avoid the German language and Nazi sympathizers. She and her fiancé, Hein Sietsma, formed a Resistance group with some friends. At first, they just listened to the forbidden BBC broadcasts together and spread what they heard to as many people as they could. But when the Nazis began to enact laws against Dutch Jews, Diet's Resistance work began in earnest.

She had a Jewish friend named Herman, who, because of a new Nazi edict, was not allowed to visit Diet's family anymore because of his race. When Herman was ordered to report to the train station with other Jews so that they could all be "relocated" in the east, he asked Diet what he should do. When Diet asked Hein, Hein reminded her that many German Jews had committed suicide when Hitler had conquered the Netherlands. They obviously knew that the promises of relocation were a lie. Herman must hide. But where?

Hein said that he knew of many famers in an area of the Netherlands called the Veluwe who would be willing to hide Herman. Herman then asked Diet and Hein if they could also find a place for Herman's fiancée, his mother, and his sister. News spread quickly that there were hiding places in the Veluwe and that Diet and Hein were taking people there. Within two weeks Diet and Hein were trying to find safe places for 60 people among the farmers of the Veluwe.

Soon Hein and Diet were both busy with Resistance work, usually apart from each other. Diet would deliver false identification papers and extra ration cards to whoever needed them, whether they were on a farm or in the city. There was one very small apartment in The Hague, rented by a middle-aged woman named Mies, which was being used to hide 27 Jews, an incredibly dangerous number. Even in the country, which was much safer than the bustling, populous city, there were never that many Jews hidden in one place. Diet regularly delivered extra ration cards to Mies but warned her repeatedly that it was just a matter of time before they were all discovered. Mies allowed Diet to move some of the Jews out of the apartment and into safer locations, but the next time Diet visited, Mies had taken in more Jews.

For her own safety, Diet decided to always phone the apartment before knocking at the door, to avoid being arrested herself. One day when Diet called, a strange man's voice answered the phone. Diet hung up and tried again. Again, the man answered. After calling a third time and hearing the same voice, Diet went to the grocery store across the street from the apartment. Surely, if the Gestapo had raided the apartment, people in the store would be talking about it.

They were. Mies and all the Jews she had been hiding were now in the hands of the Gestapo. Mies had not only made the mistake of hiding too many Jews in her apartment, she had also kept a daily journal that included detailed descriptions of Diet's visits.

Diet had given herself the code name Toos for safety's sake, and the Gestapo soon connected the dots between the Toos of Mies's journal entries and Diet. It was no longer safe for Diet to go home.

She soon found refuge at a farm named Watergoor just west of Nijkerk, Gelderland. It was run by Aalt and Alie Lozeman, who used their farm to hide downed Allied pilots, *onderduikers*, and Jews. Some of the Watergoor guests, such as the Allied pilots, stayed only temporarily on their way out of the country, but others were permanent residents. Now Diet was one of these, and she had a new identity—Willie van Daalen.

Diet's outward reason for staying with the Lozemans was to help Alie with the farmwork, and she did help whenever she was there, but she was usually on the road doing Resistance work. She traveled to and from all the farms in the Gelderland area that were hiding Jews, delivering ration cards and false ID cards. A man who was involved in collecting military information for the Dutch Resistance and the Allies asked Diet if she would help him collect this information while she traveled from place to place. She readily agreed, sending coded notes detailing Nazi troop movements and stores of military equipment.

Diet and Hein did not have much opportunity to be together since they were both very involved in Resistance work. But on one rare occasion, they finally got to spend an entire day together, biking and sharing a picnic. A few days later, on April 26, 1944, Hein was arrested. He had been caught carrying stolen ration cards and other items that clearly identified him as a member of the Resistance. He was able to smuggle out a note to warn everyone of his arrest, telling Diet to change her name again because the Gestapo had found papers on Hein that pointed them to a person named Willie van Daalen. Now Diet became Willie Laarman, an uneducated maid.

A few weeks later, Diet woke up certain that she would be arrested. But she couldn't just stay home; she had work to do. She needed to deliver ration cards and blank ID cards, some of them for recently downed Allied airmen who needed to get back to England. She hid the envelope in her blouse.

Diet was traveling by train that day. While aboard the train, a German officer asked Diet for her ID. It was a new ID showing Diet's identity as Willie Laarman. The officer could tell that it was false. Diet was asked to get off the train and waited on a bench with six officers sitting in a half-circle around her.

She knew that she would be searched, and upon the discovery of the packet of illegal documents in her blouse, she would be arrested, probably be shot, and then many others would likely be arrested. She needed to get rid of the envelope when the officers weren't looking, but that was clearly impossible. She was surrounded.

She prayed, "If it is at all possible, grant that those six men give me half a minute so that I can get rid of this envelope." Suddenly, one of the officers stood up, and another officer asked him about his raincoat, which was made of plastic, a material that was new at the time. The man with the coat opened it up so that they could all see the inside pockets of the coat. All six officers turned to look at the inside of the plastic raincoat. Diet pulled the envelope out of her blouse and threw it as far as she could.

Because she had been caught with a fake ID, Diet was taken to the prison in Scheveningen and then to the Vught concentration camp, where she was to be questioned. Knowing all along that she might be caught someday, Diet had always planned to remain silent. But while imprisoned in Scheveningen, she met an Allied spy, Beatrix Terwindt, who had been interrogated before and advised Diet to create a completely new story with a new identity and to carefully memorize the facts of this false story. Diet did this carefully for four months.

At Vught, Diet was given a job: cleaning bloody civilian clothing. As she was handed more and more garments, day after day, she made enquiries and discovered that she was cleaning the clothing of executed Dutch Resistance men. She examined the clothing more closely and discovered that the bullet holes were at the abdomen level. The resistance men had been deliberately shot in a manner that would cause a long, agonizing death.

At this point Diet's hatred for the Nazis ballooned until it threatened the very core of her Christian identity. It seemed that the painful execution of these Dutch men was the only reward she would ever know for all her Resistance work and her fervent prayers for everyone's safety. She began to doubt God's goodness and became physically paralyzed for three days.

Soon afterward it was time for Diet's hearing. A good friend and fellow prisoner had promised to "storm the gates of heaven" for Diet so that her hearing would go well. As Diet went through the hearing, pretending to be uneducated Willie Laarman, she gradually realized that the healthy German officers seated comfortably in that room, who were there to decide her fate, were the real prisoners, not she. She became convinced that God was on her side. Her hatred for these Germans melted into pity, and she was filled with an overwhelming peace.

She answered all of the questions asked of her with her carefully memorized details. Finally, when she was finished, one of the Germans who hadn't said a word during the session looked at her closely and said, "I have done nothing else my whole life but hearings and interrogations. That is my area of expertise . . . and I have developed a sixth sense. I can *feel* what is true and what isn't true. I can't put a needle in your story. It fits—all the way through. But my sixth sense tells me that it's all made up."

Whether or not the Germans truly believed Diet's story, they eventually decided to release her. She returned to the Lozemans' farm, where she continued her Resistance work until the end of the war, more determined than ever to fight the Nazis.

Diet was overjoyed when Canadian troops eventually rolled past the farm, signaling the end of the Nazi regime, and she eagerly awaited news of Hein's return. But he didn't come back. She received news that he had died at the Dachau concentration camp after surviving two previous camps. Diet was heartbroken. She was comforted somewhat when she received letters from Hein's fellow prisoners, telling Diet how inspirational and spiritually encouraging Hein had been. Nevertheless, Diet moved away from the Netherlands and didn't speak of her Resistance work for many years.

Then, in 1978, Diet heard Corrie ten Boom (see page 136) speak about her wartime experiences and began to sense that she had a responsibility to tell her own story. After she spoke at a "Suffering and Survival" convention, she met Dr. James Schaap, who offered to help write her memoir, *Things We Couldn't Say*, which was first published in 1994.

Diet received a certificate of appreciation personally signed by General Eisenhower in 1946, which expressed gratitude "for

Hein Sietsma.
Diet Eman

gallant service in assisting the escape of Allied soldiers from the enemy." In 1982, she received a letter from President Ronald Reagan that stated: "In risking your safety to adhere to a higher law of decency and morality, you have set a high and fearless standard for all those who oppose totalitarianism." In 1998, she was granted the Righteous Among the Nations award by Yad Vashem.

Diet lived in the United States for decades, became a U.S. citizen in 2007, and until she died in 2019 at the age of 99, continued to receive many letters of gratitude from the families of those she helped rescue.

★★★ LEARN MORE ★★★

The Reckoning: Remembering the Dutch Resistance (Vision Video, 2007). This DVD contains interviews with several former Dutch Resistance workers, including Diet Eman.

Things We Couldn't Say by Diet Eman and James Schaap (Eerdmans, 1994).

Hannie Schaft
THE SYMBOL OF THE RESISTANCE

THE WINTER OF 1944–45 was a particularly cold one that would become known in the Netherlands as the *hongerwinter* (hunger winter). Certain areas of the Netherlands had already been liberated by the Allies, but the western sections were still in the control of the Germans when, on March 21, 1945, a dark-haired, bespectacled young woman on a bicycle was stopped at a checkpoint—a concrete wall with a narrow opening built over a street—in the northwestern city of Haarlem. The guards searched the girl's bag and found a bundle of illegal newspapers. She was obviously part of the local Dutch Resistance. This didn't surprise them; they had discovered many women working for the Resistance during the occupation.

Hannie Schaft.
National Hannie Schaft Foundation (Nationale Hannie Schaft Stichting)

But they found something else in the bag that did surprise them: a pistol. Most female resisters in the area didn't use weapons. If this woman's hair hadn't been so dark, the soldiers might have thought she was "the girl with the red hair," who had been spotted during several assassinations but who had thus far evaded capture. They arrested the woman and took her away for questioning.

Auburn-haired Hannie Schaft was born Jannetje Johanna Schaft on September 16, 1920, in Haarlem, the capital city of the Dutch province of North Holland. She was a shy child, perhaps because she was teased by schoolmates for her reddish-brown hair and freckles or perhaps because her parents became protective of Hannie after the death of her older sister.

But though the Schaft family kept to itself, mother, father, and daughter engaged in lively discussions regarding politics and social justice. As a result, Hannie grew up planning to obtain a law degree focusing on human rights. Her dream was to eventually join the League of Nations (an organization later replaced by the United Nations).

While Hannie was a law student at the University of Amsterdam, the Netherlands was invaded by Nazi Germany. Life in the Netherlands didn't change right away under the Nazi occupation. But when anti-Semitic laws were enacted a few months later, gradually stripping away the rights of Dutch Jews, Hannie had to do something. Her sense of justice was, of course, offended by the new laws, but because her two best university friends, Sonja and Philine, were Jewish, her desire to help was all the greater.

Hannie became involved in small acts of resistance. She went to a public swimming pool and stole two identification cards for her Jewish friends. The ID cards of Jews were stamped with a huge *J*, easily identifying the bearers as Jewish and making them vulnerable to the ever-increasing anti-Semitic laws. Hannie began to do this type of work sporadically for other Dutch Jews who were desperately in need of false IDs.

In the spring of 1943, the Nazis passed a law that forever altered the course of Hannie's life. All Dutch university students were required to sign a loyalty declaration to Nazi Germany, promising, among other things, to spend a certain amount of time working in Germany after graduation.

Hannie, like 80 percent of Dutch university students, refused to sign the declaration. She left the university and went back home to live with her parents in Haarlem. It was there that she became involved with a Resistance organization called Raad van Verzet (the Council of Resistance), or RVV, that had ties to the Dutch Communist Party.

The RVV was a militant Resistance group, one that used explosives and bullets to fight the German occupiers and Dutch NSB agents who were being paid to betray Dutch resisters and Jews. Women were always in demand as couriers for the RVV because they generally wouldn't be stopped and searched as much as their male counterparts. But Hannie wanted to do more than courier work: she wanted to fight with weapons.

The RVV agreed to her request. Her first assignment was to connect with another resistance worker and assassinate a certain target. At the designated spot, the contact handed Hannie a pistol. Together, they waited for the target to pass by.

"Now!" called the contact. Hannie took aim and squeezed the trigger. But instead of hearing the "bang" of a bullet, there was only an empty click. Another empty click and then another. Suddenly, the person, who should have been dead, walked over to Hannie and introduced himself as the head of the Haarlem RVV. Hannie had been given a test, and she had passed.

Hannie was initially furious for having been deceived about the man's true identity and wouldn't shake his extended hand, but she eventually calmed down. It was unusual for Dutch Resistance women to be directly involved with explosives and weapons, yet Hannie, along with sisters Truus and Freddie Oversteegen, began to do sabotage and assassination work for the RVV.

The RVV was working to avenge the deaths of Resistance workers and also to protect more of them from betrayal, imprisonment, and death. Most of its assassination targets were members of the NSB—Dutch Nazis—who were being paid by the Germans to locate hidden Jews and betray Dutch Resisters. The NSB agents, along with the Germans, tortured captured resisters for information, then either sent them to a concentration camp or killed them. The RVV didn't have the means to capture these Dutch traitors and had nowhere to imprison them. So they stopped these betrayals in the most effective way they knew. And Hannie helped them in this effort.

Hannie, Freddie, and Truus had no qualms about shooting Germans or Dutch traitors, but they didn't accept every assignment. One day they were told to kidnap the children of Reich Commissioner Seyss-Inquart, the Nazi official in charge of the occupied Netherlands, so that the RVV could exchange them for Resistance prisoners. All three women refused. If the plan failed, they'd have to shoot the children. "We are no Hitlerites," Hannie said to Freddie and Truus as they walked away together. "Resistance fighters don't murder children."

While participating in one particular assassination attempt, Hannie was spotted by witnesses who claimed that they had seen a red-haired girl involved. The Girl with the Red Hair was now put high on the Nazis' most wanted list.

Hannie sometimes also did sabotage and assassination work with Jan Bonekamp, another RVV member. One night, Hannie knocked on Truus's door. Truus pulled her inside, very glad to see her good friend. Hannie burst into tears.

"I messed up my job and Jan got caught," she sobbed. "I rode away and Jan was shot down." Truus tried to calm Hannie by handing her a glass of water, but Hannie was shaking so badly the water spilled all over.

Hannie and Jan had just attempted to assassinate a traitorous Dutch police captain, William M. Ragut. All three were on bicycles. Hannie cycled up next to Ragut and took the first shot. Then she quickly cycled away. Jan cycled by next to make sure that Ragut was dead. He wasn't. Just as Jan came near him, Ragut pulled out a gun and shot Jan in the abdomen.

Hannie and Truus waited outside the hospital where the badly injured Jan was going to be treated. They saw an ambulance arrive. Two armed SS guards accompanied the nurses who carried Jan into the hospital on a stretcher. "Oh Jan, Jan," was all Hannie could whisper. There was no way to save him.

Jan's injuries had blinded him, damaged his spine, and caused him excruciating pain, but he still refused to give out any information under questioning. Finally, NSB agents sent in two nurses posing as Resistance workers. They quietly asked Jan if there was anyone they could contact on his behalf since he was dying. He gave them Hannie's name.

The day after Jan's death, Hannie's parents were arrested and sent to Vught, the Dutch concentration camp. The Germans were laying a trap for Hannie that her friends begged her to avoid. Hannie was deeply grieved that she had put her parents in such a situation, but she did not turn herself in. She became ill and depressed and temporarily ceased all Resistance activities. (When the Nazis saw that their plan had failed, they eventually released Hannie's parents.)

When she recovered enough to resume her work with the RVV, Hannie was determined to take the most dangerous jobs available. She took the new name of Johanna Elderkamp, dyed her hair black, and began to wear fake glasses. In addition to participating in more assassination and sabotage work with Truus and Freddie, Hannie also busied herself with courier work, transporting weapons and illegal Resistance newspapers from place to place.

On the evening of March 21, 1945, Hannie was on her bicycle transporting a packet of underground papers, *De waarheid* (The Truth). She was stopped by German soldiers at a checkpoint in Haarlem. They found the newspapers and a pistol in her bag. They arrested her. After they brought in pro-German Dutch witnesses who claimed to have seen Hannie in action, they noticed the auburn roots of her hair. They had finally captured the Girl with the Red Hair.

Hannie was interrogated, tortured, and placed in solitary confinement, but she refused to give any information on her fellow resisters. Truus concocted a desperate rescue plan, but it failed.

On April 17, 1945, three weeks before the liberation of the Netherlands, Hannie Schaft was taken to the sand dunes near Bloemendaal. A German SS officer took a shot, but only grazed Hannie's temple. "I am a much better shot!" Hannie cried. Then a Dutch NSB agent took out a submachine gun and fired. Hannie was dead. Her body was buried in a shallow grave.

After the war, the bodies of more than 400 resisters were found in those dunes, all men and one woman—Hannie Schaft.

On November 27, 1945, Hannie's body was reburied in a state funeral presided over by Queen Wilhelmina, who called Hannie "the symbol of the Resistance." Hannie received several posthumous awards, including the Wilhelmina Resistance Cross and the Medal of Freedom from General Eisenhower.

Because Hannie had worked with the communist RVV, she became a heroine of the Dutch Communist Party. After the war, when it became clear that the Communist Soviet Union was as oppressive as Nazi-occupied Europe had been, and that country became an enemy to the democracies of Western Europe, the Communist Party fell out of favor in the Netherlands. All commemorations for Hannie were banned.

But in 1982, a memorial sculpture dedicated to Hannie, created by Truus Oversteegen, was displayed in Kenau Park in Hannie's home city of Haarlem. Several Dutch-language books were also written about her. One of them, *Het meisje met het rode haar* (The Girl with the Red Hair) by Theun de Vries, was made into a film starring Renée Soutendijk as Hannie.

In the early 1990s, due to the work of the Hannie Schaft Memorial Foundation, commemorations for Hannie resumed, and she again became a valued symbol of Resistance. Every year, on the last Sunday of November, there is an annual commemoration to Hannie's life and sacrifice, which is attended by hundreds of Dutch citizens.

★★★ LEARN MORE ★★★

Seducing and Killing Nazis: Hannie, Truus and Freddie: Dutch Resistance Heroines of WWII by Sophie Poldermans (SWW Press, 2019).

"Hannie Schaft: Symbol of Resistance"
Haarlem Shuffle (English language resources for Haarlem, Netherlands)
www.haarlemshuffle.com/history/topic.php?id=12.

Hannie Schaft Memorial Foundation website (in the Dutch Language)
http://www.hannieschaft.nl/.

Johtje Vos

A GROUP EFFORT

JOHTJE AND AART Vos didn't sit down one day and decide to begin rescuing Jews from the Nazis in their Dutch village of Laren. Their rescue work began with a piano, a child, and a suitcase.

When their good friends, professional musicians Nap and Alice de Klijn, were ordered to move into the Jewish quarter in Amsterdam, the de Klijns signed over ownership of one of their pianos to Johtje to protect it from the Germans. The de Klijns also had a child who was hiding with another family, and when that hiding place suddenly became unsafe, Johtje and Aart took the child into their home, no questions asked. And when another good friend received word that he was also being forced to move to the Jewish

Johtje and Aart Vos.
The United States Holocaust Memorial Museum

section of Amsterdam, he asked the Voses if they would hide a suitcase of valuables for him. They agreed.

Before long the Voses had joined a Resistance organization composed of other like-minded people in the Laren area. The members of the Laren Resistance called themselves the Group. The Voses agreed to work for the Group by using their home as a hiding place for anyone on the run from the Nazis.

The Voses' house was at the end of a dead-end street, just a few kilometers outside of Laren. Beyond that was an acre of woods where it would be easy for people to hide if they had the time to get there. A local police officer, also part of the Laren Resistance, would warn the Voses by telephone before the suspicious Gestapo conducted a raid on their house, but there often wasn't time to get the fugitives out of the house and safely into the woods. So Aart built a tunnel, approximately 55 yards in length, which led from a studio in the back of the house to the woods, so that anyone trying to travel between the two would not be seen.

The Laren Resistance Group was well organized, and when people would come to the Voses requesting a hiding place, they always came with proof—names and papers—that showed they had been first screened by the Group and were truly people in need and not informers on the Germans' payroll.

One day a Jewish man came to the Voses' door and begged Johtje to hide him. He said he knew Johtje was hiding Jews in her home and he desperately needed a place to stay because he was going to be arrested that night.

Johtje wanted very much to help him, but it was too dangerous. He had no identifying names or papers from the Group. Johtje repeatedly denied having a hiding place for Jews in her home while the man kept insisting that she hide him, telling her that he understood why she was "playing innocent."

After half an hour of conversation with the man, Johtje finally closed her door with a heavy heart. She was haunted by this incident for days afterward. What had happened to him? Had he been arrested? Shot? Sent to a concentration camp? If so, it was all her fault for not taking him in.

One night about a week later, Johtje asked Aart if he would go out with her to get a cup of coffee at a nearby restaurant. After they had been seated, Johtje looked up in shock. There, a few tables away, was the same Jewish man who had come to her door only a week before. He wasn't in a concentration camp, and he wasn't dead. Instead, he was socializing calmly with a group of German officers. He was an informer! If Johtje had agreed to hide him, she and Aart and their children would be dead, and the Jews they were hiding would be on their way to concentration camps. Johtje and Aart quickly left the restaurant.

But the Gestapo didn't give up on the Voses. They would often come to their home and question Johtje, hoping to tire her into making an incriminating mistake that would prove that she and Aart were part of the Resistance. Johtje would become exhausted during these sessions, but she didn't slip.

One day the Gestapo officers stationed in Laren finally got the break they were looking for. With the help of a Dutch collaborator, they arrested a man named Jan who was part of the Laren Resistance. Unfortunately, it had been Jan's turn to hide a package of dangerous items that the Group referred to as "the arsenal." The package included the names of all the Jews who were hidden in the Laren area, where they were hidden, and several stolen rubber forgery stamps—one with the signature of Reich Commissioner Seyss-Inquart, the Nazi official in charge of the occupied Netherlands, and the other with the German eagle—both used for creating false ID papers for those on the run from the Gestapo. The package was never kept in one place for long but was constantly moved from house to house.

The night before Jan was arrested, he had left this package at his mother-in-law's house. When Aart received the news of Jan's

arrest, he knew that Jan's relatives would be searched and questioned first, so Aart raced over to the mother-in-law's house and
offered to hide the package.

A short time later, Johtje looked outside into the garden and
saw Aart and one of the Jewish men living with them digging a
hole in the garden. She went outside and asked them what they
were doing.

Aart wasn't planning to tell her about the package, since it
would be safer for her if she didn't know.

"I'm burying a dead rabbit," he answered.

The package was wrapped in special paper, so Johtje was suspicious. "That's quite an honorable funeral for a dead rabbit," she
said. Aart finally told her what it was.

A few hours later, Aart, Johtje, and their hiders were sitting
around a table discussing the pros and cons of moving everyone
to alternate hiding places, at least temporarily. Jan might have broken under interrogation, and the Gestapo now might finally have
proof that the Voses were hiding Jews. Lying on the table in front
of them were the real identification cards of everyone currently
living there.

Suddenly a black Gestapo car pulled up in front of the house.
Aart and the hiders ran for the tunnel. The ID cards were still on
the table. What was Johtje to do? Their nine-year-old son Peter had
just come running down the stairs when he heard the commotion.
Johtje stuffed the cards into his sweater and then told him to walk
away quietly. Peter clearly understood what was going on, so he
took a ball outside and began to bounce it up and down. When he
passed the officers, he played his part well, greeting them politely
as he walked farther and farther away.

Johtje was horrified that she had put her son in such danger,
but as the men walked in, she watched Peter out of the corner of
her eye until she knew that he was safe. Now she had other things
to worry about. Standing in her house were a German SS officer,

a Dutch NSB officer, and Jan, his face bruised and swollen. He begged Johtje to tell the men the location of the rubber stamps. If she handed them over, they would spare his life.

Johtje didn't know what to do. Should she save her Resistance friend and tell the truth? Or should she deny any knowledge of the stamps, thereby saving everyone in the Laren Group, both hiders and resisters? She told them she didn't know what Jan was talking about.

When the SS officer said that he had some business to attend to in the nearby town of Baarn, Johtje, the NSB officer, and Jan were left alone. The Dutch officer tried to convince Johtje he was on their side. "If you only trust me," he said, stretching out his hand to Johtje, "if you tell me where the stamps are, I can help Jan. I can get him his freedom, believe me." When that didn't work, the officer warned her that if she didn't cooperate by the time the SS officer returned, she would surely be interrogated and sent to a concentration camp. Johtje was trembling with fear, but she continued to play dumb.

Just then, the telephone rang. It was Aart, seeing if Johtje was safe. In a puzzled voice, in front of the NSB officer, Johtje told Aart that the officers and Jan had all been asking about some forgery stamps. Did he know anything about these stamps? Aart wasn't sure what to do. He claimed ignorance but then suggested that perhaps Jan's brother Dick knew something about them. Aart was sure Dick would be hiding somewhere safe at this point and thought it best to keep the Germans running from place to place instead of staying focused on Johtje.

Jan's wife, Mieke, suddenly rushed into the house, heedless of the danger, wanting to see her husband. Johtje quickly asked her if she knew where Dick was and if she could find him and get the stamps the Germans were looking for. Mieke said she knew where he was and turned to go. Then, as she walked Mieke to the door, Johtje suddenly got a flash of inspiration, a brilliant idea. She whispered to Mieke to meet her outside in a few minutes.

Johtje came back into the house and told the NSB officer that perhaps she could find her husband and that he might be able to help them find the stamps. He let her go, knowing that her two little girls were sleeping upstairs and that she would surely come back for them.

Johtje met Mieke, then they both crawled past the window to the garden. With their hands, they dug up the package containing the forgery stamps. Then Johtje told Mieke to come back on her bicycle in 20 minutes, pretending to have retrieved the stamps from Dick. Meanwhile, Johtje ate the dirt off her hands, wiped them clean on her underwear, and came back into the house, saying that she hadn't been able to find her husband after all. Mieke came in 20 minutes later, panting as if she had just made a strenuous trip, and

Aart, Johtje, their children, and some of the people they rescued during the war. Back row, left to right: Ilona Schroeder, Aart Vos, Johtje Vos, Peter Vos, Koert Delmonte. Front row, left to right: Teto Schroeder, Barbara Vos, Hetty Vos, Moana Hilfman. The photograph was taken during the time of the liberation, and Aart is pointing at some Allied planes.
United States Holocaust Memorial Museum

tossed the stamps onto the table. A short while later, the German officer returned. He was apparently satisfied and didn't go after Dick. Jan's life was spared, and those hiding in Laren remained safe.

One night over the radio the Voses heard their prime minster speaking from London. With a tearful voice he said the words they had been longing to hear: "Patriots, you are free!" The war was over!

Johtje and Aart had saved the lives of 36 people—including 32 Jews—during the course of the occupation. They were both honored by Yad Vashem with its Righteous Among the Nations award.

In 1951, Johtje and her family moved to the United States, where she and Aart ran an international children's camp in Woodstock, New York. They were often asked to speak to various groups about their Resistance activities, and in 1999, Johtje wrote a book about their experiences called *The End of the Tunnel*. Aart died in 1990 and Johtje in 2007.

★★★ LEARN MORE ★★★

The End of the Tunnel by Johtje Vos (Book Masters, Inc., 1999). Available by writing to the following e-mail address: bandb@ hvc.rr.com.

"Johtje Vos, Rescuer: Choices of Courage"
Living Histories: Seven Voices from the Holocaust
USC Shoah Foundation Institute for Visual History and Education
A 30-minute video interview of Johtje conducted in 1996 by Naomi Rappaport.
http://college.usc.edu/vhi/education/livinghistories/lesson .php?nid=717.

Rescuers: Portraits of Moral Courage in the Holocaust by Gay Block and Malka Drucker (Holmes & Meier, 1992) includes a chapter interview of Johtje and Aart Vos.

Corrie ten Boom

WATCHMAKER, RESCUER, RECONCILER

CORRIE TEN BOOM, her sister Betsie, and their father Casper were listening to the radio. It was the evening of May 9, 1940, and the prime minister had just assured the Dutch people that Hitler would not invade the Netherlands. In spite of the growing rumors of war, and despite the fact that he had already invaded Norway and Denmark, Hitler was going to honor the Dutch for remaining neutral during the previous war.

Suddenly, Casper walked up to the radio and turned it off with an anger that his daughters had never seen in him before. "It is wrong to give people hope when there is no hope," he said. "There will be war. The Germans will attack, and we will fall."

Corrie ten Boom in the 1940s.
The Corrie ten Boom House Foundation

Corrie and Betsie were shocked. Their elderly, devout father was normally so optimistic, so patient, and so kind. Before Corrie had become involved in their family watch shop, it made almost no money. Casper was so fascinated by the intricate beauty of watches that he would usually forget to bill his customers for the repair work he did for them.

When Corrie decided to learn watchmaking—becoming the first female licensed watchmaker in the Netherlands—she also took over some of the bookkeeping work from her father and helped the shop to make some money.

But if Corrie had a practical streak, unlike her father, in other ways she was as gentle and kind as he was. She and Betsie often took in foster children, and Corrie cared deeply for the developmentally disabled. She organized special outings and regular church services just for them.

By the time that Corrie, Betsie, and Casper ten Boom heard the prime minster's assurances over the radio, Corrie and Betsie were both unmarried middle-aged women: Corrie, 48, and Betsie, 54. They lived with their father in the city of Haarlem above their watch shop in the home they had grown up in, which they called the Beje.

In the middle of that night, Casper was proven correct. Explosions and brilliant flashes of light lit up the sky in the early hours of May 10, 1940. During the next five days, as the Dutch army fought the Germans, frightened neighbors flocked into the Beje, asking Casper ten Boom to pray for them and finding strength in being near the man they referred to as Haarlem's Grand Old Man.

Several months after the Dutch surrender to the Germans, when the Netherlanders in Haarlem were almost becoming used to the German uniforms, tanks, and trucks everywhere, Corrie and Betsie noticed that laws were being enacted against Dutch Jews. Jews had to wear yellow stars and were forbidden to walk in public parks and shop anywhere but Jewish shops. Soon, Jews were disappearing without a trace after being rounded up by the Germans. One day when Corrie and her father were out for a walk, they saw a group of people wearing the yellow star being forced into the back of a truck by a large group of Nazis.

"Father! Those poor people," Corrie cried.

"Those poor people," repeated Casper, as the truck drove off and the Germans marched away. But to Corrie's surprise, he was not looking at the truck full of Jews but at the Germans marching away. "They have touched the apple of God's eye."

The ten Booms' devout Christian beliefs were already well known in Haarlem. That this devotion extended a deep respect toward all Jewish people spread quickly through the Jewish community. One day a Jewish woman visited the Beje, asking for help. By this time it was against the law to provide shelter to any Jew. Police headquarters were half a block away. But none of that mattered. The ten Booms hurried the Jewish woman into their house and quickly made her part of their family.

After more Jews found their way to the Beje, Corrie realized that she needed extra ration cards, which were the only means by which people in Nazi-occupied countries could legally obtain groceries. A man named Fred Koornstra kept Corrie supplied with extra ration cards. His developmentally disabled daughter had been attending Corrie's church services for 20 years and he worked in the Food Office,

A Dutch ration card.
Diet Eman

where ration cards were issued. Corrie shared these cards with others who were sheltering Jews and other refugees, and soon the Beje became the center of a network of local Resistance workers seeking to hide Jews.

The Beje became a permanent home for several Jewish refugees and a temporary one for many more (never more than 12 at one time) who would pass through on their way to find a safer hiding place out in the country.

Members of a national Dutch Resistance network heard about the refugee work at the Beje and sent an architect to create a secret room adjacent to Corrie's bedroom, big enough to hide all the refugees living at the Beje at any one time. Then an electrician was sent to install a buzzer warning system that would alert everyone to go to the secret room in the event of a Gestapo raid.

Betsie's poor health prevented her from being as active as Corrie was outside the home, but she worked hard to create a comforting environment for the refugees living at the Beje. She organized poetry readings, plays, and musical evenings. And while the ten Booms continued their Christian devotions and celebrations, they now tried to make their guests feel comfortable by also observing Jewish rituals and holidays. The ten Booms never sought to convert any Jews to Christianity, although they had many lively discussions with their guests regarding their differing faiths.

One night, Corrie was sick and took a briefcase filled with important Resistance papers with her to bed. These papers had the names and addresses of refugees who would need extra ration cards that month. She was so ill, however, that the briefcase soon slipped from her hand and landed on the floor as she fell asleep.

In her dreams, she kept hearing the buzzer go off, the sound of feet running by, and nervous whispering. She woke up. Why were people running into the secret room? There was no drill planned for that day. Then she suddenly realized what was happening. It was a raid! They had been betrayed! The Gestapo was at the door! Every refugee had slipped into the secret room, and Corrie dropped the secret panel down. She could hear loud footsteps coming up the stairs, approaching her room. Suddenly, she looked down at the briefcase on the floor. It was stuffed with the names and addresses of local refugees. Corrie quickly opened the panel and threw the briefcase into the secret room just as the bedroom door flew open. A Gestapo officer was standing there and demanded her name.

Corrie tried to sound sleepy and confused. "What?" she asked. "Your name!" he repeated.

She told him. He took a piece of paper out of his pocket, read it, and then looked at Corrie again. "Tell me now, where are you hiding your Jews?"

Corrie pretended she didn't know what he was talking about.

The Gestapo agent laughed and took her downstairs, where another Gestapo agent began to slap her hard across the face when she wouldn't answer his questions. In between slaps, Corrie could hear the trained searchers trying to locate the secret room where the Jews were hiding. After a long while, the man in charge of the search gave up, saying, "If there's a secret room here, the devil himself built it." Resistance materials and extra ration cards were found in the house, so Corrie, Betsie, and Casper were taken away to the Scheveningen prison. The Gestapo posted guards at the back and front of the house, determined to catch more Resistance workers (they eventually arrested 30 people who tried to visit the Beje that day) and "starve out" the Jews they knew were hiding there.

When they arrived at Scheveningen, Corrie and Betsie were separated from their father. They discovered later that he died in prison 10 days after their arrival.

While in prison, Corrie received a letter that said, "All the watches in your closet are safe." Corrie understood the code: all their refugees had managed to escape the house and get to safety.

After three months in solitary confinement, Corrie was escorted to her first hearing. There she was questioned by a German named Lieutenant Rahms, who treated her in a polite manner, hoping to gain information regarding her Resistance activities and fellow Resistance workers. He obviously thought that she was a leader, but it soon became clear from her answers that she was not. However, he kept asking her about her other activities. She told him about her activities for people with developmental disabilities.

The Nazis had been "mercy killing" the mentally disabled for years, and so the lieutenant scoffed at Corrie's efforts, telling her that she had wasted her time and energy because "one normal person is worth all the half-wits in the world."

She responded by saying that in God's eyes, one "half-wit" might be more valuable "than a watchmaker. Or—a lieutenant."

Corrie and Betsie were sent to the Vught, the Dutch concentration camp, and from there they went on to Ravensbruck, the infamous women's concentration camp in Germany. There, after completing their nigh-impossible daily workload in the midst of Nazi cruelties, starvation, and cold, they would gather in their barrack to hold secret Christian devotions with anyone who wanted to join them, whatever their denomination, faith, or language. Portions of the Dutch Bible that Corrie had smuggled into the camp were sometimes translated into many different languages during the devotional time. Praying and hearing the Bible read gave many women in the barrack hope, peace, and faith. It seemed to Corrie as if God were shining spiritual light into a very dark place. She often wondered why no guards ever stopped these meetings, but she eventually found out: the excessive fleas in the barrack kept the guards away and the meetings private.

During their time at Ravensbruck, Betsie began to visualize and discuss plans for a home that she and Corrie would organize after the war as a place of healing for all those wounded by the war.

But Betsie didn't survive to implement those plans. She became ill and died on December 16, 1944. A few weeks later, on December 28, Corrie was released due to a clerical error. The following week all the women her age were killed. She came home during the "hunger winter" and opened the Beje to the mentally disabled, who had been hidden away by their families during the war, unable to attend school or any other activities for fear that the Nazis would kill them.

After the war, Corrie helped to organize and run several homes, just like those Betsie had envisioned, designed to help victims of the war heal from their emotional wounds. She also began to travel and speak of her and Betsie's experiences and how she had seen God use them.

Corrie was reluctant to make Germany part of her speaking itinerary, but she felt compelled to do so. While there, Corrie met two Germans who had been employed at Ravensbruck: a guard and a nurse, both of whom had been extremely cruel, one of them to Betsie in particular. They had come to hear Corrie speak because they realized their desperate need to be forgiven. Corrie found it difficult at first to forgive them, but when she did so, she tapped into a power that she would speak of for the rest of her life as she visited over 60 countries: the healing power of forgiveness, both human and divine.

Corrie also wrote many books. Her most famous, *The Hiding Place*, based on her wartime experiences, was made into a film in 1975. Corrie was granted the Righteous Among the Nations award by Yad Vashem and was also knighted by the queen of the Netherlands. She died in California in 1983 at the age of 91.

The Beje is now a museum (above an actual watch shop), and visitors can see the secret room where the ten Booms once hid Jews.

★★★ LEARN MORE ★★★

The Hiding Place by Corrie ten Boom, John Sherrill, and Elizabeth Sherrill (Barbour, 1971).

A Visit to the Hiding Place: The Life-Changing Experiences of Corrie ten Boom by Emily S. Smith (The Corrie ten Boom House Foundation, 2005).

Corrie ten Boom Museum
www.CorrietenBoom.com
The Official website of the Corrie ten Boom House Foundation contains information about the ten Boom house and museum, including exhibitions, photographs, and history.

PART V
Belgium

ALTHOUGH THE BELGIAN government had built a line of defensive fortifications on its border with Germany after World War I, on the morning of May 10, 1940, German glider planes silently flew over the fortress and began the invasion of Belgium. After 18 days of fighting, Belgium's King Leopold III surrendered on behalf of his country.

Unlike most other countries invaded by Nazi Germany, Belgium had been occupied by Germany before, during World War I. Many Belgians clearly remembered the first German occupation, when German soldiers had brutally massacred Belgian women and children and destroyed entire villages. During that occupation, Germans were first referred to as Huns, named for some particularly brutal fourth-century warriors.

The Germans tried to show a different face to the Belgians during this new occupation, as they were anxious to keep the Belgian economy running for their own gain. But most Belgians were not fooled by the Germans' outward politeness.

The strict ration cards the Germans forced the Belgians to live on was enough to prove that the German expression of concern for Belgians was a lie. Belgians lived on meager rations while their German occupiers ate heartily. The only bread available to Belgians was a thick, dark, sticky, black substance that could not be cut with a knife and that contained very little nutritional value. The only way to get extra food without using the German-issued ration cards and stay moderately healthy was to buy or barter for groceries on the illegal black market.

There were stiff German penalties for buying food without using ration cards, yet many hungry Belgians took that risk. Other Belgians took additional risks by joining Resistance groups that engaged in numerous activities made illegal by the Nazis. One of the first acts of Belgian Resistance was the printing and distribution of underground newspapers. *La libre Belgique* (Free Belgium) was a Belgian paper that had been printed secretly during the first German occupation. The first World War II edition was published on July 1, 1940, approximately two weeks after Belgium's surrender.

Some of the information printed in *La libre Belgique* was obtained by those associated with information-gathering Resistance networks, such as Zero, Luc, and many other smaller local groups. On information-gathering missions, members of these networks often escorted a trapped Allied serviceman or two to safety. At first, these were Allied servicemen who had been trapped while fighting on Belgian soil. But soon they included many British and, later, American airmen who were shot down during missions over Nazi-occupied Belgium (and the neighboring Netherlands). Many who survived were quickly rescued by Belgian civilians, given civilian clothing, and hidden. Several escape lines were created to escort

★★★ ANDRÉE GEULEN ★★★

Andrée Geulen was a young Belgian schoolteacher in 1943 when she was recruited by the Committee for the Defense of the Jews to escort Jewish children from their homes into hiding. Andrée personally helped approximately 300 Jewish children to safety, often right under the noses of the occupying Germans. After the war she worked to reunite Jewish families, and to this day she keeps in contact with many of the children she rescued. She received a Righteous Among the Nations award from Yad Vashem, and in 2002 a French-language film called *Un simple maillon* (Just a Link) was made about her wartime rescue activities. When

Yad Vashem awarded her honorary Israeli citizenship in 2007 for her rescuing activities, she accepted the award saying that she had merely done her duty.

Andrée Geulen in occupied Brussels, 1944, with German officers behind her.
United States Holocaust Memorial Museum, courtesy of Andrée Geulen

these Allied servicemen from one safe house to another, across Belgium, through France, and over the Pyrenees Mountains, the border between France and Spain. From there, it was relatively easy (most of the time) for the men to get back to Great Britain.

The two main Belgian escape lines for Allied servicemen were the O'Leary Line and the Comet Line, the latter named because travel on it was unusually swift. The Comet Line was created and organized by a 25-year-old Belgian woman named Andrée de Jongh. Many Belgians assisted the work of both the O'Leary and Comet lines, some by opening their homes as safe houses and others by forging false documents and ration cards for the servicemen on the run. Many women, like Andrée de Jongh, personally accompanied the men as they traveled because women were less likely to come under suspicion and be stopped for questioning by Germans than men were.

Anti-Jewish laws began several months after the invasion of Belgium, and in the summer of 1942 many Jews without Belgian citizenship were rounded up by the Germans and shipped to concentration camps. But when the Germans moved against Belgian Jews, rescue organizations worked very hard to try to prevent the deportations.

The efforts of the Committee for the Defense of the Jews (CDJ) saved approximately 3,000 Jewish children during the Holocaust. Rescuer Andrée Geulen, who worked with the CDJ, escorted hundreds of children to safety during the war.

Belgian nuns were also heavily involved in rescuing Jewish children, often working closely with the CDJ, escorting and housing children in convent boarding schools and orphanages. Mothers superior often made the decision to accept or deny a child, and very few Jewish children were refused a hiding place at these institutions. After the war, nearly 50 Belgian nuns were honored as Righteous Among the Nations by Yad Vashem.

The Battle of the Ardennes, more commonly known as the Battle of the Bulge, fought between the Allies and Germany began in December 1944 in Belgium's Ardennes forest. It was a near-victory for Germany, but by the end of January 1945 it was over, and the Allies had successfully pushed the Germans out of Belgium.

Andrée de Jongh

THE COMET LINE

A WOMAN CRAWLED silently through the tall grass on the banks of the Somme River. She could almost reach out and touch the beams of light emanating from the German patrol searchlights. Had she been seen? No, not yet. She and the man who was with her continued to crawl through the grass, searching for the rowboat they needed. Finally they saw it. It was exactly where it was supposed to be, but some campers had suddenly pitched their tents just a few yards away. The man and woman had to change their plans. They could have easily swum across the river, but a good portion of the 11 people traveling with them could not, and they were there to help those people. But how could they help them without a boat?

Andrée de Jongh.
Sherri Greene Ottis

The woman suddenly had an idea. She told the man to search the farmhouses in the area for something that could be used as a lifebelt. As she waited for him to return, the woman kept a wary eye on the German patrols and on the group of travelers who were hiding nervously in the nearby bushes.

Hours later, the man returned with an inner tube and gave the woman a signal to send the first passenger. The woman helped the first passenger, a very large man, onto the tube and pushed it from behind. Her view was blocked, but she knew she had reached the other side of the river when her foot finally touched bottom. Then she took the inner tube back for the next passenger.

After one and a half hours, the woman had safely pushed all 11 travelers across the river. This river crossing was a small part of a larger and very important journey, and not only for these travelers who were seeking to escape the Germans. It was also the trial run for an escape line—spanning from Brussels, Belgium, all the way into Spain, a total of 1,200 miles—that would enable Allied servicemen to escape Nazi-occupied Belgium. The woman's name was Andrée de Jongh, and the escape line she was testing that night in the cold waters of the Somme River would eventually be called the Comet Line, so named for its unusual swiftness.

Andrée de Jongh was a native of Belgium, a 23-year-old artist and a nurse-in-training when the Germans overran Belgium in the spring of 1940. She had been inspired to study nursing by Edith Cavell, the heroic British nurse who was executed in Brussels by a firing squad during World War I because she had helped British servicemen escape from German-occupied Belgium.

Andrée's father, Frederic, who had lived through that previous war, broke down in tears of rage and despair when he saw the Germans march into Brussels, Belgium's capital city. Andrée, who had never seen her father cry before, comforted him by saying, "You'll see what we'll do to them. You'll see, they are going to lose this war. They started it, but they are going to lose it."

When Andrée realized there were Allied servicemen trapped inside Belgium because they had attempted to assist the Belgian army against the Nazi invasion, she organized a series of safe houses in and around Brussels where the servicemen could hide, receive civilian clothing (to disguise the fact that they were Allied servicemen), and secure false identity papers. They couldn't stay there forever, though; they had to get back to England somehow. The path back to England was through France, over the Pyrenees Mountains, into neutral Spain, then home to Great Britain.

After the trial run that had taken her back and forth across the cold waters of the Somme River, Andrée was determined to try

★★★ SPAIN DURING WORLD WAR II ★★★

Spain was officially a neutral country during World War II, but its government was Fascist. Its leader, General Franco, had emerged triumphant from the Spanish Civil War (1936–1939) after receiving military help from the Fascist governments of Germany and Italy. Franco didn't want to anger Hitler by openly allowing Allied refugees into Spain, but he also didn't want to offend the Allied countries who supplied him with certain domestic products. This caused a hit-or-miss situation for those trying to escape from Nazi-occupied France into Spain. If Allied refugees could get past the German guards on the French side of the border, they were sometimes arrested by Franco's men on the Spanish side. And while some of these refugees were handed over to the Germans, others were able to get out of jail more easily than if they had been arrested by the Germans on the French side. If they were placed in Spanish refugee camps, British diplomats working at the British embassy in Spain were sometimes able to free them.

again. She and Arnold Depée, the man who had helped her in the trial run, couldn't agree on the relative safety of the main route, so they split up, intending to meet just south of the Belgian-French border. Andrée waited and waited at the appointed meeting place, but Arnold didn't come. Andrée felt she had to continue on with her "parcels," as she called the servicemen.

Andrée soon discovered that all of the people in the Comet Line's trial run had been arrested shortly after crossing the Spanish-French border. She realized that for the escape line to be effective, she would need direct contact with the authorities at the British consulate in Spain: they would certainly ensure the Allied servicemen's safety.

But there was one problem: the mountain guide who had been hired to escort Andrée and the soldiers across the Pyrenees on this second trip did not want to take Andrée with him. He didn't think that a slim, petite young woman would be able to keep up with him, an experienced hiker, on the two 10-hour treks necessary to cross the Pyrenees. But Andrée refused to be denied, and the mountain guide reluctantly set out with his travelers across the Pyrenees.

Several days later, Andrée appeared in the offices of the British consulate in Balboa, Spain, telling the British official there who she was and why she was there.

"I am a Belgian, and have come all the way from Brussels. I have brought you two Belgians who want to fight for the Allies, and a Scottish soldier. We left Brussels last week and crossed the Pyrenees two nights ago."

The British vice consul looked at tiny Andrée, neatly dressed in a blouse and skirt. He didn't believe her story, especially about her having crossed the rough Pyrenees Mountains. He was convinced that she was a German spy. He asked her how she had gotten over the Pyrenees.

She explained that she had hired a mountain guide, and then she continued: "There are many British soldiers and airmen hidden in Brussels, most of them survivors from Dunkirk [the final point of the Allied retreat during the Battle of France]. I can bring them through to you if you will let me. With money, we can find guides to cross the mountains." Andrée wanted no pay except to be reimbursed for the mountain guide fee and for the food the men had eaten.

The vice consul was still incredulous. "But you—you are a young girl. You are not going to cross the Pyrenees again?"

Andrée patiently explained that she was as strong as a man and, besides, girls attracted less attention from police in that area, given that no one would believe that females could possibly be part of an escape line. She continued: "With your help I can bring through more Englishmen. I beg of you to let me."

The British official eventually agreed. He asked how soon she could come back with another group of men. She said it would take three or four weeks.

"Then bring three more men with you," he said.

Andrée did just that. During 32 crossings back and forth through the Comet Line, she personally escorted 118 Allied servicemen to safety. She was finally stopped on January 15, 1943, at a safe house in the foothills of the Pyrenees, the last stop on the

A U.S. air crew that flew missions over occupied France and Nazi Germany. When Andrée and her team found Allied servicemen, they had to get civilian clothing for them.
Teune family collection

Comet Line, where she and three Allied servicemen were arrested by the Germans. When interrogated, she wouldn't surrender any names but eventually admitted that she had been in charge of the Comet Line. The Germans didn't believe her. But because she wouldn't cooperate by betraying anyone else, she was sent to the Mauthausen and then to the Ravensbruck concentration camps.

The Comet Line was so well organized that it continued successfully in Andrée's absence, eventually helping approximately 700 Allied servicemen, including many Americans, reach freedom. Hundreds of people working the line, including Andrée's father, Frederic, who had taken charge of the Belgian portion of the line, were captured and murdered by the Nazis.

Andrée survived her ordeal in the concentration camps and received numerous awards from the governments of Belgium, France, Great Britain, and the United States. After regaining her health, she went to work as a nurse in a leper colony in the African Congo. When her health and sight began to fail, she returned to Brussels, where she died in 2007 at the age of 90.

★★★ LEARN MORE ★★★

"Airmen Remember Comet Line to Freedom"
BBC News Online
http://news.bbc.co.uk/1/hi/world/europe/988881.stm
This article quotes former Allied airmen who escaped through the Comet Line.

Little Cyclone by Airey Neave (Hodder and Stoughton, 1954, reprinted by Coronet Books, 1986). A biography of Andreé and the Comet Line.

Silent Heroes: Downed Airmen and the French Underground by Sherri Greene Ottis (University Press of Kentucky, 2001) contains a lengthy section on the Comet Line.

Hortense Daman

PARTISAN COURIER

A TALL OFFICER in an SS uniform stepped onto a train car loaded with female prisoners, their hands and feet chained to their train seats. He glanced around the car until he noticed one particular prisoner, a pretty 17-year-old girl. He walked over to her.

"I'll give you one last chance," he said.

"I don't understand," the girl replied.

The officer almost smiled. "I'll give you your freedom, set you free, if you can tell me where I can find your brother."

"I can't help you," the girl replied.

"Can you hear what I'm saying to you?" he asked again. "Do you understand?"

Hortense Daman.
Courtesy of Mark Bles

"I've nothing to say," she replied.

The officer knew that this girl had been subjected to 30 days of beatings and interrogation by the Belgian SS. They were all looking for her brother, François Daman, a leading member of the local Resistance who had thus far skillfully evaded their grasp. The girl had taken beating after beating but repeatedly refused to reveal her brother's whereabouts.

This officer was an experienced interrogator who had seen grown men break down and betray their associates under similar treatment. This young woman had been beaten day after day but had remained silent. He had great respect for her conviction.

"A pity, Hortensia," he said. He stepped back, snapped his heels together, and saluted her. "I wish you had been a German." Then he stepped off the train. The wheels of the train began to squeak. It was headed for Ravensbruck, a place called L'Enfer des Femmes or "the Women's Inferno." It was a concentration camp for women.

During the four-day journey, in which she was never unshackled from her seat, Hortense Daman had plenty of time to reflect on the events that had put her on this train.

Hortense had been only 13 when Germany had invaded Poland in 1939. Her brother, François, then 26, was a sergeant in the Belgian army. When Germany invaded and conquered Belgium in May of the following year, François began to work for the Red Cross, but that work was just a cover. In reality, he had joined the Belgian Army of Partisans, one of several large militant Resistance organizations in Nazi-occupied Belgium.

François asked Hortense to join the Partisans for two reasons. He knew that its work would not be successful without the help of female volunteers. He could also see that if he didn't give her something to do, Hortense might get involved on her own. Francois would rather that Hortense worked closely with him so that he could keep an eye on her.

He asked her to distribute copies of Belgium's most popular underground newspaper, *La libre Belgique* (Free Belgium). Then he asked her to deliver a letter to someone she would find sitting on a park bench. Soon, Hortense was doing regular courier work for Francois, delivering important items from place to place. Their mother owned a grocery store in their hometown of Louvain, so Hortense could perform these duties while riding her bike, supposedly delivering groceries. Some of the time she was actually delivering groceries, but they were black market groceries—obtained illegally, without ration cards—used to feed Allied airmen who were being hidden until they could be safely escorted back to England.

Soon, Hortense's bike basket was filled with more than just groceries: she began delivering explosives for the Partisans. One day while transporting a load of grenades in her basket, barely hidden under a load of eggs, Hortense pedaled directly into a raid. The Germans were checking identification papers, looking for young men who had thus far avoided the enforced draft into German munitions factories. They were also checking for black market groceries. Hortense was stopped by an officer who gruffly asked her what she was carrying. As she came to a sudden stop, she struggled desperately to keep her balance as the front of her bike threatened to topple over at any moment.

"Just eggs," she said. Eggs were rare and expensive in Nazi-occupied Belgium, even for the Germans. When she noticed that his eyes were fixed on her basket, she saw her opportunity and pulled a few of the eggs out. "Would you like some?" He snatched them from her hand before impatiently waving her away. She pedaled away from the raid until her legs began to shake uncontrollably and she had to stop to regain her composure.

After Hortense had delivered the grenades to their destination, she considered the circumstances carefully: while she knew she had escaped being more thoroughly searched largely because she was female, she also realized that she had kept her head in a very tense situation. This realization gave her the confidence necessary to take another, even more dangerous, mission. The Germans were moving successfully against the Partisans in the Louvain area. Leaders were being betrayed and then either arrested and interrogated or just assassinated on the spot. Changes needed to be made, plans altered, and files—which included the names and addresses of Partisan members—needed to be moved quickly and quietly before they fell into the hands of the Germans.

Hortense was to bicycle to a certain house to collect a bundle of these files. Then, in case she had been followed, she was to take the train back home instead of bicycling back. Francois knew by now that Hortense was very capable. Still, it was such a dangerous mission that he couldn't help fearing for her safety.

"It's vital that you don't get caught," said Francois to his sister as she was preparing to leave.

She smiled at Francois's warnings. "Don't worry, I'll be all right. I've memorized all the contact details."

"Well, anyway, they'll think it's Christmas if they find those papers. There's everything about the Partisans in this whole sector. If you're picked up with them you'll be in real trouble."

She smiled confidently as she straddled her bicycle.

"For God's sake, be careful," he said as he watched his young sister pedal away.

After Hortense had made the contact, received the package, and boarded the train, she noticed, to her horror, that the GFP (Geheime Feld Polizei, or Secret Field Police) were checking not only identification papers but also parcels and suitcases. The GFP was a branch of the German armed forces that, in Belgium and France especially, was used for stamping out Resistance activities.

She couldn't let her package be inspected. There was only one thing to do: move to another train car. She ended up in a car full of German officers.

A German officer politely offered Hortense a seat beside him. He took her parcel and set it on the rack above their heads. The letters *GFP* were emblazoned on his shoulder straps. He was obviously a senior officer.

"My word, that is a heavy thing to carry about. What's in it to make it so heavy?" he asked.

"Magazines," Hortense replied quickly.

For one terrifying moment, Hortense thought he was going to ask her to show him what kind of magazines they were. Instead, he began a friendly, if extremely one-sided, conversation with Hortense. He asked her where she was going.

She answered truthfully that she was headed toward her home in Louvain.

He became very excited and told her that he was traveling there too: he had been sent to take charge of the Geheime Feld Polizei there, and he was planning to have the area's "terrorists" wiped out within two months. Then he warned Hortense that she should be careful to avoid them for her own safety.

"I don't think they'll bother me, will they?" Hortense asked, trying to make her eyes look wide and frightened.

"I doubt it," said the officer. But to ensure her safety, and also to ask her out to dinner, he insisted on driving her home from the train station, politely handing her the package as she left the car and smiling when she told him that her mother wouldn't approve of her going out with a German officer.

Although Hortense took some time off after her successful mission, the officer who had given her a ride home did not. He was successful in one respect: Hortense and her parents were betrayed and arrested one day when soldiers came crashing into their home at dinnertime. François was not there.

But the Germans were determined to find him. Hortense was interrogated every day for 30 days and beaten severely every time she refused to tell François's location. This refusal landed her on the train headed for Ravensbruck.

Not only did Hortense survive the horrors of the Women's Inferno for nearly a year—including attempted sterilization and being injected with gangrene as part of a medical experiment—but after her mother arrived there too, Hortense did everything in her power to see that her mother also survived, endangering her own life several times.

After the war Hortense married Syd Clews, a British army sergeant, and moved with him to England, where they had two children together. The Belgian government honored Hortense with top awards, and in 1989 Mark Bles wrote her biography, titled *Child at War*. Hortense died in 2006 at the age of 80.

★★★ LEARN MORE ★★★

Child at War: The True Story of a Young Belgian Resistance Fighter by Mark Bles (Hodder & Stoughton, 1989).

"Hortense Clews: Belgian Resistance Courier Who Was Captured by the SS but Survived the Cruelties of Ravensbruck Concentration Camp."
Times Online, 2007. www.timesonline.co.uk /tol/comment/obituaries/article1299135.ece

Fernande Keufgens

THE TEEN WITH THE BOLD VOICE

THE TEENAGED GIRL walked hand-in-hand with the five-year-old boy through the edge of the Ardennes Forest in southern Belgium. Their destination was the tuberculosis sanatorium (hospital) in Banneux. The little boy was going there, supposedly as a patient, and the girl had a false work permit for the hospital in her pants pocket. She carried a red handkerchief containing the boy's clothes. Inside the bundle of clothes was hidden a packet of false identification cards that was to be delivered to the nuns at the sanatorium. The nuns were planning to distribute the cards to the English spies that would be landing nearby that very night.

Fernande Keufgens during the war.
Girl in the Belgian Resistance: A Wakeful Eye in the
Underground *by Fernande K. Davis.*

As they turned a corner, a beautiful meadow came into view. The girl was very tired. She and the young boy had already walked five miles together. She knew that he must be even more exhausted than she was, but she didn't feel strong enough to carry him at that point. She tried to distract him from his fatigue by singing all the children's songs he might know. The little boy joined in and seemed strengthened and buoyed by the singing.

She was greatly relieved when she finally saw the sanatorium in the distance.

"*Oui, c'est ça!*" (Yes, that's it!) said the little boy, as enthusiastically as he could.

Suddenly, two Gestapo agents jumped out from behind a mound of dirt and pointed their guns at the travelers, screaming in German, "Halt!" and "Work card!"

The girl remembered what her father had said when she told him she wanted to join the Resistance: "Never show fear to your enemy [the Germans]," he had said. "In your best German speak louder than they do."

Now, as two Gestapo agents shouted orders at her, she tried to heed her father's words and stay very calm. She took as long as possible to fish the fake work permit out of her pants pocket as the small boy sobbed beside her.

The agent took the work permit and examined it. He asked the girl where she worked. The girl responded loudly in German, to the obvious surprise of the Gestapo agents. "Can you not read German? The answer is written on the card, in German. I work over there," she said, pointing to the sanatorium.

The agent then demanded to know what was inside of the red handkerchief and who the boy was. The girl responded, "This child has tuberculosis. In the bundle are his dirty clothes. Do you wish to see them?" she asked, gesturing toward the handkerchief. The Gestapo agent quickly stepped backward and waved his arms nervously while screaming, "*Rause! Rause! Schnell!*" (Get out! Fast!)

The teenager and the sobbing five-year-old were back on their way to the sanatorium while the Gestapo agents returned to hide behind the mound of dirt.

The girl's legs suddenly felt like rubber. Although she had fooled the Gestapo agents, she now had a tremendous urge to run away as fast as she could. But she knew that she was still in view of the agents, so showing any fear was out of the question.

Although she was only 17, Fernande Keufgens had already successfully fulfilled one mission for the Army of Liberation, a branch of the Belgian Resistance stationed in the city of Liége. This was her second mission, and she must not fail. If those Gestapo agents had discovered the false identification cards in the boy's bundle of clothes, the nuns' work at the sanatorium would certainly have been crushed and the British spies captured, tortured, and imprisoned or shot. So she remained as calm as possible, walking steadily with the boy until they reached the entrance of the sanatorium. The nun opened the door to them immediately. She had seen the entire episode. Fernande handed her the identification cards. Then she left within half an hour.

What chain of events had led this teenaged Belgian girl to this terrifying situation where she had successfully fooled two adult men—trained Gestapo agents? Two things: the Nazi invasion of her country and an absolute refusal to assist the Nazi war machine.

Before the war even began, Fernande's father had foreseen the Nazi invasion *and* the forced draft into munitions factories that would certainly occur afterward. So he arranged for 15-year-old Fernande to move farther away from the German border, to work in the town of Verviers.

Then in 1942, two years after the invasion, Fernande was summoned back home to Montzen. The Nazis had finally caught up with her, and she was ordered to report to the local train station to be shipped to a German labor camp/munitions factory. If she failed to do so, her father would be imprisoned. Fernande would do anything to save her father, but nothing would make her create bullets and bombs for the Nazis. What to do? In Fernande's mind it was simple: she would report to the station, board the train, and then jump off it before it left Belgium. She would then join the Belgian Resistance.

After jumping from the train, Fernande walked for miles through fields and farmland, carefully avoiding paved streets and Nazi border guards, until she arrived at the home of her uncle, Hubert. He was a devout priest who was working in the Army of Liberation, a branch of the Belgian Resistance movement stationed in Liége. At first he tried to talk Fernande out of joining the Resistance, telling her how dangerous it would be, how she was too young, how she would most likely not be given any important assignments anyway.

But he finally saw that Fernande would not be swayed. She didn't care about the quality of the assignments or the possible dangers of the work: she just wanted to do something—anything—to fight the Nazis. Uncle Hubert gave Fernande a false identification card and a roll of counterfeit food stamps, and, with tears in his eyes, he sent her to a contact in the Army of Liberation, where she became a courier.

Thousands of young Belgians in the city of Liége were regularly being stopped on the street at gunpoint and forced onto trucks headed for German munitions factories. Avoiding these forced deportations was like a dangerous game, one that Fernande—now a full-fledged Resistance worker—could not afford to lose.

The Germans took all the best Belgian goods and food for themselves, leaving the Belgians to survive on what meager items they could buy with ration cards. Fernande couldn't afford to buy any luxuries, but she did like to spend some of her free time in Liége's small city square. Called Place de la Liberté, the square was filled with shops and was popular with young Belgians.

One day Fernande was wandering through Place de la Liberté in a somewhat distracted fashion. She had just been handed a treasured éclair by a kind baker who had seen her gazing longingly at the treats in his window.

Suddenly she looked up. German trucks had rolled into the square, blocking the streets in all directions. Guards poured out of each truck, blocking each sidewalk with guns while others grabbed every teenager within reach and forced them into the backs of the trucks. Screams and wails pierced the air. The scene was one of terror and confusion.

Fernande could not afford to be caught. As a member of the Resistance, she was now an official enemy of the Reich! She remembered her father's words once again and calmly walked up to a young-looking German soldier. She put her hand on his gun, smiled at him, and in perfect German shouted, "You can't hold up a compatriot, my friend. I am running for my train to Aachen [Germany], where I work."

The young soldier's partner aimed his rifle at Fernande as she walked past, but the first soldier stopped him from shooting Fernande. She was, after all, obviously a German. The second soldier asked to see her ID, but she flirtatiously answered him over her shoulder, "No time, but thank you, darling, I must catch my train." She darted around the corner, thanking God for her escape and more ready than ever to fight the Nazis for their treatment of the young people who hadn't been so fortunate.

Fernande survived the war, fighting with the Belgian Resistance to the end. She married an American soldier named Bill Davis, who had been stationed in Belgium, moved with him to the United States, and became a university professor of French. In 2008 she wrote a book detailing her experiences during the war years called *Girl in the Belgian Resistance*. Fernande continues to give talks regarding her Resistance work.

★★★ LEARN MORE ★★★

Girl in the Belgian Resistance: A Wakeful Eye in the Underground by
Fernande K. Davis (Beach Lloyd, 2008).

PART VI
Denmark

JUST BEFORE DAWN on April 9, 1940, numerous German ships docked in several Danish harbors. German soldiers quietly disembarked from these ships and spread throughout Denmark. German troops were also dropped via plane to various locations, and the invasion was on. Although the commander-in-chief of the Danish armed forces wanted to defend Denmark, it was obvious that the tiny country would be quickly overwhelmed in a fight with the Germans. When the German ambassador to Denmark handed the government in the capital city of Copenhagen a demand for Danish surrender, Luftwaffe (German air force) airplanes circled overhead as a visible warning. The surrender was granted, and the fighting was stopped just a few hours after it had begun.

Hitler planned to use Denmark as a geographical buffer between Great Britain and Germany, but the German occupiers took pains to tell the Danish people something quite the opposite: that the point of the invasion was to "protect" Denmark from a possible British invasion. The German occupiers were unusually polite to the Danes—whom they considered to be perfect Aryans—and allowed the Danish government to remain in place and make many independent decisions. One of these was the insistence that Jews living in Denmark be free from any German harassment. Not a single law was passed against the Jews of Denmark.

From the start, there was a large difference in Danish opinion regarding the German presence. Some thought that since the German occupiers were polite, were not interfering with the government, and were not harming the Jews in Denmark as they were in other countries, that Danes should cooperate with the Germans as much as possible.

Other Danes argued that polite or not, the Germans were still occupying Denmark and that Danes should fight back in any way they could. Some became involved with printing illegal underground newspapers. Others were in communication with the British Resistance organization, the Special Operations Executive (SOE); some Danes gathered information for the SOE regarding German military activities in Denmark. The SOE provided sabotage-oriented Danes with explosives and weapons to fight the German occupiers. Other Danes were able to secretly manufacture their own guns at great risk—the Germans had ordered that all firearms be relinquished.

In November 1941, the Danish foreign minster was forced by the Germans to sign the Anti-Comintern Pact. Although the Danish government had already been forced to imprison some leading Danish Communists a few months before, signing the pact took this one step further: it meant that Denmark was being forced to declare war on international communism.

This obvious loss of political independence sparked angry protests—not only against the Germans but against the too-

★★★ THE JEWS OF DENMARK ★★★

At the time of the German occupation, there were slightly more than 7,000 Jews living in Denmark. Approximately 1,600 came from families who had been there for centuries. Nearly 3,400 were Jews who had fled to Denmark during the turn of the century or after World War I to escape persecution in Russia and other Eastern European countries. Others were recent immigrants from Nazi Germany, and several hundred were in Denmark specifically to learn agriculture before they went to live and work in Israel. Nearly 200 more were German Jewish orphans. But no matter how long they had lived in Germany or what their future plans, all the Jews living in Denmark were fiercely protected by the Danes. When a Danish Nazi (a very small political party during the occupation) tried to set fire to a synagogue, Danish officials sentenced him to three years in prison.

cooperative Danish government. These protests turned violent when Danish police attacked and arrested the protesters.

Acts of sabotage steadily increased until the occupiers finally had had enough. On August 28, 1943, the Germans delivered an ultimatum to the Danish government: if the Danish government would not make an effort to control its people, then the Germans would. The Danish government resigned rather than cooperate with the Germans any longer.

The following day, the Germans issued an edict that severely limited the Danish government's powers and installed martial law on the population. The edict enforced a strict sundown curfew, a ban on public gatherings, and death for anyone caught in any act remotely related to sabotage.

The majority of Danes were finally united against their German occupiers. And not a moment too soon, for the Danes were informed by a German civil servant that the Germans were secretly planning a roundup of Denmark's Jews on October 1 and 2.

Danes responded immediately. Jews were warned and hidden in private homes and hospitals until arrangements could be made for their escape by boat to neutral Sweden. All other resistance activity halted temporarily while Denmark's Resistance organizations worked together with the rest of the population to rescue Denmark's Jews and send them to Sweden.

Most of the rescue operations took place in the first two weeks of October, and by the month's end, nearly all of Denmark's Jews were safe in Sweden. Only 481 were caught and sent to the Theresienstadt concentration camp in Czechoslovakia, but these Jews were more fortunate than most other prisoners at that camp. The Danish government was allowed to send the Danish Jews in Theresienstadt food packages and vitamins. The Danes also convinced the Nazis to allow the Danish Jews to remain in Czechoslovakia instead of being transferred to harsher camps in Poland or Germany. Because of this intervention, nearly all of them survived.

After the Jews were rescued, Danish sabotage against the German occupiers continued, with harsh German reprisals, sometimes ending in the saboteur's death and other times in a trip to a German concentration camp. Approximately 6,000 Danes—mostly Resistance workers—were in German concentration camps during the last year of the war, and many of them died.

On May 4, 1945, the BBC announced over the radio that Germans had surrendered in Denmark and the Netherlands and that the surrender would become official on the following day. Some Germans and Danish Nazis continued to fight, but officially the Danes were free as of that date.

Monica Wichfeld

IRISH HEROINE OF THE DANISH RESISTANCE

A WOMAN CARRYING a large, heavy bag walked quietly onto a pier where a rowboat was tied, awaiting her use. It was past midnight, but the moon was bright and lit her way as she rowed silently through the still waters of the lake. On these quiet, moon-lit nights, this lake reminded her of her childhood, when she used to create magical imaginary worlds with her beloved brother Jack on the lake of their beautiful estate in Northern Ireland.

She still couldn't bear to speak Jack's name aloud, even though he had been killed many years before, during World War I. That war had been started in part, as the current one had been, by the Germans, and she would never forgive them for the conflict that

Monica and Jorgen Wichfeld on their estate, Engestofte, September 1942. *Museum of Danish Resistance*

took her brother's life. That is why Monica Wichfeld was now risking her life and safety by rowing the two miles across the lake with
a bag full of explosives to be used by the Danish Resistance.

Monica owned the lake that she was now rowing across. She
had met Jorgen Wichfeld, a wealthy, land-owning Dane, in London during World War I. She had traveled there from Northern
Ireland in 1915 to support the British cause by working in a soldiers' canteen. At that time she also became part of the wealthy
young London society of which Jorgen was a part. They were married the following year.

A few years after the war ended, Monica and Jorgen moved onto
Jorgen's Danish estate. Named Engestofte, the property contained
a mansion, a lake, and thousands of acres of farmland. Shortly
after Monica's arrival at Engestofte, a fire broke out, destroying
much of the farmland and causing financial disaster for the Wich-
felds. To save Engestofte, they would have to lease it to tenants and
live elsewhere.

Monica took control of the family finances, starting her own jew-
elry and cosmetics business in London and Paris during the 1920s.
She eventually situated herself and her family part of the time in
Italy, where her own mother was living in modest comfort. During
the 1930s, Monica's European business travels allowed her to wit-
ness the rise of Hitler's Nazi regime. She saw the hysterical Nazi ral-
lies and watched France and England do nothing as Hitler defied
the terms of the Treaty of Versailles and geared his country for war.
Monica also saw many Jewish refugees desperately trying to flee
Nazi Germany.

Monica was determined to do what she could to stop the Nazis'
progress. She began to gather information for British intelligence
organizations regarding the Italian attitude toward the approaching war. Some of this material was broadcast by BBC radio, the
London radio station that reported official Allied news. Monica's
espionage activities—and pro-Allied sympathies—soon came to

the attention of the Italian authorities, and she began to be treated in a hostile manner. When a close friend of Monica's was interrogated exclusively about Monica's activities, Monica realized it was time to return to the safety of Denmark.

Denmark had already been occupied by Germany for over a year when Monica came back. The Germans allowed the Danish government to remain in control, made no laws against Denmark's Jews, and treated the population with gentleness unheard of in any other Nazi-occupied country.

Many Danes felt relatively fortunate, but others, like Monica, were furious that the country was being occupied. She felt distinctly out of place among the other contented Danish landowners. She quickly tried to find others who were involved with the small but growing Danish Resistance movement.

Her opportunity came when she rented the cottage on her estate to Hilmar Wulff, a Communist, who had answered the ad only after being reassured that the lady of Engestofte was British by birth and openly pro-Allied. On her second visit to her new tenant, after they had been discussing books and politics, Monica suddenly turned to Wulff and asked him if he read *Frit Danmark* (Free Denmark), the most popular and influential underground Danish Resistance newspaper. He said that he did. She told him that she wanted to help the Resistance. He told her that she could begin collecting funds for a distribution network he was trying to establish for *Frit Danmark* and *Land og folk* (Country and People), the official paper of the Danish Communist Party.

An unlikely friendship developed between this communist, whose belief system involved the ultimate overthrow of private landownership, and Monica Wichfeld, the owner of a vast estate. But they were united in their desire to fight the Nazi occupation, and Monica not only began to raise funds for the distribution of *Frit Danmark* and *Land og folk*, she also began to occasionally distribute the papers herself.

Monica soon became involved with additional Resistance work. In 1943, she was introduced to Flemming Muus, a Dane who had been trained by the British SOE Resistance organization to strengthen the Danish Resistance, unify the Danes against the Germans, and cause them to embrace the Allied cause. (Flemming later married Monica's daughter, Varinka, in June 1944.)

When Flemming first met Monica, he was amazed that some of her ideas were exactly those being discussed by the most brilliant men in the RAF (Royal Air Force) of Great Britain. She agreed to help build a network of Danish Resistance workers who would receive and distribute weapons and explosives being dropped into Denmark from Great Britain, as well as establish a series of safe houses for spies and others who were running from the Germans.

Monica used her estate, Engestofte, to hide explosives, often rowing them across the two-mile-wide lake in the middle of the night to the cottage where Hilmar Wulff lived. She also told her family that she wanted a new bedroom, one away from the rest of the family (who, with the exception of her daughter, Varinka, had no idea of her Resistance activities), so that she would not be disturbed while writing letters and sewing. Above her new room, she could hide several spies, saboteurs, and others who needed temporary shelter until safe transport to England could be arranged.

In late August 1943, a team of four men who had been trained by Flemming Muus blew up the Forum in Copenhagen, the largest public hall in the city. Four days later, the Germans gave the Danish government an ultimatum: control the Resistance, or else. When the Danish government refused to cooperate and resigned, the Germans took over.

Part of that takeover was a long-delayed movement against Denmark's Jews. The leaders of the Danish Resistance had forbidden Monica to shelter Danish Jews, fearing it might lead to the collapse of the entire network and certain that there were plenty of Danes who would be willing to take in Jews. But when Monica

was approached by Jewish people in need, she agreed to hide them
and pass them off as her servants. During the mass rescue operation of Denmark's Jews, Monica was also able to secure safe pas-
sage to Sweden for the Jews living with her.

In December 1943, Jacob Jensen, a Resistance worker whom
Monica never completely trusted, ignored security precautions
and made several long-distance calls, which were intercepted by
the Gestapo. He and a radio operator were arrested and, in spite
of his being armed, he surrendered without a fight. He told the
Gestapo everything, handing over the names of 44 prominent
Resistance members, including Monica and her group.

Monica was urged to flee Denmark before she was arrested.
She refused, saying, "As I have joined the struggle for Denmark,
I am willing to pay the price." On January 13, 1944, Monica was
woken by two heavily armed Gestapo agents who pointed their
revolvers in her face and ordered her to get up immediately. As she
dressed, she looked out the window and noticed German soldiers
outside the window, pointing machine guns at the house.

Monica dressed slowly, then walked downstairs under the
watchful eye of the Gestapo agents and ordered the cook to make
breakfast. She turned to the Gestapo agents, who were now filling
the room, and asked them calmly if she could get them tea or coffee. They declined. One of them found a pile of maps that had red
circles around the cities that had been captured by the Allies.

"You are obviously pro-Allies?" he asked.

Monica laughed. "Two of my brothers are fighting in the British army; a third was killed on the Somme in the First World War.
What do you expect me to be, pro-German?"

Monica was taken to the Vestre Faengsel, the West Prison, in
the center of Copenhagen. There she was interrogated. Jacob Jensen had not only revealed names but also minute details of the
whole operation; he ultimately was responsible for the arrests and
deaths of over 100 Danish resisters. Because of the information

Jensen had provided, the Gestapo was certain that Monica had tremendous stature in the Resistance, so they interrogated her night
and day. She told them nothing. When they discovered that she
was a smoker, they tempted her with a packet of cigarettes if she
would talk. She flicked the packet away with contempt.

After four months of fruitless interrogation, Monica stood trial
with 10 other members of the Danish Resistance. She was sentenced to death along with four of the men. Because she was well
known and because she was a woman, Monica's sentence sparked
outrage. The threat of violence regarding her death sentence was
so extensive that the Germans in Denmark, afraid that they would
have to call in additional troops (which were desperately needed
to battle the invading Allies) to quell a possible riot, promised
Monica a life sentence if she would only ask for clemency (official
forgiveness).

Monica refused. If the others who had been condemned to
death wouldn't be spared, why should she be? She was, however,
finally convinced by her friends and family and wrote up a short
defense of her case. In return, she received a sentence of life imprisonment. Her three Resistance colleagues were executed several
days later.

Monica's imprisonment was to take place in Germany, where
conditions were surely going to be severe. Her reprieve obviously had been designed to stave off a violent Danish protest, not
to spare her life. After enduring grueling prison conditions while
simultaneously being a source of strength and inspiration to her
fellow prisoners, Monica fell ill, and she died on February 27, 1945,
a little over one year after her arrest and only months before the
Allies defeated Germany. Her death was widely mourned in Denmark. Because of her Resistance efforts and her courageous refusal
to give the Nazis any information, she became an inspiration and
a symbol of the Danish Resistance.

★★★ LEARN MORE ★★★

Monica: Heroine of the Danish Resistance by Christine Sutherland (Farrar, Straus and Giroux, 1990).

Ebba Lund

THE GIRL WITH THE RED CAP

IT WAS AUGUST 1943. Twenty-year-old Ebba Lund read the words on the poster. It stated that, due to the increased acts of violence against the occupying German forces in Denmark, the Danish government was now dissolved. Germany was taking complete control of Denmark. After three-plus years, Germany had had enough of Danish rebellion.

Ebba could remember clearly the day that Denmark had been invaded. She had been woken by a heavy, humming sound, but since she had no idea what it was and it was too early to get up for school, she had gone back to sleep. Riding her bike to school hours later through the streets of Copenhagen, Ebba saw a crowd

---

Gilleleje Harbor, where many Danish Jews began their escape to Sweden.
The Museum of Danish Resistance

of Danes formed around a smaller group of German soldiers who were holding weapons. She stopped to see what was going on.

A young man standing next to her said, "I just can't believe it."

"What's happened?" Ebba asked.

"We've been occupied!" he answered.

Ebba didn't quite understand. Was Denmark at war? She kept riding until she came to the British embassy. Trucks pulled up in front of the building. German soldiers got out, entered the building, and came out with people whom they forced into the trucks. They were British diplomats, now under arrest, since Germany and Great Britain had declared war on each other months before.

The sympathetic Danes standing by began to chant, "Hurrah for the Britons!" Suddenly, a German shouted, "Anyone attempting to escape will be shot." His grim warning temporarily silenced the encouraging chants. Then, they began again, "Hurrah for the Britons!"

The Germans didn't want the Danes to think that the British were their friends. Part of the reason the Germans had invaded Denmark was so that Denmark might serve as a geographical buffer between Germany and Great Britain in case of a British invasion. But the Germans told the Danes the lie that they were protecting the Danes from a possible invasion of their tiny country by Great Britain.

Many Danes were content with the polite German occupation, but others were deeply offended and joined Resistance organizations. Some of these organizations were involved with explosives, weapons, and acts of sabotage and assassination. Others, like the ones Ebba Lund and her sister, Ulla, joined, published illegal underground newspapers. By 1942, two years after the invasion, there were 48 different underground papers in Denmark (and by the end of the war there were 166). *Frit Danmark* (Free Denmark), the paper for which Ebba Lund worked, was the most popular of all Denmark's underground presses because of its lively writing

Frit Danmark. "Events Draw Closer to Denmark: Parliament Must Act Now." *The Museum of Danish Resistance*

style and its inclusion of many different political opinions, both liberal and conservative. By the end of the war, over six million copies of *Frit Danmark* had been published.

The debate over the necessity for illegal groups and newspapers ended with the publication of another paper, the public one that Ebba had just read. It stated that because of the rise of sabotage activities, the Danish government had lost its ability to maintain order and was being shut down.

The Danish government had resigned the day before the edict, on August 28, rather than cooperate with the Germans any longer. The Danes were finally united and not a moment too soon; shortly afterward plans for a roundup of all Danish Jews became known. The Germans ran Denmark now, and nothing was going to stop them in their quest to destroy all of Europe's Jews.

Nothing except the Danes. They quickly took action. Sweden had promised to accept any and all Danish Jews who could be brought there. All over Denmark, rescue plans were set in motion.

★★★ THE EDICT OF AUGUST 29, 1943 ★★★

Recent events have shown that the Danish Government is no longer in a position to maintain Law and Order in the country. . . . I am ordering the following to take place with immediate effect:

Crowds and meetings involving more than five persons on the street or in a public place are prohibited, as are all assemblies, even in private.

Closing time is decreed to occur at sundown. From this point onwards, traffic on the streets will also cease.

All the use of the Post, Telegraph, and Telephone is prohibited until further notice.

All strikes are prohibited. Fomenting strike action which causes damage to the German Wehrmacht assists the enemy and will normally be punished by death.

Any encroachment of the above edicts will be punished according to standard German law. Any acts of violence, assembly of crowds, etc., will be ruthlessly suppressed by force of arms . . . —The Commander-in-Chief of the German Forces in Denmark.

A German soldier posts the Edict of August 29, 1943. *The Museum of Danish Resistance*

Ebba joined the sabotage-oriented Resistance group Holger Danske (named for a legendary Danish hero), which was planning to work its rescue operation out of Copenhagen. Members of Holger Danske planned to secure as many fishing boats as possible, raise money to pay the fishermen, then take the Jews to Sweden in these boats.

Since Ebba's family regularly vacationed on the island of Christiansø, and she knew many fishing families from that island, she was given the task of securing the boats. She contacted the son of a fisherman who knew of an eccentric Danish fisherman called "the American" (because he had once spent some time in the United States). She found him by his fishing nets outside the hut where he lived near a Copenhagen harbor. She approached him and offered to pay him well if he would take some Jews to Sweden. He agreed. Then she asked him if he knew of any other fishermen who would be willing to transport Jews. He did, and soon Ebba and her group had almost a dozen boats at their disposal.

Now they needed money. Most of the fishermen who agreed to rescue the Jews were very willing to help, but they needed money to participate in the rescue operation. If they were caught by the Germans or if anything else happened to their ship during the trip to Sweden, they would lose their livelihood. Ebba and the others working with her managed to find enough money in a matter of days. Wealthy landowners were asked for donations, and most gave generously. Ebba also helped raise money from people in Copenhagen.

They had the boats. They had the money. Now they needed the refugees. Again, word got out quickly, and safe houses were set up in Copenhagen—including Ebba Lund's home—where the Jews could hide until they could be taken safely to the harbor.

Soon hundreds of Jews were flocking to Copenhagen and being sent to Sweden in the group of boats that Ebba had organized. Most of the other Danish rescue missions operated only under cover of darkness, but Ebba did her work by the light of day. Her reasoning was that the Germans had established a sundown curfew and she didn't want to invite extra trouble. Plus, who would suspect an illegal rescue operation to be occurring in broad daylight?

During the rescue operations, Ebba became known as the Girl with the Red Cap, Red Cap, or Red Riding Hood because she would wear a red cap as a silent signal to the Jews who would be escorted to the port with directions to look for her. Ebba would then walk them down to the boats, pay the fishermen, and make sure the Jews got away safely. The boats used in Ebba's operation could hide approximately 25 to 35 people at one time below the deck in the passenger cabins.

One day, after Ebba had helped a group of Jews into a boat and had already taken off her red cap, she was standing on the pier about to pay the fishermen when five Germans in grey Wehrmacht uniforms began walking toward her. If they asked to search Ebba's bag, they would find a large amount of money there—10,000 kroner—which was enough to raise serious suspicions about what Ebba was doing on the pier. She had to think fast.

The fishermen looked up at the approaching Germans. Ebba quickly walked up to one of the fishermen, hooked her arm into his, and smiled at him lovingly. The fisherman took the hint and smiled right back at Ebba. The Germans stared at the loving couple for a moment, then turned and walked away.

There were many reasons why Ebba didn't have more close calls. One reason was that members of the Holger Danske group and the Danish coast guard kept an armed patrol on the rescue operations out of the port where Ebba was working. The Germans, many of them Wehrmacht soldiers and not the Jew-hating SS, knew this and apparently didn't want to get killed over a rescue operation. Others had been bribed to look the other way. Some of them would even tell the Danish coast guard exactly when they were going to patrol the port and when they would be gone.

But still, Ebba was taking a great personal risk in helping the Jews. One day it became graphically clear to her what fate she had been rescuing them from. A passenger who had escaped from Germany showed Ebba a photo of piles of dead bodies from a Polish concentration camp. Ebba was extremely disturbed by the images—in her wildest imagination, she could not have pictured such horror when she set out with her friends to rescue the Jews.

Ebba felt compelled to become involved in the Jewish rescue before she knew the particulars because, as she said many years later, "For me it was not a Jewish problem, it was a simple humanity problem." The Holger Danske group helped approximately 700 to 800 Jews escape from German-occupied Denmark in just a few weeks.

After the war, Ebba studied chemical engineering and immunology (the study of how the body fights disease) and did important research regarding the polio virus. She later became the head of the Department of Virology and Immunology at the Royal Veterinary and Agricultural University in Copenhagen. She was heavily involved in scientific research and served on many science-related committees all her adult life. She died in 1999.

★★★ LEARN MORE ★★★

Darkness over Denmark: The Danish Resistance and the Rescue of the Jews by Ellen Levine (Holiday House, 2000) includes the story of Ebba Lund's rescuing activities.

"'Girl in Red Cap' Saved Hundreds of Jews"
San Diego Jewish Press-Heritage
www.jewishsightseeing.com/denmark/copenhagen/1994-01-14_
red_cap_girl.htm
An interview with Ebba Lund dated January 14, 1994.

PART VII
Great Britain

MANY BELIEVE THAT World War II could have been prevented if the Allied leaders, including British prime minster Neville Chamberlain, had stopped Hitler in 1938. That was the year the governments of France and Great Britain both agreed to allow Hitler to seize the Sudetenland, a section of Czechoslovakia in which many Germans lived. Hitler promised in writing, in what became known as the Munich Agreement, to take no more land after being given the Sudetenland. Chamberlain came back from Munich with the signed paper and claimed that it assured "peace for our time." He feared—correctly so—that stopping Hitler would have meant war for Britain, something his country wasn't ready for.

That "peace" was made pointless six months later when Hitler invaded Czechoslovakia, annexed the Czech half of the state to Germany, and made Slovakia a German puppet state (meaning

Germany allowed the Slovakian government to exist but had easy and ultimate control over it). And the peace was completely shattered when German tanks rolled over the Polish border the following year, on September 1, 1939. France and Great Britain, who were allies of Poland, declared war on Germany, and in turn, Germany declared war on both of them. But neither France nor Great Britain did anything to help the Poles against Germany. This was the beginning of the eight-month Drôle de Guerre, the Phony War, so called because during this time these countries, though officially at war, didn't make a significant move against the other. The Phony War became real, however, when Hitler began conquering western Europe in the spring of 1940. By the summer, his troops had conquered Norway, Denmark, the Netherlands, France, Luxembourg, and Belgium.

Hitler now turned his attention to Great Britain. He knew that the British Royal Navy was superior to that of Germany, so crossing the English Channel for a land attack was initially out of the question. He also viewed the British as fellow Aryans and didn't want to humiliate them. He decided that securing a voluntary surrender was the best route to take. To obtain this, he waged an air battle with his German Luftwaffe against the British Royal Air Force (RAF) during the summer and autumn of 1940 in what was called the Battle of Britain.

Hitler knew the RAF was powerful, but initially he didn't understand the character of Britain's new prime minster. Winston Churchill refused to surrender, and the RAF successfully prevented a German air victory. By autumn of 1940, Hitler switched strategies and ordered the Luftwaffe to bomb civilian and military targets during what was called the Blitz. By the spring of 1941, thousands of British civilians had been killed in the bombing, but still Britain refused to surrender. Hitler finally decided to focus his attention elsewhere, although German bombs would continue to explode in Britain for most of the remainder of the war—especially after Germany developed so-called *Vergeltungswaffen* ("vengeance weapons"). The buzz bomb (V-1) and the A4 rocket (V-2) could be launched from occupied France into Britain.

Churchill's radio broadcasts and strong stance stimulated patriotism among the British, and many of them—including women—responded by volunteering for the armed services. In 1941, Great Britain required that all women aged 18 through 60 be registered for a military draft. By 1943, nearly 90 percent of all single women and 80 percent of all married women were employed in some type of war effort.

The Women's Land Army (WLA) was made of young women who generally came from British cities to work on farms so that the male farm workers could be free to join the armed services. The work of the women in the WLA prevented a national famine during the war. Idle Women, most inappropriately named, worked long grueling hours transporting cargo along Britain's inland waterways.

Female air raid wardens provided first aid and organized emergency measures when a German bomb struck. The women in the Women's Voluntary Service (WVS)—which had over one million members—supported the work of the air raid wardens, organized evacuations, and ran mobile canteens that provided refreshments and entertainment for soldiers. Female air raid wardens and the women in the WVS were often in considerable danger.

Each branch of the British military had a section for women, and nearly 500,000 British women were involved in the branches. The Auxiliary Territorial Service (ATS) was attached to the army. Women could also join the Women's Royal Naval Service (WRNS) or the Women's Auxiliary Air Force (WAAF). Some of these jobs were clerical and far from the fighting, but others were closer to danger. For instance, some women involved with the ATS assisted men who operated antiaircraft guns, working searchlights and radar equipment that would help the men hit their targets. The women in these jobs were exposed to the same dangers as the men.

The First Aid Nursing Yeomanry (FANY) was the first women's voluntary corps in Great Britain. It was created in 1907, utilized during World War I, and continued during World War II (attached to the ATS). Women involved with FANY drove ambulances and jeeps and worked in canteens, hospitals, and military headquarters. Many women who signed up for the FANY, however, did so only to provide a cover—a false reason—to be away from home. They had really been recruited for the Resistance organization the Special Operations Executive (SOE).

Almost immediately after France fell to the Germans in June 1940, Winston Churchill began to form the SOE, an organization that he claimed would "set Europe ablaze." The agents of the SOE waged a clandestine (secret) war in Nazi-occupied countries that involved espionage, sabotage of German military equipment and transportation methods, and the assassination of German officers

ATS worker operating a searchlight.
Getty Images

and soldiers. The SOE accomplished these activities by training agents who were native speakers of a particular Nazi-occupied country and then sending them into those countries to locate, organize, fund, and assist the Resistance fighters already working there.

When the SOE first discussed the possible inclusion of women in the ranks of agents, who would be on equal footing with the men, the idea was met with strong opposition. But that was soon forgotten in light of the obvious fact that female agents would have more freedom to move about than would their male counterparts since most able-bodied men in occupied countries were supposed to be working in German munitions factories.

Thousands of men and women (more women than men) worked at an English country estate called Bletchley Park (code named Station X), trying to break the German Enigma code that enabled the German military to communicate top-secret messages to each other. Polish mathematicians, who had already broken the initial Enigma code, provided Enigma machines to the Bletchley Park workers and helped them crack the updated Enigma codes. Because the work at Bletchley Park eventually succeeded, the Allies were able to intercept crucial messages regarding German military plans, which, it is believed, significantly shortened the war. Despite the fact that the staff eventually numbered 9,000, none of these workers ever told anyone outside the organization what he or she was working on, even for decades after the war. Winston Churchill praised the Bletchley Park staff members, calling them "the geese that laid the golden egg but never cackled."

By March 1945, the Germans had stopped bombing Great Britain, and in May, the Germans surrendered to the Allies.

Noor Inayat Khan

ROYAL AGENT

NOOR INAYAT KHAN, the daughter of an Indian-born father and an American mother, was born in Moscow, the capital city of Imperial Russia, on New Year's Day, 1914. It was fitting that Noor should have been born within steps of the Kremlin, a building that had been built for the royal tsars of Russia. Her great-great-great-grandfather was the royal Tipu Sultan, called the Tiger of Mysore, a Muslim ruler who had fought bravely for his lands and people.

Noor grew up in France, just a few miles from Paris, where she lived in a house called Fazal Manzil, or the House of Blessings. There she learned music, art, and poetry. She also learned a great

Noor Inayat Khan.
Shrabani Basu

deal about Sufism, the religious and meditative philosophy that her father and his friends followed.

After graduating from the University of Sorbonne, Noor began to write and illustrate children's stories. She was planning to create an illustrated children's newspaper, which would be called *Bel Age*—"the Beautiful Age"—when Hitler's tanks rolled into Poland on September 1, 1939, and the whole world changed.

Noor abhorred Hitler's anti-Semitic ideals and was determined to hinder him in some way. She joined the British Women's Auxiliary Air Force (WAAF), an organization that provided support to the Royal Air Force (RAF). It was here that she was trained as a radio operator, communicating through a special type of radio by Morse code. After a while, Noor realized that she would not be content until she could be more directly involved in the battle against Hitler. What she didn't realize was that she had already been noticed by an organization that was waging a very different type of war.

The Special Operations Executive, or the SOE, was a Resistance organization that sent its agents into many different Nazi-occupied countries to fight a secret but deadly war. There was always a need for a radio operator among the agents; that is, someone to transmit messages via Morse code from France to London. Noor was an excellent candidate for this type of work since she had already been trained in radio transmission.

Hand-drawn illustration
for a children's story by
Noor Inayat Khan.
Shrabani Basu.

And because she was a native French speaker, she was perfect for work for the F (French)-Section of the SOE, the section that worked directly with Resistance workers in Nazi-occupied France.

Although Noor's skills were impressive, some of her SOE instructors had serious doubts about her personality. She seemed very fragile, and she miserably failed her fake Gestapo interrogation in which she was woken in the middle of the night, splashed with cold water, and roughly questioned. She didn't seem strong enough to withstand a real interrogation. What would happen if she was caught by actual Gestapo agents? Would she break under torture and give out important information?

Despite Noor's apparent fragility, others in the SOE were certain she would be a good agent. And even those who doubted her knew that there was a desperate need for more radio operators in France. They really had no choice but to send her in. So Noor became the first female radio operator to be sent into Nazi-occupied France.

She chose to work out of Paris, a dangerous place for any member of the Resistance but especially for those doing radio work. Teams of Germans, many of them dressed in plain clothes, were using a device called a listening machine to locate and capture radio operators. The German teams worked out of vans that were disguised as laundry vans, bakers' vans—anything to hide who they really were. Because the radio operators traveled from place to place to avoid being detected by the listening teams, they had to carry their radios with them, which was very dangerous: people were often stopped and searched by suspicious Gestapo agents, especially on the busy streets of Paris.

Many of Noor's new Parisian associates also thought that her shy, naive personality seemed at odds with that of a successful agent. But whatever doubts they may have had about Noor, they soon had more pressing issues to worry about. Ten days after Noor arrived in Paris, their whole circuit (Resistance group) fell apart.

Several agents had been arrested, and the information that the Gestapo had found with them included names and, most important, addresses of current French Resistance members. Almost immediately, the Gestapo arrested hundreds of Resistance workers including most of those involved with Noor's circuit. The SOE office in London, which found out about this catastrophe from Noor's radio transmissions, urgently asked her to return to London for her own safety and told her that a plane would be sent right away. She refused, believing that if she left, there wouldn't be a single radio operator left in Paris. All the others had been arrested.

Officials at the SOE agreed, and when it was relatively safe to resume operations, Noor began to transmit radio messages again. Communication between the French Resistance, and the SOE offices and French leader General Charles de Gaulle, both in London, was absolutely critical at this time. The Allied invasion—D-day—was less than one year away. Between July and October 1943, Noor sent and received messages that helped 30 Allied airmen escape, arranged for four agents to obtain false identity papers, pinpointed exact positions for airplane drops, helped obtain weapons and money for members of the French Resistance, and communicated the exact spot where the Nazis were hiding a supply of torpedoes.

The Gestapo knew there was a radio operator in Paris, but for months Noor successfully eluded them. They failed to track her down because Noor was careful to transmit from many different locations and because she was a very fast radio operator. She also possessed a keen intuition that alerted her to the dangers of being followed or the overtures of too-friendly strangers. Her fellow agents knew that the Gestapo was closing in on Noor and urged her return to London. But she was still hesitant to leave until the SOE could send a replacement. Once she was assured that this would happen, she would make plans to return to London.

One day when Noor opened her apartment door, a French man named Pierre Cartaud, who was working for the Gestapo, was there to meet her. A woman the Germans referred to as "Renée" had contacted the Gestapo and agreed to betray a British agent she knew into their hands if they would pay her 100,000 francs. They agreed.

If Cartaud thought it would be easy to arrest this slim, petite woman, he was very wrong. She fought him violently, clawing and biting at his wrists until he was bleeding heavily. Finally, he pulled out a gun and threatened to kill her while he made a phone call, asking for assistance. When help finally came, Cartaud was standing as far away from Noor as possible. She was taken by car to 84 Avenue Fochs, the Gestapo headquarters in Paris.

Housed in a cell in the headquarters, Noor was a difficult prisoner. She demanded the privilege of taking a bath and screamed at the guards when they wouldn't allow her to close the door. The Gestapo agent in charge of interrogating Noor thought her request for a bath seemed suspicious, so he went into the bathroom next to hers and looked out the window. There was Noor, walking on the roof, trying to escape. He persuaded her to come in, telling her that a slip off the roof would mean certain death. She complied but was immediately angry with herself for doing so. She then refused, throughout an entire month of questioning, to betray her fellow resistance workers.

One day Noor decided to tap a Morse code message on the wall of her cell to see if she would get a response. She discovered that there were two SOE agents also imprisoned at the headquarters, and together they planned a daring escape. They managed to get a screwdriver and passed it between them until they had gotten all the bars of their cells loosened. Eventually they all reached the roof and were ready to let themselves down to the ground using some sheets they had tied together.

Suddenly Allied planes flew overhead, and the air-raid siren went off. Whenever that happened, the guards at 84 Avenue Fochs would rush to check that the prisoners were still in their cells. They also flashed searchlights all over the roof where Noor and her fellow spies were lying flat, hoping that no one would see them. Perhaps Noor and the others were not visible, but their cells were found empty. The escapees looked down the road and saw that it was closed off. Gestapo agents were everywhere. Desperate, they made one last attempt by swinging down by the sheets and crashing into a nearby house. The Gestapo burst in and captured them.

Back inside her cell at 84 Avenue Fochs, Noor scratched a V symbol (for victory) and an RAF symbol on her wall. She was asked to sign a promise that she would never try to escape again. She refused. It was her duty, she said, to try to escape if at all possible. A call was made to Berlin, the German capital: Noor was to be transferred to a high-security prison in Germany called Pforzheim.

The Pforzheim warden was ordered to keep Noor in solitary confinement, her feet and hands handcuffed and both sets of cuffs chained together. She became quite depressed but tried to encourage herself by meditating and thinking of her father. She and several female prisoners exchanged messages by scratching words onto the bottoms of their food bowls.

On September 11, 1944, after having been chained at Pforzheim for nearly 10 months, Noor scratched one final message on her bowl: "I am leaving." She was taken from the prison that night and moved to Dachau with three other female British agents. They were all shot the next day and their bodies burned so that there would be no trace of them.

But Noor was not forgotten. France awarded her the Croix de Guerre (Cross of War), and Great Britain awarded her the George Cross, Great Britain's highest award for courage shown somewhere other than on a battlefield. There are also many plaques and memorials in Germany and Great Britain dedicated to Noor and the other SOE agents who lost their lives during the war. Just outside of Fazal Manzil, Noor's happy childhood home, is a plaque dedicated to Noor. And every Bastille Day, July 14, a military band plays outside the house in honor of the artistic, gentle woman who grew up there, a woman who turned out to be one of the most courageous agents of the SOE.

★★★ LEARN MORE ★★★

Flames in the Field: The Story of Four SOE Agents in Occupied France by Rita Kramer (Michael Joseph, 1995) contains information on Noor's Resistance work.

Spy Princess: The Life of Noor Inayat Khan by Shrabani Basu (Omega Publications, Inc., 2007).

Nancy Wake

THE WHITE MOUSE

A BEAUTIFUL WOMAN pedaled her bike furiously along the quiet French road. Her legs were numb with exhaustion. Her seat was very sore. Although she desperately wanted to stop and rest, she knew that if she did, she might not be able to make herself get back on the bike. And it was of the utmost importance that she continue. She was responsible for the arming and the welfare of 17 different maquis groups including 7,000 *maquisards* (rural French Resistance fighters) whose lives and work against the Nazis now depended solely on her bike ride. And so she pedaled on, blocking out the pain and wiping the sweat from her brow as best she could.

Nancy Wake in her FANY uniform.
Australian War Memorial

When she passed German soldiers on the road, she forced a sweet smile and waved. Little did the soldiers know that this pretty woman whose smiles and waves they returned was the woman the Gestapo had named the White Mouse, who was near the top of its "most wanted" list and had an enormous price on her head. She had several code names as an agent of the Special Operations Executive (SOE), such as Andrée and Helene, but the name her parents had given her when she was born in New Zealand was Nancy Grace Augusta Wake.

When Nancy Wake had come to Paris from Australia, where she had grown up, as a young woman in the 1930s, she found work as a journalist and was tremendously curious about the horror stories that were coming out of Germany and Austria. Jews were streaming out of those countries with nearly unbelievable tales of brutality. She and her fellow journalists decided to see for themselves if those stories were true.

They were. When Nancy witnessed firsthand the bizarre and openly cruel behavior of the Nazis toward the German and Austrian Jews, she was revolted and extremely angry. She later said, "I resolved there and then that if I ever had the chance I would do anything, however big or small, stupid or dangerous, to try and make things more difficult for [the Nazis]."

Soon after falling in love with and marrying the wealthy Frenchman Henri Fiocca, Nancy got the chance she had been looking for. Several of them, in fact. She befriended some Allied officers who were imprisoned nearby but who were free to walk about by day. Through these connections she became a courier. She also learned of the Garrow and the O'Leary escape lines that led out of Nazi-occupied France, across the Pyrenees Mountains on the border of France and neutral Spain, and, finally, to England and freedom.

Nancy became key in helping escaped Allied servicemen and Jewish refugees cross these lines. She would discreetly pick up the refugees or Allied servicemen from the train station, find a hiding place for them, and then accompany them, via train, to their next destination.

Because Nancy was so successful in helping Allied prisoners and refugees escape, a description of her circulated among Gestapo officials. They didn't know exactly who she was, but they gave her the code name the White Mouse because she was able to elude their grasp so well, especially when they thought they had her cornered. The Gestapo offered a reward in the amount of five million francs for information leading to her capture.

It worked. The Gestapo was closing in on her. Nancy's phone line was tapped, her mail was inspected, and she was being followed. She was coming under suspicion of being the White Mouse and knew it was time to leave Marseille. She packed her bags, bid a sad farewell to Henri, got on a train, and tried to follow the Garrow Line into Spain, hoping to eventually reach England.

If Nancy thought that her trip across France and the Pyrenees Mountains was going to be as trouble-free as it had been for most of those she had assisted, she was very wrong. On her seventh try, she finally crossed into neutral Spain but not before being imprisoned twice, once in France and once in Spain; jumping from a moving train; being shot at by German soldiers; going several days without food; spending some nights in a sheep pen; and almost freezing to death while crossing the frigid Pyrenees Mountains.

When she arrived safely in England, eager to start fighting Hitler again, Nancy joined the SOE under the cover of the First Aid Nursing Yeomanry (FANY). The SOE was eager to recruit her, having already heard about her successful Resistance work in France. After she completed her SOE training, she was parachuted right back into France with her work partner, Major John Farmer, whose alias was "Hubert." They were eventually joined by their radio operator, Denis Rake, who provided them with direct radio contact with the SOE headquarters in London. This radio contact would enable the agents in France to tell the SOE exactly what they needed, and in return, the SOE could tell the agents when and where supplies and money would be dropped. Without this communication the SOE agents would have been unable to assist the maquis they had come to help.

The first maquis leader they were supposed to work with, Gaspard, a man in charge of 3,000 to 4,000 men, mistrusted Nancy. In his mind, there were two things wrong with her: she was from England, and she was a woman. He didn't trust the SOE either. He decided to have one of his men get Nancy drunk, seduce her, murder her, and then take her money. Nancy overheard his plans, and after boldly confronting her would-be assassin she walked away unharmed and soon began to work with a different and more friendly maquis leader, Henri Fournier.

Because of the radio transmissions provided by Nancy's radio operator, Fournier's band of maquis soon became the best-supplied group in the area. The good news quickly spread, and although Nancy lived with Fournier's band, she was soon regularly visiting and supplying 17 different bands, which included 7,000 men in total, and eventually Gaspard's men as well. They came to greatly respect Nancy and value her judgment. She worked day and night to keep the steadily increasing number of *maquisards* supplied with the weapons and explosives received by air-drop from London and then trained them to use those weapons and explosives effectively. She also provided them with SOE money so they could pay local farmers for provisions instead of stealing from them.

Although these *maquisards* were usually outnumbered by the Germans in the area, they often put up incredible fights that inflicted large numbers of German casualties. This made the Germans more determined than ever to wipe them out. The Germans sent in 22,000 troops, 1,000 military vehicles, and 10 airplanes.

Nancy raced to the area of the fighting. After she had unpacked, prepared, and distributed all of the ammunition and arms from the last plane drop, Nancy was so exhausted that she fell asleep for a few hours under a tree.

An order came to withdraw from the battle. As Nancy left the area in her car, one of the German planes spotted her and began to chase her down. The pilot was close enough that Nancy could see his helmet and goggles. She could hear the whizzing of the bullets he was firing at her coming closer and closer. She flung herself out of the car and landed safely by the side of the road.

Then, in the midst of the retreat, Nancy's radio operator got rid of his radio and radio codes to keep them from falling into the hands of the pursuing Germans, leaving Nancy without SOE contact. She and all the *maquisards* in the area would soon run out of supplies and weapons. It was essential to obtain a radio and new codes, and Nancy knew that there was only one way to do it. She would have to get on a bike and pedal to the nearest radio operator to ask London to send, via the next parachute drop, a new radio and new codes. The nearest radio operator was 200 kilometers (approximately 125 miles) away.

When Nancy presented her idea to the *maquisards*, they tried to talk her out of it. They reminded her that she had no identification papers. When she would be stopped at checkpoints, she would surely be suspected as part of the maquis. And furthermore, she—a woman—would be alone and unprotected for all those miles.

That was precisely the point, Nancy replied. She was a woman. If any of the men tried to pass a German checkpoint, they would be immediately identified as a member of the maquis and arrested, or possibly shot, on the spot. But as a single woman, alone on a bike, Nancy could easily pose as a housewife, simply out shopping for her family. And as Nancy knew from past experience, a pretty woman had ways of getting past German soldiers without any trouble. Despite their misgivings, the *maquisards* knew that without a radio they would all be useless in the fight against the Germans. So Nancy obtained a new outfit, applied the last remnants of makeup she had, and rode off on her bike.

Whenever German soldiers passed her on the road, Nancy smiled and waved. When she had to stop at a checkpoint, she would ask innocently, "Do you want to search *moi* (me)?"

The response from each officer was basically the same: "No, mademoiselle, you can carry on."

She was finally able to find a radio operator who agreed to contact the SOE offices in London and ask them to send another radio and more codes. When she finally got back to camp, several days later, she could barely move. The bike ride had rubbed away the skin from her inner thighs. She was in terrible pain, unable to stand or sit. She couldn't walk for days. But the radio and the codes came soon, with the next parachute drop. It had been worth it. Nancy's *maquisards* were again organized and armed.

After she recovered from her bike ride, Nancy continued to fight the Germans with her *maquisards*. While making a raid on a munitions factory, Nancy killed a German guard with her bare hands before he could sound an alarm. Another time she and several other maquis interrupted a meeting of German officers by hurling hand grenades into the room. And after the war, Nancy became one of the most highly decorated women from World War II, receiving numerous top awards from the governments of France, Great Britain, and the United States.

But what made Nancy the most proud was that bike ride that ended up totaling 500 kilometers and that she had accomplished in just 72 hours, one of the most difficult things she ever did and a key moment in the maquis' fight against the Germans.

In 1985 Nancy wrote her memoir, called *The Autobiography of the Woman the Gestapo Called "The White Mouse."* She died in London on August 7, 2011, at the age of 98.

★★★ LEARN MORE ★★★

The Autobiography of the Woman the Gestapo Called "The White Mouse" by Nancy Wake (Sun Books, 1985).

Nancy Wake: The Inspiring Story of One of the War's Greatest Heroines by Peter Fitzsimons (Harper Collins, 2001).

The White Mouse: Nancy Grace Augusta Wake
www.diggerhistory.info/pages_heroes/white_mouse.htm is a website with information on Wake and includes photos of her numerous medals.

Pearl Witherington

THE COURIER WHO BECAME A LEADER

THE ALLIED INVASION of Nazi-occupied France—D-day—had finally come. Urgent orders had come from London to obstruct the roads to hinder German troops from getting to the Normandy coast, where the Allies had just landed. Pearl Witherington, an SOE agent, and the rural French maquis fighters she was working with had been very busy for two days following these orders, blocking the roads in their area with felled trees and large pieces of debris.

A young man who had just bicycled in from Paris, 120 miles to the north, was outside the gatehouse of the chateau property where Pearl and her team of maquis were living. Pearl questioned him about the condition of the roads to the north.

Pearl Witherington and Henri Cornioley.
Hervé Larroque

She was shocked by what he told her: the only obstructions he had seen were in their immediate area. None of the other networks had obeyed the order. The Germans, always trying to weed out bands of maquis, would certainly come looking for whoever had created these obstructions.

Two days later a low-flying reconnaissance plane (referred to by the maquis as the Snoop) flew over Pearl's area. Had the pilot seen them?

Apparently so. At 5:00 A.M. on June 11, 1944, five days after D-day, a group of maquis leaders in a truck near their headquarters ran right into a group of Germans. They were able to get away, with German bullets flying after them.

About 2,000 German troops moved in, attacking both Pearl's maquis network and a Communist one to the south. Pearl grabbed her small sack of personal items and a cocoa box in which she kept the network's money. With bullets whizzing by her ears, she biked to where the weapons and explosives were kept. She began to assemble the guns, fill them with ammunition, and put fuses on the grenades.

A young *maquisard* suddenly rushed in and told Pearl to get out because the Germans were already there. Pearl dropped the weapons, took her sack of personal items and the cocoa box—which contained approximately 500,000 francs—and ran into a wheat field, where she hid for the rest of the day.

Were these the actions of a hero? Why didn't she stay and fight?

Pearl always had good reasons for her choices, and no wonder: decision making had been forced upon her very early. Her English father, who brought his family to Paris for his work, was an alcoholic who wasted his family's money. Because of this, and the fact that she spoke French well, certain responsibilities fell on Pearl's young shoulders. Even at the age of 12, she often had to speak to creditors and landlords on behalf of her family.

When Pearl was 17, her father left. Pearl then went to work to support her three younger sisters and her mother, who was in poor health and could barely speak French. Pearl held various secretarial jobs and also taught English in the evenings. Eventually, she obtained a very good desk job at the British Embassy with the Air Ministry.

Then, in June 1940, the Germans invaded France. All embassy employees were boarded on a train and sent to Normandy to catch a boat to England. But at the last minute it was announced that only employees who had been brought over from England would be shipped out. No provision was made for employees who had been hired locally, like Pearl. She and her family were stranded in Normandy without money or even a place to go. Pearl went to the American embassy in Normandy and through her connections with her former embassy job, she was given some financial help to allow her and her family to get back to Paris, now occupied by the Germans. Then, a few months later, when they heard rumors that Germans were rounding up English people in Paris, Pearl guided her family through a seven-and-a-half-month exodus from France, managing all the tedious customs and embassy details herself.

When they finally arrived in England, Pearl and her sisters joined the Women's Auxiliary Air Force (WAAF), where they worked as office staff and secretaries. But Pearl was not content with her desk job. Memories of German-occupied Paris—the swastika banners flying in the streets, the posters announcing the murders of innocent Parisians—filled her with anger. She wanted to take a more active role in fighting the Germans.

Pearl had heard that there were people, fluent in French, who were being trained in England to work with the French Resistance. She asked her superior at the WAAF about it, but he said this organization was composed of "amateurs," and he forbade her to apply. However, when Pearl related her frustration to a friend, she discovered that this friend worked for the head of the secret operation. He contacted Pearl, and she was in.

What Pearl had joined was the Special Operations Executive (SOE), an organization that trained agents to work in Nazi-occupied countries. Pearl was a good candidate for the F (French)-Section, but some of her instructors thought she lacked leadership qualities, suggesting she would do well only under the guidance of a strong leader. She was assigned to work as a courier under Maurice Southgate, a man whose code name was Hector Stationer. The Stationer network was collecting intelligence (information) regarding German activities, training local French fighters—the maquis—in the use of weapons and explosives, and conducting selective acts of sabotage.

She parachuted into France on the night of September 22, 1943, after being forced back to England on two previous occasions due to bad weather. Her suitcases ended up in the bottom of a lake, and she didn't get them back for weeks. Then, from September 1943 until May 1944, posing as a cosmetics representative, Pearl functioned as a courier for the Stationer network, delivering important messages from place to place.

The area covered by the Stationer network was very large, so Pearl spent most of her time on night trains, using a special pass that precluded her from most Gestapo searches. French railways at that time didn't have private sleeping cars—men and women were thrown together haphazardly—so Pearl often chose to sleep in her seat, in the unheated cars. This took a toll on her health, and early in 1944 she became ill for several weeks.

Courier work was often dangerous, sometimes in surprising ways. Once Pearl was sent to collect money from a certain maquis leader, but she had been given no password with which to identify herself. She was greeted coldly. She tried to give code names of

★★★ THE MILICE ★★★

The Milice Française (French militia) was established in Vichy, France, to locate and arrest French Resistance workers and Jews. Members of the Milice had a particularly brutal reputation and, in a way, posed more danger to Resistance workers than the Germans did, since as French natives they could detect small differences in French accents that the Germans could not. Members of the Milice were also expert at recruiting local informers. By the beginning of 1944, the Milice had spread from Vichy to the entire country.

other agents. This did nothing. The leader became more hostile. Pearl sensed she was in serious danger. Finally, she mentioned the name of the farmer on whose property she had landed the night she parachuted into France.

Suddenly, several large men came into the room. They had been listening and were under orders to strangle Pearl if it turned out that she was an agent of the Milice, the traitorous French militia. They were now convinced that she wasn't. She was safe, but she thought later, "If I had not managed to convince him with the last name, I don't know how I would have got out of it. . . . Being killed by another Resister, that would have been the end!"

Just a month before D-day, Pearl's leader, Maurice Southgate, along with his radio operator, was captured by the Gestapo at his residence in Montluçon. The Gestapo found the radio in the house, along with lists of the various drop fields and the network's money. Germans surrounded Montluçon the next day. Pearl, her fiancé Henri Cornioley (who had joined the network), and some others escaped the area by small back roads before splitting up.

Pearl, Henri, and a radio operator fled to the chateau, several miles to the northwest, where they established a new base of operations.

With Maurice Southgate gone, who would take over the leadership of the Stationer network? Pearl, now using the code name Pauline, was the obvious choice. She was SOE-trained, she had expertise in all the weapons and explosives, and she had communication with London.

The Stationer network was split in three. Pearl directed the northern section, which was now called Marie-Wrestler. She further divided Marie-Wrestler into four parts, each led by its own lieutenant who answered to her. They reestablished contact with London and received fresh shipments of arms. They were just beginning an escalated campaign of harassing German troops, cutting German communication lines, and causing damage to a major railroad line that ran through their area when the Germans attacked the area on June 11. Pearl escaped into the field with the box of money.

The battle lasted for 14 hours. Two small maquis groups—100 people in a different (Communist) group and 30 in Pearl's—put up quite a fight, killing over 80 Germans. But the Germans killed over 30 of them. By nightfall, when the trucks had all left, Pearl emerged from the wheat field to find that they had no radio and no weapons, and the Marie-Wrestler group was now down to about 20 people (including—happily—her fiancé, Henri).

Pearl and her group had been trying to recruit more fighters to their ranks before the Germans attacked. When she had run into the field with the cocoa box, Pearl had this thought: with the money she had saved, she could pay each new recruit a small salary and feed them until more money could be dropped from England. By late July the Marie-Wrestler network had grown to almost 1,500 maquis and had received drops from 60 planes totaling over 150 tons of arms.

From late June 1944 to the end of August, when France was liberated, the Marie-Wrestler network staged more than 80 acts of sabotage on the rail line, frequently attacked German convoys on the road, and killed about 1,000 Germans. They provided information to London that enabled the Royal Air Force to attack a 60-tank train of gasoline bound for Normandy (after D-day). And at one point, a column of 18,000 Germans surrendered to the Allies as a direct result of being harassed by the maquis in Pearl's area.

She went to France with the misgivings of her SOE instructors, and her efforts there were plagued with setbacks. Yet Pearl emerged from her difficulties to become one of the only women to lead a maquis group during the war. And in the end, it was clear-headed thinking—such as leaving the guns and grabbing the money—that enabled Pearl to succeed. The maquis of her network loved her and called her "our mother" and "our National Pauline."

In September 1944, Pearl and Henri went to London, where Pearl concluded her service with the SOE, turned over reports of her activities, and returned all the remaining money with a detailed accounting of how the rest had been spent. (She seems to be one of the few agents to have done this.) A few weeks later, practically penniless and unemployed, Pearl and Henri were married in London. Then they returned to Paris at the end of the year to begin civilian life.

Pearl was granted numerous awards by the governments of Great Britain and France, and in her later years she was approached by many writers who wanted to help write her memoir. She always refused because she didn't want to see her life story transformed into a dramatic fiction. But in 1994, French journalist Hervé Larroque convinced Pearl to grant him an interview that would be published. She agreed because she realized her story might encourage young people to persevere in difficult circumstances; she knew that her own hardships had prepared her for successful Resistance work. The result was the French-language memoir, *Pauline*.

Pearl died in February 2008.

★★★ LEARN MORE ★★★

Code Name Pauline: Memoirs of a World War II Special Agent by Pearl Witherington Cornioley, edited by Kathryn J. Atwood (Chicago Review Press, 2013).

"Pearl Witherington: SOE Officer Whose Leadership of French Resistance Fighters Was a Thorn in the Side of the Germans Before and After D-day."
Times Online
www.timesonline.co.uk/tol/comment/obituaries/article3432757.ece
An obituary of Pearl Witherington Cornioley.

Hannah Senesh

BRITISH PARATROOPER

ON THE NIGHT of March 13, 1944, a group of armed Yugoslavian partisan fighters were waiting for the arrival of several British paratroopers. Shortly after midnight, they saw the paratroopers drop from the sky. One of them was being blown far from the others. The fighters separated so they could locate all the paratroopers before the Germans or local Fascists did.

Two partisans came upon a stranger, their weapons ready. One put down his weapon and took out his flashlight to have a better look. The stranger was wearing the uniform of a British paratrooper. The second partisan then put down his weapon, but the first kept his flashlight on the stranger. He was surprised to

Hannah Senesh.
Collection of the Senesh family

see the face of a young woman. So were the other partisans, who walked over after locating the other paratroopers. The partisans showed their surprise by smiling and laughing in a friendly way. The young woman understood and smiled back. Her name was Hannah Senesh, and she was on a rescue mission.

Hannah wasn't far from Hungary, the nation of her birth. Her father, Bela, a successful playwright in Budapest, had died when Hannah was only six. She then became especially close to her widowed mother, Catherine, and older brother, Giora.

Hannah loved literature and aspired to become a writer, like her father. By the age of 16 it seemed that she was well on her way toward that goal. Some of her classmates noticed, and nominated her to be secretary of the school's literary society. But she couldn't be elected. Why? A new rule stated that society officers must be Protestant. Hannah was Jewish. "Only now," wrote Hannah after this incident, "am I really beginning to see what it is to be a Jew in a Christian society."

Giora's opportunities were also narrowing, due to his race, so after he graduated from secondary school in 1938, he left Budapest to study in France. Meanwhile, Hannah was making her own plans. She wrote in her diary, "I've become a Zionist. . . . To me it means, in short, that I now consciously and strongly feel I am a Jew, and am proud of it. My primary aim is to go to Palestine, to work for it. . . . I'm convinced Zionism is Jewry's solution to its problems and that the outstanding work being done in Palestine is not in vain."

Zionism—the idea that Jews should have their own nation in Palestine, the same general area once inhabited by the Israelites— had been considered throughout history but was set into serious motion during the late 19th century as a reaction against European anti-Semitism.

Hannah arrived in Palestine in September 1939, just weeks after the start of World War II. She attended the Agricultural School for

Girls at Nahalal for two years, where she studied, cared for farm animals, and harvested crops. It was exhausting, but she was determined to work with her hands instead of attending a university, as her mother had suggested, so that she might make a tangible difference in Eretz—the Land—as the Jews in Palestine referred to it.

In December 1942, the first news of the Holocaust made its way to Palestine when Jews fleeing Europe began arriving. Before then, most people believed Hitler's anti-Jewish laws had been meant to isolate and humiliate the Jews. Now it was clear that he intended to kill them all, if he could. The headlines of every Jewish newspaper in Palestine shouted the horrible news. Most Palestinian Jews had family members still in Europe, and they desperately wanted to do something.

Hannah was no different. Now living on the Sdot Yam kibbutz (communal farm) at Caesarea, working in the kibbutz kitchen and doing laundry, Hannah became seized with a determination to return to Hungary to rescue her mother. And soon she found a way to try.

★★★ "HARVEST" ★★★

Hannah wrote this poem in Palestine in 1940:

Our people are working the black soil,
Their arms reap the gold sheaves,
And now when the last ear its stalk leaves
Our faces glitter as with gilded oil.

From where comes the new light and voice,
From where the resounding song at hand?
From where the fighting spirit and new faith?
From you, fertile Emek, from you, my land.

In February 1943, she met Yonah Rosen, a young man who had been born in Hungary. He was now part of the Palmach, the elite fighting force of the Haganah, the Jewish military in Palestine.

The Haganah (Hebrew for "the Defense") had been formed secretly in 1920 in response to the violent outbreaks between the Jews and the Muslims in Palestine, the latter who resented the steady influx of Jews into the area. The Jews realized that even though the British controlled Palestine, their military presence was not enough to protect Jewish settlers.

As the Haganah grew and became more organized, it operated with the knowledge—but not the blessing—of the British, even as the Haganah High Command formed an elite fighting force in 1941 named the Palmach (Hebrew for "striking force").

When Palmach leaders heard the shocking news of the Holocaust, they asked the British for help to train agents for rescue missions. The British weren't interested—at first. But when the Allies began to bomb a major source of Axis fuel—the oil fields in Ploieşti, Romania—and their fliers were being shot down, the British and the Palmach made a deal: if the Palmach would provide young Jewish agents, natives of the nations near Romania, to create escape lines for the downed Allied fliers, they would be free to rescue European Jews afterward.

The Palmach accepted, and Hannah began her training for the Hungarian mission.

The young agents learned various forms of sabotage and combat from the Palmach, both armed and unarmed. The British made them officers in the Royal Air Force and trained them in parachuting and intelligence gathering, which included the use of a radio and Morse code.

When asked why she was training for such a dangerous mission, Hannah answered, "In my heart there are two great loves: one is of my nation, and my second love is my mother."

Hannah and Giora pose for a street photographer in Tel Aviv, 1944. *Collection of the Senesh family*

But just before leaving for intelligence training in Cairo, Egypt, Hannah learned that a third love had just arrived in Palestine: her brother, Giora. He had been arrested in Spain after crossing the French-Spanish border trying to escape occupied France. He had been released from prison and had come to Palestine to be reunited with Hannah.

The two spent hours together walking through the streets of Tel Aviv. Hannah didn't tell him that she was on her way back to Hungary. She only said that she was leaving the following day to receive special training in Cairo and that she couldn't talk about the details.

While the Hungarian team trained in Cairo, their ultimate destination—Hungary—was on the verge of major change. Although technically allied with Germany, Hungary's antifascist leaders—the prime minister Miklós Kállay and the royal regent Miklós Horthy—had delayed Hitler's order to deport Hungary's Jews.

Jewish refugees from other nations had flooded into Hungary because of its relative safety. The entire nation was simmering with tension, especially when, as British intelligence learned, the impatient Germans were planning to invade Hungary and deport the Jews themselves.

The exact date of the German invasion was unknown, but it was too dangerous now for the young agents to enter their homeland without precise information. Yoel Palgi, a member of the team, noticed that Hannah seemed the most disappointed and frustrated of them all at this delay. She was, he said later, "totally unconcerned about her own safety."

The British decided to drop the team into neighboring Yugoslavia. Although the Germans had conquered it, two warring partisan groups were keeping the Germans and the fascist Yugoslavian puppet government constantly off-balance and were in control of large stretches of territory.

Because the British were supporting these partisans with air drops of supplies and weapons, the Yugoslavians were in their debt and agreed to receive the paratroopers. When the British had more information, the Hungarians might cross the border.

On the night of May 13, 1944, a plane took off carrying the first members of the Hungarian team, including Hannah and Reuven Dafne, a young Palmach man who had fought with the British Army and was the team's leader.

Reuven had his doubts about the ultimate success of the mission, but Hannah's intense optimism affected him. As they flew to Yugoslavia, Reuven saw that her face "exuded happiness and excitement."

The roar of the plane's motor made conversation impossible, but just before Reuven jumped, Hannah, her face "wreathed in a smile," gave him a thumbs-up. She jumped right after him but was blown far from Reuven's landing spot because she was lighter than he was.

After the partisans found them, the team walked four days to headquarters, where they learned the German invasion of Hungary had just occurred. Their rescue mission now seemed impossible.

"We are late, we are late," Hannah cried. "What will happen to all of them . . . to the million Jews in Hungary? They're in German hands now—and we're sitting here . . . just sitting."

But they weren't just sitting. They had orders from the British to assist the partisans. Sometimes they participated in raids against the Germans. Often they just marched with them from place to place. Hannah caused a stir wherever she went among the partisans, and not just because she was a young, attractive woman in a British uniform, weapon at her side. There was something electric about her, Reuven said later, "a special, mysterious quality that excited their wonder and respect."

None of this admiration affected Hannah. She focused on her duties but grew more restless with every new report of German atrocities in Hungary. While the Nazis had implemented anti-Semitic laws gradually in other occupied European countries, the Hungarian Jews got the full force of the anti-Semitic laws all at once, beginning with the rural areas. Budapest, where Catherine Senesh lived, was still relatively safe. But for how long?

Hannah became gripped by the idea that the members of this small team were now the only ones who could rescue the Hungarian Jews. When Reuven argued that their chances of success were slim, Hannah countered that the attempt—even if it cost their lives—might at least give hope to any Jews who heard that someone had come all the way from Palestine to rescue them.

Reuven finally agreed to escort Hannah to the border. The partisans led them to a village near the border where they met three men who agreed to cross with Hannah. Two were Jewish Hungarian resisters, one named Kallos and the other Fleischmann. The third man was a French POW, Antonin Tissandier.

Reuven cautioned Hannah to wait in the village. He had sent one team member into the Papuk Mountains of Yugoslavia, where Yoel was in contact with the British, to gain up-to-date information on the border area. Once they had that, they might find a relatively safe way into Budapest, where they could possibly connect with resistance workers.

Hannah refused, and Reuven, tired of arguing, let her go with the three men. Before she left, Hannah handed Reuven a piece of paper, telling him that if she didn't return, to bring it to her kibbutz

in Palestine. On the paper was a poem Hannah had written one
month earlier:

> *Blessed is the match consumed*
> *in kindling flame.*
> *Blessed is the flame that burns*
> *in the secret fastness of the heart.*
> *Blessed is the heart with strength to stop*
> *its beating for honor's sake.*
> *Blessed is the match consumed*
> *in kindling flame.*

Hannah and the three men crossed the border on the night of
June 9. When they came to the outskirts of a village, the Hungarians went on ahead to contact some smugglers who, they thought,
might give them travel permits. Hannah and Antonin waited in
the woods.

The smugglers weren't at home, and a Hungarian police patrol
stopped Kallos and Fleischmann on their way back. Local villagers told the police they had seen two other young people with the
Hungarians. The police found Hannah and Antonin, who, when
Kallos and Fleischman didn't return, realized the mission was
doomed and had buried their transmitter.

After two days of digging in the woods, the soldiers found
it. They interrogated Hannah and Antonin separately. Hannah's
interrogator tricked her into admitting the radio was hers. He
asked her for the codes. If he had them, he could pretend to be
Hannah, receiving details about the mission while communicating false information to her team and the British.

Hannah refused to give the codes.

She was put on a train to the military prison in Budapest, where
she was brutally beaten for days. While she maintained her silence
regarding the codes, she did finally admit her real name.

★★★ "ONE—TWO—THREE" ★★★

Hannah wrote the following poem in June 1944, while imprisoned in Budapest.

One—two—three . . .
*   eight feet long,*
Two strides across, the rest is dark . . .
Life hangs over me like a question mark.

One—two—three . . .
*   maybe another week,*
Or next month may still find me here,
But death, I feel, is very near.

I could have been
*   twenty-three next July;*
I gambled on what mattered most,
The dice were cast. I lost.

On June 17, Catherine Senesh was escorted to the military prison in Budapest, where a Hungarian interrogator named Rozsa asked about her daughter's whereabouts. Surprised, Catherine told the detective that Hannah was in Palestine. He told Catherine that her daughter was in the room next door.

When the guards brought Hannah into the room, a very shocked Catherine almost didn't recognize her daughter—her face was a mass of bruises and welts and her hair was tangled and dirty.

Hannah ran into Catherine's arms. "Mother!" she sobbed, "forgive me!"

"Speak to her!" Rozsa shouted. "Convince her she had better tell us everything. Otherwise you'll never see each other again."

Both women refused to cooperate.

Catherine was imprisoned in a cell with other women. As the days passed, she didn't know whether Hannah was alive or dead. One of the prisoners, who had more freedom to move about than others due to her office work, came into Catherine's cell one night and told her to look out her window. When Catherine did, she saw Hannah waving to her from another cell. They began to communicate with hand signals and pieces of paper cut into letters.

Hannah asked her mother why she and the other prisoners were all wearing a yellow Star of David. Catherine told her that now all Hungarian Jews were forced to do so. Another prisoner in Catherine's room communicated to Hannah that she was lucky she didn't have to wear one; she wasn't "branded."

Hannah immediately traced a large Star of David on her dirty window. It stayed there for several weeks until someone washed the window.

Catherine was released in September. Hannah remained imprisoned.

On October 28, 1944, as the Allied bombers pounded the city and the shrieks of approaching Soviet artillery grew ever louder, Hannah was given a military trial by the Hungarian fascists now in control of Budapest. When allowed to speak on her own behalf, Hannah warned the men deciding her fate that they would soon be facing their own trials from the victorious Allies. She wasn't a traitor to Hungary, she said. They were.

Her verdict was postponed. This news spread like wildfire through the prison. Yoel, who had by this time also been arrested, was convinced that it meant the Hungarian fascists were afraid to execute her.

On November 7, he and the other prisoners heard shots. They all banged on their cell doors, demanding to know who had just been executed.

"Don't worry" the guard said. She wasn't one of yours. Just some young girl . . . a British parachutist. But that's surely a lie. Whoever heard of a young girl being a British officer?"

Hannah had just been shot.

With the Soviet troops only days away, Hungarian fascists now forced the Jews of Budapest, including Catherine, out of the city on a death march toward Austria. The fascists provided very little food, water, or rest to the Jews, and many died along the way. On the sixth day of the march, Catherine escaped during the confusion caused by falling Soviet bombs. She ripped off her yellow star and made her way back to Budapest, where a friend helped her find shelter in a convent hospital until it was safe to emerge at the end of the war.

She was then reunited with Giora in Palestine, where Hannah's writings were published and translated into many languages. Some of her words were even set to music.

In 1950 Hannah's body was moved from Hungary and reburied in a public ceremony in the new state of Israel, where she was considered a national hero. Streets, schools, and forests were named for this young woman who had been the heart and soul of the only attempted military rescue for Jews during the Holocaust.

★★★ LEARN MORE ★★★

Blessed Is the Match: The Life and Death of Hannah Senesh (Katahdin Films, 2008).

Hannah Senesh: Her Life and Diary by Hannah Senesh (Jewish Lights, 2004).

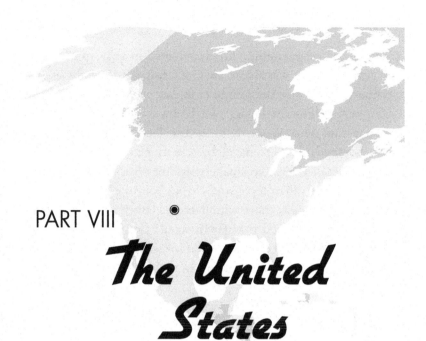

PART VIII

The United States

WHEN HITLER'S TANKS rolled into Poland on September 1, 1939, the reaction in the United States was largely one of upholding the same isolationist policy that had made the country initially hesitant to become involved in the previous world war. The America First Committee (AFC), whose spokesman was aviation hero Charles Lindbergh, believed that getting involved with a European war would destroy, not strengthen, the American way of life.

But when the Axis powers began to conquer country after country—Germany in Europe, Italy in North Africa, Japan in the Far East—many isolationist Americans began to change their thinking: the Axis was creating a very lopsided world.

The U.S. Congress, which in the 1930s had passed many Neutrality Acts to prevent President Franklin D. Roosevelt from allowing the United States to contribute money and arms to the growing European conflict, finally relented in 1941. In March of that year Roosevelt was able to aid Great Britain in its fight against Germany by passing the Lend-Lease Act, which supplied Great Britain with billions of dollars' worth of war equipment.

Americans became largely unified on December 7, 1941, when Japan bombed the U.S. naval base stationed at Pearl Harbor, Hawaii (part of a massive Japanese assault on American, British, Dutch, and Australian territories throughout the Pacific Ocean). Americans, especially those who lived in Hawaii and on the West Coast, became terrified that Japan would now begin a ground invasion. That terror faded when the invasion didn't occur, but it was replaced with a fervent patriotism and desire to fight the Axis powers.

The United States declared war on Japan, and then Germany, Japan's ally, declared war on the States. American men and women signed up for the armed services by the hundreds of thousands. For the first time in U.S. history, women had their own branches of the armed services. The first—and largest—of these divisions was the Women's Army Corps (WAC), which had approximately 140,000 women in its membership. The female branch of the navy was called Women Accepted for Volunteer Emergency Service (WAVES), the female coast guard branch was called SPAR (Semper Paratus, Always Ready), and the female marines were simply called the female marines; they had no special designation.

Two female pilots, Jacqueline Cochran and Nancy Love, began two different pilot training programs for women that eventually merged into the Women Airforce Service Pilots (WASP). The WASPs' main job was to fly newly manufactured planes to military bases within the United States, where air force men would then fly them out of the country into combat zones. WASPs also helped train antiaircraft crews by flying back and forth with a target trailing 25 feet behind the plane. Yet the WASP organization was not technically part of the armed forces—its members received no armed service benefits aside from pay, and the program was shut down in 1944, before the war ended.

Many civilian women also supported the war effort. When American men left farms and factories to join the armed services, there was a huge labor shortage. The Women's Land Army hired thousands of women—from the cities and the country—to work U.S. farms to prevent a national famine. And manufacturing companies, given government money to produce airplanes, ships, and weapons, encouraged American women to work in factories to help the war effort. American women responded enthusiastically to the call for well-paying factory jobs, and eventually their numbers reached into the millions. These women became associated with a fictional character named Rosie the Riveter, who was the subject of a new popular song about a patriotic girl working in a munitions factory using a riveting machine out of love for her marine boyfriend.

Women Airforce Service Pilots (WASPs).
National Museum of the United States Air Force

The Office of Strategic Services (OSS) was a U.S. organization devoted mainly to espionage, created in 1942 by World War I veteran William J. Donovan at the request of President Roosevelt. Most of the 2,000 women employed by the OSS (out of a total 16,000 employees) worked far from danger. Others, such as Virginia Hall (see page 197), were dropped into enemy territory and worked as agents, gathering vital information for the U.S. government and the Allies and helping to organize Resistance workers.

On June 6, 1944, Allied forces composed mainly of American, British, and Canadian troops landed on the beaches of Normandy under the leadership of U.S. General Dwight D. Eisenhower. The German forces who met the Allied forces at Normandy (determined though greatly depleted in number from their costly battle against the Soviets) were severely hindered in their rush to the Normandy coast by numerous maquis groups and other Resistance workers, some of whom were being supplied by the OSS and the British Resistance organization, the SOE.

The Allies were eventually able to push the Germans out of France. The following year, on May 7, 1945, the German armed forces formally surrendered to the Allied forces in a schoolhouse where General Eisenhower kept his headquarters. The United States would remain in the war until Japan, the country that had gotten the States involved in the war in the first place, formally surrendered to the Allies on September 2, 1945.

Virginia Hall

THE MOST DANGEROUS ALLIED AGENT

AN OLD FRENCH woman, lugging a heavy suitcase, shuffled through the busy train station, her husband beside her. The German soldiers standing about in the station didn't take a second glance at them. They were preoccupied with more important matters. It was March 1944, and they knew that the rumored Allied invasion of Nazi-occupied France (D-day) would soon be a reality. Members of the French Resistance, emboldened by the impending invasion, were increasing their acts of sabotage. Trains were being blown up, German soldiers were being shot, phone lines were being cut, all with increasing frequency. Public executions of those suspected of sabotage did nothing to deter the destructive work of the French Resistance.

Virginia Hall.
Lorna Catling

The Germans were especially concerned with capturing a certain woman whom they called, in French, La Dame Qui Boite—the Limping Lady. There were posters all over France portraying a sketch of the woman, believed to be Canadian, and including the following warning: "The woman who limps is one of the most dangerous Allied agents in France. We must find and destroy her." The Germans knew that the Limping Lady had been a leader in the French Resistance, but so far she had successfully—and infuriatingly—eluded their grasp.

They would have been quite shocked to discover that this old French woman, shuffling past them with her heavy suitcase, was the very woman they had been searching for. Her disguise was extremely clever, for she was neither old nor French. She was an American, working for the American espionage organization called the Office of Strategic Services, or the OSS. Her name was Virginia Hall.

Virginia Hall was born in 1906 in Baltimore, Maryland, to a family who could afford to send her to the best schools, where her favorite subjects and activities were sports, drama, and languages. Virginia's love of languages drew her to Europe to finish her university studies, where she became fluent in both French and German. She found Europe so fascinating that she stayed there after graduation and found work at different American embassies, eventually hoping to land a job in the State Department, a high-level foreign affairs agency of the U.S. government.

While employed at the American embassy in Turkey, Virginia had an accident that was to affect the rest of her life. While on a hunting party with some embassy friends, her gun went off accidentally, shooting her in the left foot. By the time she was able to receive medical help, the wound had become gangrenous, and part of her left leg had to be amputated, just below the knee. She returned to the United States and had a wooden leg made. She practiced with the new leg (which she nicknamed Cuthbert) until she could do almost everything she had done before. She just couldn't run very well, and she walked with a slight limp.

But Virginia's accident destroyed all hopes of a career in the State Department (because they wouldn't hire anyone with a false limb), and she quit embassy work and began to travel through Europe. After Germany invaded Poland, Virginia eventually found her way to Paris where during the tense but peaceful period known as the Drôle de Guerre, she enlisted in the French Army as an ambulance driver.

She noticed Jewish refugees frantically streaming into Paris from Germany and Austria and knew that the Nazis must be doing something terrible in those countries. After the Battle of France ended with the French surrender and severe anti-Semitic laws were enacted against French Jews, including some of her close friends, it became clear to Virginia that Hitler must be stopped. But how? And what could she do to help?

Virginia's path became clear when she was recruited by a British Resistance organization known as the SOE, or the Special Operations Executive. The SOE recruiters were very impressed with Virginia's intelligence, her desire to fight the Nazis, and her impressive command of French and German. After three weeks of intense training, Virginia arrived in France on Saturday, August 23, 1941, as the first female field agent that the SOE would send into France.

Posing as a journalist, she went to the southern area of France (known as Vichy), which was officially unoccupied by the Nazis. Yet it was still a dangerous place, filled with French collaborators, those eagerly cooperating with the Nazis. Virginia had to be extremely careful when she went to the town of Lyon, the largest city in unoccupied France, to locate, help organize, and fund groups of people who were willing to become involved in the Resistance. She also located safe drop zones, or good places to air-drop new agents, supplies, money, and weapons from London. She helped escaped prisoners of war and downed Allied airmen evade arrest and find their way safely back to England. She successfully planned and executed a daring escape for a group of SOE agents who had been imprisoned in one of France's worst prisons.

Virginia was disappointed when, after 13 very productive months, the SOE called her back to Great Britain to take a mandatory break. There was so much more work to be done, and many Resistance workers had come to depend on her. But when she heard that Allied forces were getting ready to invade Nazi-occupied North Africa, she understood why she had to leave Lyon. Because of the impending North African invasion, the Gestapo was headed directly for southern France (geographically across the Mediterranean Sea from North Africa) not only to defend France from a possible Allied invasion but also to crack down on Resistance members whom they knew were working there. They were especially eager to find the Limping Lady, whom they knew to be a ringleader in the Lyon Resistance. The Gestapo would be arriving in Lyon by midnight. The last train out of occupied France left at 11:00 P.M., and Virginia was on it.

Part of the trip included a 30-mile trek, which had to be taken on foot, through the frigid Pyrenees Mountains bordering France and Spain. Virginia's leg stump became sore and blistered during this hike, but she couldn't complain or stop to rest. The mountain guide had been reluctant to take her along because she was a woman. What would his reaction have been if he knew she had a false leg?

After an eventful trip, which included a brief jail stay for not having correct entrance papers at the Spanish border and a lengthy stopover in Spain, Virginia finally returned to the SOE offices in London. While she had waited in Spain, she had been quietly given a notable award for her work in France, the Most Excellent Order of the British Empire, or the MBE. Back in England, she was trained as a radio, or wireless, operator. She thought that every agent should be able to convey his or her information directly to London and not have to wait for one of the already overworked wireless operators.

Virginia also joined a new American espionage organization called the Office of Strategic Services, or the OSS. She decided that this new organization might be able to utilize her experience. It was as an agent of the OSS that she found herself back in France, disguised as an old woman, trudging through a French train station right under the nose of the Gestapo who were searching for her.

Living with a poor French farmer and his elderly mother, Virginia maintained her disguise and posed as an elderly cook who also tended the farmer's cows. Taking the cows to pasture every day was a perfect ruse for finding fields that could be utilized for agent and supply drops. And as the Allied invasion of France approached, Virginia had a brilliant idea for obtaining needed information on German troop movements. She began to help the farmer's mother make cheese and then sold it to the Germans. They had no idea that the old French cheese peddler understood German and would

transmit their comments regarding German plans directly to London as soon as she returned to the farmer's cottage.

Painting of Virginia transmitting
messages via Morse code
with her radio.
Jeff Bass

Once, just after reporting to the OSS office on her radio, Virginia heard a car drive up to the cottage. She thought it was probably an agent coming to see her, but out of practiced caution she hid her radio and went downstairs. When she opened the cottage door, she was shocked to find a group of German soldiers.

The commanding officer asked her why she was there. In her best "old woman" voice, she explained that she worked for the farmer and his mother. Apparently not satisfied with her answer, the officer sent three of his men into the cottage and upstairs to her room. Virginia could hear them knocking things over. If they found her radio, she would certainly be arrested. Her heart was beating so wildly, she was sure the soldiers could see it. Would they find the radio? Should she run? How far could she get before she was shot? Wild questions passed through her mind, but she remained outside with the soldiers as seconds passed into minutes.

Finally, one of the men came down and handed something to his commanding officer. Virginia couldn't see what it was. The officer looked at the item, then back at Virginia. He walked up to her. Virginia almost stopped breathing.

The officer then showed her what he was holding. It was a ball of cheese. He had recognized her as the cheese-peddling old woman and told her that he was going to take some for himself and his men. He tossed a few coins in her direction and then left.

Shaken though she was, this near-fatal encounter was not enough to frighten Virginia away from her work, especially not with D-day drawing closer. When it finally arrived, Virginia planned and coordinated sabotage attacks on bridges, railroads, and German convoys, greatly hindering many Germans from reaching the battle in Normandy.

After the war, President Truman wanted to publicly award Virginia in a White House ceremony. But because she didn't think her work in France merited a special award, and because she wanted to keep working in espionage (and keep her identity as an agent a secret), Virginia declined the president's request. Instead, on September 27, 1945, in a private OSS office, Virginia Hall was given the Distinguished Service Cross award, making her the only American woman and the first civilian to be awarded this honor during World War II.

After the war, the OSS was disbanded and its operations were eventually taken over by a new agency called the Central Intelligence Agency, or the CIA. Virginia was denied her request for another field job but worked in different capacities for the CIA before her mandatory retirement in 1966 at the age of 60. She died at the age of 82.

★★★ LEARN MORE ★★★

Sisterhood of Spies: The Women of OSS by Elizabeth P. McIntosh (Naval Institute Press, 1998).

The Wolves at the Door: The True Story of America's Greatest Female Spy by Judith L. Pearson (The Lyons Press, 2005).

Muriel Phillips

U.S. ARMY NURSE

WHEN MURIEL PHILLIPS heard the news, on December 7, 1941, that the United States Navy had been bombed by the Empire of Japan, she was in her final year of nurse's training at Cambridge Hospital in Cambridge, Massachusetts. The following day, all the nurses on her floor gathered around the radio in the doctor's office to hear President Roosevelt give his Date of Infamy speech, which informed the American people that the United States had declared war on Japan.

Muriel Phillips during the Battle of the Bulge, holding a blackjack in her right hand and a switchblade in her left pocket, both gifts from wounded GIs in case she was captured by the Germans.
Muriel Phillips Engelman

★★★ DATE OF INFAMY SPEECH ★★★

President Roosevelt's Date of Infamy Speech, broadcast on the day following the attack on Pearl Harbor, is one of the most famous speeches of the 20th century and was instrumental in stirring thousands of young Americans to enlist in the armed services during WWII. The following are excerpts from the speech:

Yesterday, December 7, 1941—a date which will live in infamy—the United States of America was suddenly and deliberately attacked by naval and air forces of the Empire of Japan. . . .

The attack yesterday on the Hawaiian Islands has caused severe damage to American naval and military forces. Very many American lives have been lost. . . .

No matter how long it may take us to overcome this premeditated invasion, the American people in their righteous might will win through to absolute victory. . . .

With confidence in our armed forces—with the unbounding determination of our people—we will gain the inevitable triumph—so help us God.

There was no question in Muriel's mind what she would do: right after she finished her nurse's training, she would enlist in the armed services as an army nurse. As difficult as nursing school had been, her army training at Fort Devens, Massachusetts, was even more difficult. It included hours and hours of various drills, 15-mile hikes, climbing up and down rope ladders, classroom study of various diseases, and even crawling under live ammunition.

When Muriel finished her army training and set off for Great Britain, she and the other nurses took along many things that had been given to them during their training, including K-rations (packets of canned and dried food), special clothing, gas masks, and helmets. The helmets caused more complaint than the K-rations did. They might as well have weighed a ton for how uncomfortably heavy they were. Why did the helmets have to weigh so much? Muriel would find out soon enough.

Muriel worked in Wales for six months, caring for the everyday illnesses of some of the thousands of U.S. soldiers stationed in Great Britain. For their next assignment, she and her entire hospital unit—500 enlisted men; 50 medical, dental, and administrative officers; and 100 nurses—were going to cross the English

Muriel and the other American nurses of her hospital unit with whom she trained in Fort Devens, marching in a parade in Chester, England, 1944. Muriel is the platoon leader, in front, saluting the "brass" (superior officers). *Muriel P. Engelman*

Channel to nurse the wounded of the Normandy invasion (which had taken place several weeks earlier) and await orders for their final destination.

The nurses decided to sleep on the ship's deck as the rooms below were infested with bedbugs. Muriel could hear the German planes flying overhead as she lay in the darkness; she had learned the difference between the sound of a German plane and an Allied one. But because a blackout had been ordered on the ship, all the lights had been extinguished. Muriel and the other nurses were not visible to the enemy planes as their transport ship crossed silently through the dark waters of the English Channel.

A trip across the Channel usually took only two or three hours, but all the debris in the water—remnants of airplanes and ships— had slowed the trip down substantially so that it took them three days. Finally, the coast of Normandy came into view. Muriel packed the heavy equipment onto her back and descended the rope ladder with the others in the hospital unit onto the flat-bottomed LCVP (Landing Craft, Vehicle, Personnel), which took them closer to the beach. When they were about 100 feet from land, they got off the LCVP and waded ashore, where they were loaded onto trucks.

As their trucks approached the nearest village, Muriel and the others became silent. The sights—and smells—of war were every-where. Homes and farms lay in ruins. Piles of rubble lay where build-ings had once stood. The smell of death and decay hung in the air.

Because their trucks got lost in the dark, the nurses spent their first night in Normandy sleeping under the stars in a cow pasture. It was very smelly, but they knew if the cows were still alive, the field must be free of German mines. Although they worked for some time in Normandy, the ultimate destination of Muriel's hospital unit was an apple orchard just outside the city of Liége, Belgium. Their mission was to set up and operate a tent hospital, which would be used to nurse the many soldiers who were being wounded in the Allied push against the Nazis.

★★★ TENT HOSPITALS ★★★

During World War II, any type of hospital, whether evacuation, field, or general, could be set up in tents. Muriel's hospital was a general hospital and contained almost everything a regular hospital would. Because tent hospitals were outdoors, on ground level, it was much easier to transport patients in and out than it would have been in a storied building. Each individual tent in Muriel's hospital held 30 beds and was heated by a pot-bellied stove. Liége was a coal-mining center, so it was easy to keep the stoves fueled. Muriel's hospital was spread out over several acres of an apple orchard and contained a total of 1,000 beds.

For the first few weeks, most of the tent hospital floors were dirt, which quickly turned into mud during the constant rain. During these first weeks, Muriel and the other nurses cared for their patients without the benefit of electricity or running water, working by the light of flashlights and kerosene-fueled lanterns.

After Muriel and her unit had been near Liége for about a month, the Germans began sending buzz bombs (the V-1 bomb, or the robot bomb) all over the area. A single buzz bomb contained nearly 2,000 pounds of explosives and made a "putt-putt" sound before plunging to the earth at a 45-degree angle with a loud, horrible, whining whistle. It would destroy everything within a few hundred feet, and the explosion could be felt miles away.

Liége contained a huge network of railroad lines that fanned out in many directions and connected with many different countries. The Germans knew that if they could destroy the center of these rail lines in Liége, it would greatly hinder the Allies' ability to transport soldiers and equipment. And so the buzz bombs bombarded Liége, sometimes three at once from three different directions, coming every 15 minutes for two solid months. Some of the bombs landed directly on sections of the large tent hospital where Muriel and her hospital unit were trying to nurse their patients.

Muriel wrote about this two-month bombing spree in a letter to her cousin, dated November 26, 1944:

Never in my year overseas have I put in such a hectic life as I have the past few weeks and I'm afraid if the buzz bombs continue annoying us the way they have, I won't have to worry about any postwar plans. We've been lucky so far, having had some narrow squeaks, but it can't last. It's the most awful feeling in the world when you hear the motor of the bomb stop almost above you and then wait a few seconds for the explosion. I'd rather have it all at once and get it over with, but then, Hitler never consulted me. Incidentally, keep this mum, won't you, as I wouldn't want my mother or Ruth to worry though frankly, I'm scared silly and for the first time in my life I've lost my appetite.

I'm on night duty in our tent hospital which is in a sea of mud, and with the continual rain for the past 2 ½ weeks, it will never dry out. The work has been hard and the hours long but I really feel satisfied now because we're doing the stuff we came overseas for, and they really need us. Our quarters are in the heart of a city, some miles from here, so we have to commute each night—leaving there at 5:00 P.M. and getting back at 10 the next morning—and we're supposed to sleep. Sleep, however, is out of the question when buildings all around us are being bombed and each time they get it, the force practically knocks us out of bed.

Muriel had used her helmet mainly for washing her clothes and bathing herself, but now she finally understood why it was so heavy: it provided solid head protection when the bombs came too close. She often wished she could squeeze her entire body inside its protective weight.

Despite the difficulty of the work, nothing gave Muriel more satisfaction than tending to the needs of wounded GIs. They were the most uncomplaining patients she had ever nursed. They knew their nurses were busy, so they hesitated in asking for help and always told the nurses to take care of the other patient first. Muriel felt very proud to be helping such brave servicemen.

In December 1944, six months after the Normandy invasion, the buzz bombs were still falling all over Liége, but now something even worse was on the horizon. German troops launched a sudden surprise attack that managed to push U.S. troops backward, making a bulge in the troop line, in what was called the Ardennes Offensive, more commonly known as the Battle of the Bulge.

The tent hospital became more crowded than ever with wounded GIs, and the Germans were coming closer and closer. Muriel had more to worry about than most of the other nurses. Her dog tag—the metal identification tag that every serviceman or -woman was required to wear at all times—had an *H* on it, for Hebrew. Muriel was Jewish, and she understood what the Nazis would do to her if they were able to capture her.

On Christmas Eve, the Germans were only 10 miles from Liége. The sickest patients were evacuated to hospitals in France or England, away from the fighting. The wounded GIs who remained

★★★ GI ★★★

The initials *GI* stand for *government issue*, the words that were stamped on almost everything military personnel were given. Soon the initials began to stand for the servicemen, or soldiers, themselves.

in the tent hospital were concerned for the safety of their nurses and often urged the nurses to take their places in the evacuation vehicles. None of the nurses did so, of course. Muriel received two "presents" from her protective patients that week. One was a blackjack, a type of weapon made out of rubber hosing and lead sinkers, and the other was a switchblade. Muriel had no idea if she would be able to follow the instructions that accompanied her gifts if approached by a German (the blackjack was to be slapped across his eyes and the switchblade plunged into his abdomen), but she was grateful for her patients' concern.

That night, the fog that had enveloped Belgium for over a week suddenly cleared. Muriel heard the sound of a German plane flying overhead. She went outside to look. The pilot was flying back and forth over the tent hospital, dropping flares to light his targets. Then he began flying very low and strafing (shooting at) the tent hospital while dropping antipersonnel bombs as well. All of Muriel's patients that night were able to walk on their own, so everyone took shelter under the beds. Many patients and hospital personnel died that night before an Allied antiaircraft gun finally shot down the German plane.

After Christmas week, Muriel could see and hear waves of U.S. planes overhead by day and British planes by night as they flew off toward the Ardennes Forest to combat the advancing German army. Muriel thought that she had never seen such a thrilling and beautiful sight.

Although the Germans broke through the Allied line in several places, the Allies eventually won the Battle of the Bulge toward the end of January 1945. A little over three months later, Germany surrendered, and the war in Europe was over.

After the war, Muriel—along with everyone in her hospital unit—was awarded a European Theatre ribbon and medal. They also each received three battle stars, one for each campaign, or battle, that they had been involved in. One of these stars was awarded for their work in nursing wounded soldiers during the Battle of the Bulge.

In 2008, Muriel published the memoirs of her eight-decade life, including 11 chapters on her war experiences. She called the book *Mission Accomplished: Stop the Clock*. In 2018, she was appointed a Chevalier of the National Order of the Legion of Honor by the French government for her wartime work. Muriel died in 2022 at the age of 101.

★★★ LEARN MORE ★★★

And if I Should Perish: Frontline U.S. Army Nurses in World War II by Evelyn Monahan and Rosemary Neidel-Greenlee (Anchor, 2004).

11 Days in December: Christmas at the Bulge by Stanley Weintraub (NAL Trade, 2007).

Mission Accomplished: Stop the Clock by Muriel P. Engelman, World War II Army Nurse, retired RN (iUniverse, Inc., 2008).

Marlene Dietrich

"THE ONLY IMPORTANT THING"

IT WAS DECEMBER 1944, and the Battle of the Bulge was raging across the Ardennes Forest of Nazi-occupied Belgium. A woman with a German accent, wearing an American soldier's uniform, sat shivering in the snow in the midst of some American soldiers. German troops were moving in, closer and closer. She fingered the pistol in her pocket. She now had to face the thought she had been trying to avoid ever since she had come back to Europe: Would the Germans find her, and if so, what would they do to her?

Her name was Marlene Dietrich. She had been born in Berlin, Germany, in 1901. As a young woman, she had become a stage entertainer and then successful movie star, first in her native

Marlene Dietrich, 1936.
Marlene Dietrich Collection Berlin, Stiftung Deutsche Kinemathek

Germany and then in America. Her films were so popular in Germany that in 1937, Adolf Hitler (who owned a collection of her movies) sent personal messengers to Marlene to offer her a very rewarding movie career: she could be the "queen of German film" if only she would return from the United States to Germany and make films for the Third Reich.

She told the messengers that she was currently under contract to make films in Hollywood with her longtime mentor, Jewish-German director Josef von Sternberg, but that she would gladly make a German film if he would be allowed to direct it.

There was a tense silence. Marlene finally broke it. "Do I rightly understand," she asked, "that you refuse to have Mr. von Sternberg make a film in your country because he's Jewish?"

The German messengers began to talk at once. They said that Marlene had been "infected" with false American propaganda and that there was no anti-Semitism in Germany. Marlene knew better. Hitler had drastically altered the Germany of her youth. Many of her Jewish friends in the German film industry were mysteriously disappearing. She helped many of them—not only movie stars and directors but also those who worked behind the scenes at German film studios—escape prewar Germany by giving them money to take a "vacation" in England or another country where they would be safe.

Her response to Hitler's offer to become a Nazi film star? Not just "no," but "never." As if that weren't a clear enough answer, she also immediately gave up her German citizenship to become a U.S. citizen instead. An American paper responded to Marlene's new citizenship with the following headline: "[Marlene Dietrich] Deserts Her Native Land." A Nazi-run German paper was even more accusing: "Shirt-sleeved judge administers oath to Dietrich so that she may betray the Fatherland."

Both papers, German and American, seemed to misunderstand Marlene's actions. Later, she clearly explained her motives, saying, "I was born a German, and I shall always remain German. I had to change my citizenship when Hitler came to power. I've become a good [American] citizen, but in my heart I'm German."

But Marlene wanted to do more than change her citizenship and help a few German-Jewish friends; she desperately wanted to be part of something that would defeat Nazism. When the United States officially joined World War II, she got her chance: she joined the USO.

The USO (United Service Organization) was a U.S. organization of volunteers geared to help soldiers and raise their spirits by keeping them in touch with civilian (nonmilitary) life. USO volunteers all over the country served cookies to soldiers, danced with them, sewed buttons for them, and visited military hospitals. Marlene belonged to a branch of the USO that was called Camp Shows, Inc. Camp Shows was a group of professional entertainers who put on live programs— music, dancing, jokes—for large groups of servicemen.

While American soldiers were training for war, all USO activities, including Camp Shows, took place in the United States. But when U.S. troops crossed the Atlantic, some entertainers from Camp Shows followed them into battle. Marlene was one of these courageous entertainers. One day she climbed aboard a creaky airplane with the other entertainers in her acting troupe for a frightening, stormy, and nauseating trip across the Atlantic Ocean. They first landed in North Africa, where Allied soldiers were fighting.

Marlene's shows usually consisted of her playing on a musical saw, telling jokes, and singing songs. While most of her songs were well-known American songs, when she crossed the Atlantic, she added a German song to her repertoire, a song that would forever be linked with her: "Lili Marlene." "Lili Marlene" is a love song describing the sadness of a wartime soldier separated from his girlfriend. The lyrics had been written by a German soldier during World War I, and the song was beloved among German troops although propaganda minister Joseph Goebbels tried to ban it. He

Marlene entertaining
Allied troops in Italy.
*Marlene Dietrich
Collection Berlin, Stiftung
Deutsche Kinemathek*

wanted his soldiers to be obsessed with military victories, not sigh-ing for their girlfriends back home.

Everyone knew that Marlene was part of the USO. But what many didn't know was that she was also part of an American espionage organization called the Office of Strategic Services, or the OSS. She was one of the entertainers working for their Morale Operations (MO) division. The MO sponsored a radio program in Europe called *Soldatensender West*, which consisted of Allied news and American songs translated into German. Some of them were popular songs played only so that the soldiers would stay tuned for the propaganda that would follow. Others openly mocked the Nazi leaders. Still others were sad songs designed to make the Ger-man soldiers weary of fighting.

Marlene Dietrich was one of the singers who made recordings for the MO, and one of her songs was, of course, "Lili Marlene." Although her German recording of the song was often played on *Soldatensender West*, once she was given an opportunity to sing it live for the broadcast. As soon as the microphone was handed to

Marlene in a jeep behind
enemy lines, just over
the German border in
Alsace-Lorraine.
*Marlene Dietrich
Collection Berlin, Stiftung
Deutsche Kinemathek*

her, she shouted in German, "Boys, don't sacrifice yourselves! This
war is [trash]! Hitler is an idiot!" Then she began to sing "Lili Marlene" in German.

Did any German soldiers hear her pleas and her sad German
love song? According to the hundreds of German POWs who were
interviewed after the war, a great many German soldiers listened
to *Soldatensender West* during the war even though the penalty for
doing so was death. And it is certain that the Nazi leaders heard both
her entreaty and her song. They were furious! A famous German-
American entertainer was denouncing Hitler and calling on German soldiers to give up the fight. What would they do to her if they
caught her? Marlene knew that she must never find out.

But if she was trying to evade capture, Marlene was not very
focused on that goal. Instead, her concentration was on the Allied
troops: keeping then laughing and entertained, if only for a few
moments. They couldn't believe that they were seeing the famous
film star in person, and they greatly appreciated her willingness to
come so close to the battle just to tell jokes and sing to them.

Marlene Dietrich
behind enemy lines in
the Forest of Ardennes,
December 1944.
*Marlene Dietrich
Collection Berlin, Stiftung
Deutsche Kinemathek*

For Marlene was frequently in serious personal danger. Gunfire and the sound of exploding bombs often provided the backdrop to her songs. More than once, her shows had to be stopped either because the soldiers received orders to "move out" (into battle) or enemy fire had come too close to the stage. But Marlene didn't care; she was a tireless and determined entertainer. She would often urge her fellow USO entertainers to drive as close as possible to the front lines of battle, do a short show for the servicemen there—just a few songs and jokes—and then drive back as quickly as possible.

The most dangerous event that Marlene experienced during the war occurred when she was traveling with a division of U.S. soldiers into the Ardennes Forest and entered a crucial battle of World War II: the Battle of the Bulge. The German army was trying to split and then surround the Allied army, forcing it to surrender. They managed to surround the U.S. 101st Airborne Division of soldiers—the very group of soldiers that Marlene was accompanying.

Huddled in the snow, she now had time—too much time—to consider her possible fate. What if the Germans captured her? Would they torture her? Kill her? Her biggest fear was that they would force her to make radio broadcasts to support Nazi propaganda, much like she had done for the Allies. Marlene especially dreaded the thought of being forced to say things over German radio that would hurt and confuse the Allied troops she wanted so much to help. Grateful for the risks Marlene was taking, General Patton handed her a pistol, telling her to at least shoot some Germans before she surrendered.

While she nervously pondered her fate, Marlene suddenly heard the sound of an approaching airplane. She looked up. Servicemen from the U.S. 82nd Airborne Division were parachuting toward her to rescue her. One of their commanding generals had requested that Marlene be immediately evacuated. The movie star was getting a cinematic rescue.

The 82nd Airborne Division did its job well. The 101st Airborne Division Marlene had been traveling with didn't fall into enemy hands either, and the Germans eventually lost the battle.

Marlene Dietrich was exposed to many hardships while serving the Allied troops—rats, lice, frostbite, army food, gunfire, and bombs—all because she wanted to help the Allied troops. But she would never come this close to life-threatening danger again.

When the war was over, the United States awarded her the Medal of Freedom (the highest award that can be given to a civilian), France named her a Knight of the Legion of Honor, and Belgium made her a Knight of the Order of Leopold. But her most satisfying reward was knowing that she had done her part to fight the battle against the Nazis. She would later refer to her USO and OSS work as "the only important thing I've ever done."

★★★ LEARN MORE ★★★

Marlene Dietrich: Photographs and Memories by the Marlene Dietrich Collection (of the Film Museum of Berlin), compiled by Jean-Jacques Naud and captioned by Maria Riva, Marlene Dietrich's daughter (Random House, 2001), contains many war-related photos and letters.

Marlene Dietrich
www.marlene.com
The official Marlene Dietrich website.

Maria Gulovich

SLOVAK FOR THE OSS

MARIA WAS VERY disappointed. She and a Hungarian Italian American named Lieutenant Tibor Keszthelyi had just received some terrible news. The Soviet army base, their destination, was still four or five days away on foot, and their German pursuers were swiftly approaching the area. She, Keszthelyi, and a group of Americans had been trudging through blizzarding mountains for a long time in a desperate attempt to avoid capture by the Germans. Maria and the men didn't thoroughly trust the Soviets, but since they were technically allies on the same side of the war, reaching them was the group's only possible way to avoid capture and certain death at the hands of the Germans. But the Soviet army—or

---

The identity card of Maria Gulovich, 1942.
Museum of Slovak National Uprising, Banska Bystrica, Slovakia

the "Red" army as it was sometimes called—kept moving farther and farther away, always at least several days out of reach.

Maria was prepared to go back to the others in camp with the bad news, but Lieutenant Keszthelyi stopped her. He spread his parka on the ground and beckoned Maria to sit next to him. They sat in silence together for several minutes. They had become good friends during the past months, working closely together, partly because they both spoke fluent Hungarian and could understand each other well. And he had saved her life just days before when she had slipped on a steep icy trail as they and the others in their group tried to cross the Chebenec Mountain. She had come to feel that if she allowed herself to, she could easily fall in love with this kind, handsome man who now sat beside her.

After a few moments, Keszthelyi broke the silence. "I want to tell you again how brave you are and that you deserved so much better," he said to Maria. "I keep seeing you walking down Park Avenue in New York, where a bright, beautiful girl like you belongs, and not in these godforsaken villages risking your life for us."

"You Americans are the brave ones," she answered, "because you volunteered to come here to help this little godforsaken country and the people in these villages. I had no choice."

Actually, Maria had made many choices, choices that had brought her to that very moment. No one had forced Maria to spend a month of nights sleeping in the grade school classroom where she was a teacher in the town of Hrinova, Slovakia, while two Jews hid in her own tiny room next door. When a leader in the Slovakian Resistance, Captain Milan Polak, discovered what she was doing, he gave Maria an ultimatum: either face Nazi arrest for hiding the Jews or work for him as a courier for the Resistance. She chose to become a courier after Polak promised to help the Jews find other shelter.

THE SLOVAKIAN UPRISING AND
★★★ THE DAWES MISSION ★★★

The Slovakian Uprising was waged by the CFI (Czech Slovak Forces of the Interior), a large (50,000 to 60,000) band of pro-Allied, non-Communist Slovak partisans. They were in a struggle for Slovakia's independence against the German-controlled Czech Republic *and* the Soviets who wanted to control Slovakia after the war. The headquarters of the CFI was in the Slovakian town of Banska Bystrica, and it was here that the American Dawes team was stationed in 1944 to accomplish a two-sided mission. The first, and more obvious, reason for the mission was to evacuate stranded Allied airmen in the area and also assist the CFI with intelligence operations against the Germans. The Dawes team was so successful at locating strategic Nazi bombing sites that Hitler became enraged and vowed to forsake the Geneva Conventions (which forbade the mistreatment of enemy soldiers) and shoot any Allied airmen on the spot.

The second part of the Dawes mission was top secret. The team knew of the Soviet Union's postwar plans to seize control of both the Czech Republic *and* Slovakia (known as Czechoslovakia since 1918), and they were trying to gather information regarding those plans.

But it seemed that Maria had no choice when, abandoned by the Soviets she had been ordered to work for as an interpreter in Banska Bystrica, the town that had been a center of the Slovakian Uprising, she was kindly invited to flee the oncoming German onslaught with the Americans who had been using that town as a base of operations. They were working for the OSS, a U.S.

espionage organization. Their reason for being in Slovakia was called the Dawes mission.

The Americans involved with the Dawes mission treated Maria so respectfully in comparison with the treatment she received from many of her previous associates (one of whom had attempted to rape her) that after they had escaped the Germans together in Banska Bystrica and the men formally invited Maria to join the Dawes team, Maria gladly accepted. Her direct superior, General Rudolf Viest, a Slovak commander whom Maria respected, gave her a formal release from the disintegrating CFI, telling her, "You stay with the Americans, Maria. You know the mountains, the languages, the people, and the political situation. Help them in any way you can."

While serving as a guide, interpreter, and cook to the American men on the Dawes team as they fled on foot through the snowy Tatra Mountains, always just a few hours in front of their Nazi pursuers, Maria had many chances to leave the Americans. It would have been in her best interest to do so, as she was constantly reminded by the Slovakian villagers whom she approached for food and shelter on behalf of herself and the Americans. She didn't take the villagers' advice. She stayed with the Americans.

General Viest and Maria both understood that the Americans were now running for their lives because they had come to Slovakia largely to fight against the Germans and also to help the Slovaks do so. As she walked back to the camp, hand in hand with Keszthelyi, Maria was concerned about many things: her leg, painfully infected with frostbite; her photograph, placed by the Germans on a "wanted" poster and plastered all over the area; her growing attraction to Lieutenant Keszthelyi; and their uncertain future. But she was sure that she was doing the right thing by staying with the Americans, even when a few days later, Lieutenant Keszthelyi and another member of the Dawes team, Sergeant Jerry Mican, were captured by the Germans.

Keszthelyi and Mican had been ordered to deliver a note requesting the use of some horses to a local orthodox priest, who was personally known and approved by an American woman named Margaret Kockova. Kockova had been working with a British espionage team, also on the run from the Germans. Maria had a foreboding and begged Keszthelyi and Mican not to go, but they just laughed and told her they'd see her soon.

When they didn't return and she discovered that they had been betrayed to the Germans, Maria stormed to the priest's home, risking her own betrayal and arrest, demanding to know what had happened. At first the priest denied that any Americans had been there at all, but Maria demanded to know the truth. The priest and his wife finally admitted that their female servant had betrayed the Americans.

There was nothing to do but continue on, especially because Maria and the team knew that now the Germans would be redoubling their efforts to find the rest of them. They decided to bypass the villages and instead make their way to a lodge where the British team, including Margaret Kockova, was waiting for them. They celebrated Christmas together there, but their festivities were short lived. The women's personalities clashed, and Maria couldn't bear to be under the same roof with Kockova, who had been instrumental—even if it had been unintentional—in the betrayal and arrest of Keszthelyi and Mican. Maria requested to be transferred to the hotel at the top of the mountain to cook and clean for the men who were on guard there.

The next morning, Maria and the men leaving with her turned around to see that the lodge they had left just hours before was suddenly surrounded by German soldiers. Through their binoculars they could see the British and American teams being led out of the lodge and forced onto trucks while the lodge was burned to the ground.

Maria, two Americans, and two British now walked desperately, for many weeks, toward the Soviet army lines. Their limbs became frostbitten, their clothes tattered, and they became very weak. Maria had to be carried to their final hiding place, a deserted mine shaft. It was while huddled in this mine shaft that Maria and her companions heard the good news: Soviet forces had captured a nearby town! They would finally be safe from the Germans!

But their joy was short lived. The Soviets did not trust the Americans or the British. They interrogated Maria more than the others since she was the only one in the group who spoke Russian. What had the Americans been doing in Slovakia? Why was she traveling with them? Why didn't she admit to being a spy for the Americans? Maria didn't tell them that one key aspect of the Dawes mission was to gather information on Soviet activity in Slovakia. She repeated, again and again, that the Americans had been in Slovakia to help the CFI and to wage sabotage warfare against the Germans, their common enemy. They didn't believe her and grew increasingly hostile, at last forcing her to sign a paper stating that she would now work for the NKVD, the Soviet Secret Police, for an unspecified amount of time. Maria had no choice but to sign.

When the others were ordered to be shipped to another location, Maria was told that since she was now employed by the NKVD, she would have to remain behind. She was able to escape this fate by pretending to be married to one of the men, Guilliam Davis, a British sergeant who had been protective of Maria since he had joined the retreating Dawes team.

The Soviets consented, with the stipulation that Maria would return later to fulfill her duties with the NKVD. They were all put on a train going to Odessa. When they learned that their train was going to stop in Bucharest, Romania, where there was an American army post, they devised a desperate plan.

When the train stopped in Bucharest, Maria and two other women (whom she had befriended just before boarding the train) begged their Soviet guard for permission to visit the station lavatory while one of the Americans—Sergeant Steven Catlos—snuck off the train and made a phone call to the local American army post. He was told he must stay off the train and stall for 20 minutes until some U.S. soldiers could get there. Maria and the women kept making groaning sounds from inside the lavatory, pretending to be sick, much to the dismay of their nervous Soviet guard, who kept pounding on the door. When they heard the prearranged signal—Sergeant Catlos whistling "Yankee Doodle"—Maria cracked open the door and saw a welcome sight: a group of U.S. soldiers storming the station. The Soviets insisted that the refugees get back on the train, and the leader of the U.S. soldiers insisted that they go free. The outnumbered Soviets finally relented, and Maria and the others were free.

Maria was in Italy, working at the OSS headquarter there, when she received some dreadful news: the captured members of the Dawes team, including Maria's friend Tibor Keszthelyi, had all been tortured and killed by the Germans.

For her work in assisting the Dawes team escape the Germans, Maria Gulovich was awarded the Bronze Star medal in a ceremony at West Point Military Academy, where General William Donovan, the head of the OSS, pinned the medal on Maria's dress with these words: "The dangers you courageously braved and terrible hardships endured bespeak an ardent spirit devoted to freedom and justice. Your cool and determined behavior under enemy fire is matched by skill in negotiating for sustenance in enemy infested areas. I commend you for your exemplary heroism in serving the Dawes mission and the United States of America."

Maria was given a scholarship to Vassar College and became a U.S. citizen in 1952. She died in California in September 2009.

★★★ LEARN MORE ★★★

Maria Gulovich, OSS Heroine of World War II: The Schoolteacher Who Saved Lives in Slovakia by Sonya N. Jason (McFarland & Company, Inc., 2009).

Sisterhood of Spies: The Women of the OSS by Elizabeth P. McIntosh (Naval Institute Press, 1998) contains a chapter on Maria Gulovich.

Martha Gellhorn

WAR CORRESPONDENT

MARTHA GELLHORN FIRST knew she wanted to be a writer when she was a 16-year-old student at the John Burroughs School in St. Louis, Missouri. Encouraged in her writing endeavors by two of her English teachers, she decided to send several of her poems to the celebrated poet Carl Sandburg. He wrote back saying, "If you must be a writer, you will be."

Her mother, a suffragette leader and social reformer, and her father, a medical doctor who, at the time, was one of the only whites in St. Louis to regularly invite black people to dinner with his family, had instilled a strong desire to learn in their three sons and their daughter. But after three years at Bryn Mawr College,

Martha Gellhorn in Spain in the 1930s.
JFK Memorial Library

Martha decided that her thirst for knowledge could not be satisfied in a college setting. She wanted to write novels in Europe and
thought that journalism would be a way to make a living while
doing what she loved. In the spring of 1930, when Martha was 21,
she arrived in Paris with two suitcases, a typewriter, and $75.00.
She wrote articles for the *St. Louis Post-Dispatch* regarding the
League of Nations (the precursor to the United Nations) and wrote
novels and short stories in her spare time.

In 1934, while living and writing in France, Martha was included
as part of a special delegation of young French people invited to
Berlin, Germany, to strengthen ties of friendship between France
and Germany. After the train of young people arrived in Berlin,
Martha and her friends were shocked when German border guards
walked into their train car and confiscated their books and newspapers. They responded by singing the "Marseillaise," the rousing
French national anthem.

The rest of the trip did little to change Martha's negative opinion of Nazi Germany. The Hitler Youth movement seemed too
boisterously patriotic, and everyone seemed obsessed with race,
especially the supposed superiority of the Aryan race over all others, particularly the Jews. As Martha's parents were both half Jewish, she found this very disturbing.

Martha began to see the vital role that journalism could have:
If people could clearly understand the truth of world events, they
would demand action of their leaders. Wrongs would be righted,
evil punished, and the innocent would be protected.

During the rest of the 1930s, Martha traveled throughout
Europe and the United States, reporting for a time on how the
U.S. Great Depression was affecting everyday people. She was in
Germany when she first heard the Nazis refer to the Republican
side of the Spanish Civil War (1936–39) as "Red swine dogs," both
in newspaper articles and chanted in the streets. She became so
angry that she left Germany. Martha had such a low opinion of

Nazis that she decided she would support the Republicans over the Nazi-supported Fascist Nationalists.

While in Spain, reporting the effects the Spanish Civil War had on civilians for *Collier's* weekly newsmagazine, Martha realized that Fascism had to be stopped in Spain or it would take another, larger war to do so. The Fascist Nationalists won the war.

On the evening of June 6, 1944, D-day, Martha was walking through the docks of London. By this time, she had been reporting on the world war for *Collier's* from England, Czechoslovakia, Italy, and the Far East. She no longer believed, as she once did, that public opinion could be changed by journalism. After all, she and other journalists had been reporting the dangerous rise of European Fascism for years, and it had only grown more powerful. What Martha wanted now was a front-row seat to the fall of Fascism, which she believed had just begun that morning on the shores of Normandy. She thought that being a journalist gave her that ticket.

But she was going to have to find her own ticket this time. Along with the troops that had crossed the English Channel from the very docks she was now strolling through, hundreds of writers, radio journalists, and war photographers had also crossed over into Normandy. Martha, by now a respected and renowned

★★★ FASCISTS AND THE NAZI PARTY ★★★

Fascism is a political ideology that promotes an authoritative single-party government intolerant of any other political views or parties. During the 1930s, several countries, including Spain, Italy, and Germany, developed Fascist governments, although Germany's version of Fascism was far more destructive than the others.

journalist, had not been allowed to travel with them for one simple reason: they were men, and she was a woman. Female reporters weren't allowed on the front lines of battle.

As Martha walked around the docks, she noticed a white ship that had red crosses painted on its side. It was a hospital ship that was going to cross the Channel to help the wounded. Just then, a military policeman stopped her and asked what she was doing. She pointed to the hospital ship and told him that she was a journalist with plans to interview the nurses on the ship. He let her proceed. She walked aboard and locked herself in the bathroom until she felt the ship leaving port.

The transport ships that had crossed that morning with troops and reporters were painted in shades of green and grey to hide them from view of the enemy. The hospital ship Martha found herself on was stark white, and she and the six nurses and four doctors who were on board with her, moving through the dark waters of the Channel, hoped very much that the Germans would honor the Geneva Conventions that forbade the destruction of hospital transports.

Their crossing was slow. The Germans had put mines in the water to impede the Allied invasion, and the captain of Martha's ship was being careful since the two preceding hospital ships had struck these mines. When the Normandy coast came into view, Martha was suddenly part of the invasion and wrote:

> People will be writing about this sight for a hundred years and whoever saw it will never forget it. First it seemed incredible; there could not be so many ships in the world. Then it seemed incredible as a feat of planning; if there were so many ships, what genius it required to get them here, what amazing and unimaginable genius. After the first shock of wonder and admiration, one began to look around and see separate details. There were destroyers and battleships and transports, a floating city of huge vessels anchored before the green cliffs of Normandy. Occasionally

you would see a gun flash or perhaps only hear a distant roar, as naval guns fired far over those hills. Small craft beetled around in a curiously jolly way. It looked like a lot of fun to race from shore to ships in snub-nosed boats beating up the spray. It was no fun at all, considering the mines and obstacles that remained in the water, the sunken tanks with only their radio antennae showing above water, the drowned bodies that still floated past . . . Then we stopped noticing the invasion, the ships, the ominous beach, because the first wounded had arrived.

All that day and into the night, Martha helped the doctors and nurses on the ship tend to the many wounded whom they brought on board. While waiting for the dawn, when they could cross the Channel back to England, Martha had these impressions:

If anyone had come fresh to that ship in the night . . . he would have been appalled. . . . Piles of bloody clothing had been cut off and dumped out of the way in corners; coffee cups and cigarette stubs littered the decks; plasma bottles hung from cords, and all the fearful surgical apparatus for holding broken bones made shadows on the walls. There were wounded who groaned in their sleep or called out and there was the soft steady hum of conversation among the wounded who could not sleep. That is the way it would have looked to anyone seeing it fresh—a ship carrying a load of pain, with everyone waiting for daylight, everyone hoping for the anchor to be raised, everyone longing for England. It was that but it was something else too; it was a safe ship no matter what happened to it. We were together and we counted on each other. We knew that from the British captain to the pink-cheeked little London mess boy, every one of the ship's company did his job tirelessly and well. The wounded knew that the doctors and nurses and orderlies belonged to them utterly and would not fail them. And all of us knew that our own wounded were good men and that with their amazing help, their selflessness and self-control, we would get through all right.

Martha was the first female journalist to report on the D-day invasion. But because she had crossed the Channel without the proper permission, she was deprived of her travel papers and ration cards. This didn't stop her. For the duration of the war, Martha relied on her charm and spunk to persuade many commanders to let her hitch a ride with their troops so she could see the war firsthand. She had wanted very much to fly in an Allied air mission over Germany, and one night she talked her way into becoming the first female journalist to do so.

While traveling through many European battle zones during the summer and autumn of 1944, Martha kept hearing rumors about Nazi concentration camps. The name Dachau stood out from the others, and it became a symbol of the entire Nazi regime in Martha's mind. She needed to see it for herself.

The Normandy Invasion, June 6, 1944.
FDR Memorial Library

When Martha arrived in Dachau shortly after it was liberated by the Allies and found herself interviewing one of the doctors in the camp, she met one of the former prisoners. She wrote:

> What had been a man dragged himself into the doctor's office. His eyes were large and strange and stood out from his face, and his jawbone seemed to be cutting through his skin. . . . This man had survived; he was found under a pile of dead. Now he stood on the bones that were his legs and talked and suddenly he wept. "Everyone is dead," he said, and the face that was not a face twisted with pain or sorrow or horror. "No one is left. Everyone is dead. I cannot help myself. Here I am and I am finished and cannot help myself. Everyone is dead."

Martha wanted to know everything, and she was told in detail how many people died from medical experiments and the cruel punishments inflicted by the SS guards who lived next to the camp in comfort with their wives and children. She was also given a tour where she saw the piles of dead, starved bodies that the SS had not had time to burn in the crematorium before they fled from the advancing Allied armies. As a war reporter, Martha had of course seen many dead bodies before, but to her, "Nothing about war was ever as insanely wicked as these starved and outraged, naked, nameless dead."

Dachau survivor.
Yad Vashem

★★★ THE THIRD MRS. HEMINGWAY ★★★

Martha Gellhorn was married to Ernest Hemingway, a ground-breaking and influential American novelist as well as a war correspondent, in December 1940. Gellhorn greatly admired Hemingway's novels, and he sometimes gave her advice on writing fiction. The marriage ended in 1945, in part because Martha wanted to continue reporting on World War II after their marriage and Hemingway preferred she stay home and write novels.

Toward the end of her visit, Martha was again speaking to one of the doctors when the former prisoner she had seen before came in and whispered something in Polish to the doctor. The doctor responded with "Bravo." He told Martha that Germany had surrendered and the war was over.

"We sat in that room," Martha wrote, "in that accursed cemetery prison, and no one had anything more to say. Still, Dachau seemed to me the most suitable place in Europe to hear the news of victory. For surely this war was made to abolish Dachau, and all the other places like Dachau, and everything that Dachau stood for, and to abolish it forever."

While touring Dachau, Martha lost her belief that truth and justice would ultimately prevail: man, in her opinion, had far too great a capacity for evil. But that did not keep her from reporting on wars. She continued to cover many conflicts, including Vietnam, the Six-Day War in the Middle East, and the civil wars in Central America. She died in 1998 at the age of 89, having fulfilled her earlier ambition to write novels and short stories, many of which were highly respected (and most of which were based on her own experiences). But Martha Gellhorn's journalistic skills

far outweighed those of her fiction writing, and she is widely considered to be one of the greatest war correspondents of the 20th
century.

In the year following her death, the Martha Gellhorn Prize for
Journalism was established as an annual award given to a journalist who illuminates a major news story by highlighting the human
aspect of that story.

★★★ LEARN MORE ★★★

Gellhorn: A 20th Century Life by Caroline Moorehead (Henry Holt,
2003).

The Face of War by Martha Gellhorn (Simon & Schuster, 1959;
reprinted by Atlantic Monthly Press, 1994).

*War, Women, and the News: How Female Journalists Won the Battle
to Cover WWII* by Catherine Gourley (Atheneum Press, 2007).

Hazel Ying Lee

AMERICAN FLYGIRL

WHEN JAPAN INVADED Manchuria, the large northern province of China, in September 1931, it caused great concern for people who lived thousands of miles away: Chinese Americans, many of whom had settled on the West Coast of the United States.

The Chinese Consolidated Benevolent Association in Portland, Oregon, decided to take action: it raised $20,000 and donated it to the local Chinese Flying Club in order to train young Chinese Americans to fly in Generalissimo Chiang Kai-shek's air force.

Thirty-six students applied, and they were all asked to sign a pledge promising that they would use their new skills in China. All 36 signed without hesitation. Two of them were women: Virginia

Hazel Ying Lee.
Courtesy of the WASP Archive, Texas Women's University, Denton, Texas

Wong and Hazel Ying Lee, the latter who, in October 1932, became one of the first Chinese American women to earn a pilot's license.

Hazel was born in 1912, the second oldest of eight siblings. She had attended Chinese language classes, along with her siblings, in addition to the local public school. Athletic, fun-loving, adventurous, and competitive, Hazel had her first taste of flying at the age of 19 when she rode in a friend's stunt plane during an air show.

One month before leaving to be part of the Chinese Air Force, Hazel was interviewed by a local reporter for the *Oregonian*. She told him that she was going to China to help the war effort but that her trip might also open doors for other female aviators to participate in wartime work. "Perhaps when I go up in an airplane in China," she said, "and do a couple of loops and wing-overs, they will say, 'If one girl can do that, why not others?'"

In March 1933, Hazel and 16 other Portland Flying Club trainees left for China. But when she arrived, Hazel was told that the Chinese Air Force would not allow any woman pilots to fly military missions. Why? The Chinese Air Force officers claimed "women are erratic in combat."

Hazel Ying Lee (right) and
Virginia Wong in 1932.
Courtesy of Alan H. Rosenberg,
Producer, A Brief Flight, as part
of the Hazel Ying Lee/Frances M.
Tong Collection at the Museum of
Chinese in America (MOCA)

Hazel was given a desk job with the Chinese Commission on Aeronautical Affairs and also flew for commercial flights, sometimes flying Soong Mei-ling, wife of the Generalissimo, from place to place. She also flew over highly populated areas, dropping pro-Chinese leaflets to encourage Chinese resolve against the Japanese.

Her base of operation eventually became the populous southern city of Canton, where she opened a school for her young Chinese relatives.

Hazel was still in China in 1937 when the Japanese began their campaign to conquer the entire country. When Canton was bombed in the spring of 1938, Hazel found safe shelter for herself and her family. Her friend Elsie Chang asked why she seemed so fearless. "If everybody else is afraid," Hazel replied, "there has to be somebody that could take over. And I'm the one to take over."

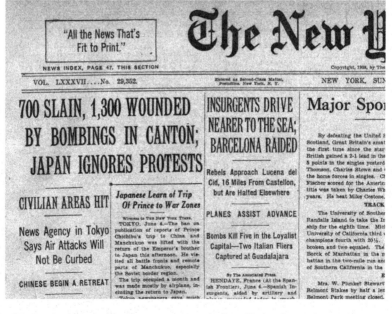

The *New York Times* headline reporting the bombing of Canton.
New York Times, *1938*

After arriving in the relative safety of Hong Kong, Hazel found little to do, so she eventually returned to Portland. Yet her heart was still in her ancestral homeland and her mind full of the war's images: death, destruction, and homeless war refugees.

The United States was still neutral at this this point and was selling scrap metal to Japan for war materials. When Hazel discovered that a ship loaded with scrap metal was about to sail from Portland to Japan, she and three friends conducted a demonstration right beside the ship.

A local reporter asked her to explain her actions. "America must stop these shipments to Japan in the interest of humanity," Hazel said. "We've seen pieces of scrap metal burst from bombs and kill or wound everyone in range."

The ship sailed anyway.

Hazel decided to move to New York City, where she stayed for four years, taking a job with Universal Trading Corporation, which was connected to the Chinese government. Hazel helped the company obtain necessary war materials for the Chinese military.

While Hazel worked at Universal, she became romantically linked with a Chinese American flier named Clifford Louie, one of her former Portland Flying Club classmates. He had been wounded while flying for China and had returned to the United States to recuperate and to take further training in the U.S. military as a Chinese officer.

Around the same time, Hazel heard about the WASP.

The Women Airforce Service Pilot program, known as WASP, merged two women's flying organizations: the Women's Flying Training Detachment (WFTD) and the Women's Auxiliary Ferrying Squadron (WAFS). Jacqueline Cochran, founder of the WFTD and then director of the WASP, had visited First Lady Eleanor Roosevelt personally, asking for increased opportunities for women who wanted to help the war effort with their flying skills. The First Lady supported the plan enthusiastically.

There was a great need for fliers in this war: the aerial attacks of Germany and Japan, right from the start of the war, had made it clear that airpower would be a game changer in this conflict. The U.S. Army, which in the early 1930s had been training only 300 pilots per year, spent the latter years of that decade and into the next scrambling to catch up.

U.S. airplane production had also been in high gear since the bombing of Pearl Harbor and America's entrance into the war. In 1939, only 921 military planes were built in the United States. In 1943, 86,000 were built.

Pilots were needed to fly all these new planes from the factories to military bases. If female pilots could be trained to do this, it would free up male pilots for air combat.

Hazel applied to the WASP program and began her training in February 1943, in Sweetwater, Texas, at an airfield called Avenger Field.

Three WASP trainees at Avenger Field. Left to right: Faith Buchner, Hazel, Grace Clark. *Courtesy of the WASP Archive, Texas Woman's University, Denton, Texas*

There were some major differences between Hazel and the other trainees. She was nearly a decade older than most of them and had seen war firsthand. Most of them were white and had never personally known a person of Asian descent. Yet Hazel had no trouble making friends with everyone in her class. One fellow trainee described her as "a wonderful, jolly, joyous, humorous person." Another said she was "a courageous, very wonderful, very witty person." She made everyone laugh when she decided to write the nicknames of her fellow trainees on their planes in Chinese letters with lipstick!

But Hazel did experience at least one incident of racial prejudice. One day when her plane engine stalled over a farm, she had to make an emergency landing there. The famer came running toward her, pitchfork in hand, yelling, "I'm going to kill you, you dirty little Jap."

Ever since the Japanese attack on Pearl Harbor on December 7, 1941, rumors and fears of a Japanese land invasion had swirled through certain parts of the country. And because the WASP flight suits were oversized—they had had been made for men—slim Hazel, with her short hair, looked almost male while training.

Doing her best to avoid contact with the farmer's pitchfork, Hazel ran circles around and under her plane, all the while trying to explain that she was an American woman training to fly for the U.S. military. This did no good. "Women don't fly in the Army Air Corps," the farmer retorted, as he continued the chase.

Finally, the man's adult son heard the commotion, came out of the house, and convinced his father to put down his pitchfork long enough to make a call to Avenger Field. Hazel was rescued and was brought back to Avenger Field.

On August 7, 1943, she graduated 43-W-4; that is, she graduated in 1943, she was a woman, and she was in the fourth WASP class.

That same month she was assigned to Romulus Air Force Base in Michigan with the Third Ferrying Group, where she flew newly manufactured planes from the assembly lines to Army Air Corps bases.

Writing to her sister Frances on April 22, 1944, Hazel described her work at Romulus: "The flying keeps me pretty busy; in fact, we hardly have any time off. We are on a seven-day work schedule. Now, we may be placed directly in the Air Corps. At present we're known as WASPS (Women Army Service Pilots) [sic]. The work is interesting and gives us many opportunities of going to all parts of the country including some parts of Canada."

Her fellow pilots at Romulus noticed that, despite their grueling schedule, Hazel was always "determined to laugh each trouble down." And when she did get time off, she always knew where to have fun: at Chinese restaurants. "[Hazel] knew somebody who had a Chinese restaurant no matter where you were," recalled one former WASP. Another remembered Hazel telling them the best dishes to order. When they felt full, Hazel would say, "Drink some more tea and then you can eat some more!"

After D-day, as the Allies pushed into occupied France, the retreating Germans were fighting fiercely and more planes were needed in the war effort. General William H. Turner, head of Air Transport Command, wanted to train a select number of WASPs to fly "pursuit" fighter planes from the factories to Army Air Corps bases, so that these planes could get into the war effort faster.

Hazel was chosen for pursuit training, and on September 4, 1944, she traveled to Brownsville, Texas, and learned how to fly the following planes (the P in their names means *pursuit*): Curtiss P-40 Kittyhawk (used in China), Republic P-47 Thunderbolt (used in the European Theater), Bell P-39 Airacobra (used by the Soviets), and North American P-51 Mustang (used by Americans in both the Pacific and European Theaters).

When a Brownsville reporter interviewed Hazel, she told him that it was "a great thrill to lift one of these thundering fighters into the air."

Training was challenging, but on October 2, 1944, Hazel and six other WASPs and 27 male pilots graduated from Pursuit Class 44-18 Flight B. And on October 9, Hazel married Clifford Louie in New York City. Then they both went back to work, Hazel to Romulus and Clifford to China.

Although it seemed that Clifford was in more danger than his new wife, the WASPs often faced serious hazards. One of the most perilous tasks for any stateside flier was ferrying what were called "war-weary" planes, those that needed repairs or replacement. No one knew if they would stay in working condition on the way to being refurbished. But someone had to fly them. And WASPs often did.

Flying seven days a week in all sorts of weather and at high altitudes could also be dangerous, or, as in Hazel's case, at least hazardous to one's health. On October 14, 1944, she was grounded due to a severe respiratory infection. Chafing with impatience, she wrote a letter to Inez Woodward—nicknamed "Woodie"—a

Three 43-W-4 WASPs: Left to right: Hazel, Alice Jean Starr, Virgie Jowell Hagerstrom. *Courtesy of the WASP Archive, Texas Woman's University, Denton, Texas*

WASP who had also graduated in the 43-W-4 class and who had worked with Hazel at Romulus until August 1944, when she transferred to a different base.

In the letter, Hazel told Inez that she had received an offer from her former employer, the Chinese Commission on Aeronautical Affairs. Hazel wrote that she hoped to recruit ex-WASPs to fly in China. They had to have new plans because by now they had all received word that the WASP program would be disbanded in December.

Although Hazel seemed filled with hope for the future, the war was taking a toll on her. Sometime in 1944, she wrote a letter to her friend Elsie Chang, telling her that "this war is going on too long. I don't know whether I will make it or not."

In late November, Hazel was ordered to report to the Bell Aircraft factory in Niagara Falls, New York, to pick up a P-63 Kingcobra and fly it to the airfield at Great Falls, Montana. From there a male pilot would fly it to the Soviet Union.

But wintry weather forced Hazel and other WASPs flying with her to stop short of their destination and land their planes at the military airfield at Fargo, North Dakota. There they waited for safer conditions. While they were there, other pilots in the same predicament landed and waited with them.

By November 23, 1944, the weather had cleared and Hazel took off for Great Falls. There were now 10 planes in the same traffic pattern, all headed for the same destination.

At approximately 2:00 in the afternoon, Hazel began to land her P-63 at the Great Falls landing field. Another P-63 was coming in for a landing at the same time, flown by a pilot named Lieutenant Charles Russel. For a few perilous seconds neither pilot could see the other—Lieutenant Russel's P-63 was slightly higher than Hazel's.

The frantic Great Falls air traffic controllers, who could see everything, ordered both pilots to pull up and come around again.

★★★ A MISSED REUNION ★★★

On October 27, 1944, Hazel Ying Lee wrote her friend Inez
Woodward:

> We're going to have a reunion at Romulus before we dis-
> band. Understand that we will report back to the base by
> the 10th of Dec. and spent the rest of the time checking
> out and packing. Kekie will come up from Cleveland &
> Pateman, Wakeham will be here also. Wish you'd come
> too. What a brawl it would be! . . . Do write, Woodie, and
> let me know what you've been doing. Best from all of us.
> Yours, Ah Ying.

Hazel obeyed the order. But the radio in Lieutenant Russel's plane
wasn't working.

Hazel's plane crashed into Lieutenant Russel's, hitting one of
his fuel tanks. Both planes then hit the ground, engulfed in flames.
Lieutenant Russel managed to get free, but the crash had knocked
Hazel unconscious and it was some time before she was pulled
from the plane, her jacket still smoldering. She regained consciousness, but died two days later from severe burns and injuries.

As Hazel's family prepared for her funeral, they received word
that one of her younger brothers, Corporal Victor Ling Lee, had
been killed in France on November 28, while his military unit was
defending the French town of Falck near the German border.

Now the family had two children to bury. But when they tried
to purchase grave plots from Portland's Riverview Cemetery, the
cemetery officials protested. Hazel and Victor weren't white and
the spot the family had chosen was in the so-called white section.

Hazel's mother, who was normally very quiet, protested, telling the cemetery officials that her children had "died in war for the United States and they are entitled to it." When they still refused, she threatened to report them to the U.S. War Department. The cemetery officials finally relented, and Hazel was buried there, as was Victor after the war.

All told, 38 WASPs lost their lives in the line of duty over the course of the program. Hazel Ying Lee was among the last to die. One of the most beloved of all her fellow pilots, she was deeply mourned by everyone who had known her.

★★★ LEARN MORE ★★★

A Brief Flight: Hazel Ying Lee and the Women Who Flew Pursuit (LAWAS Productions, 2002).

Seized by the Sun: The Life and Disappearance of World War II Pilot Gertrude Tompkins by James W. Ure (Chicago Review Press, 2017).

To Live and Die a WASP: 38 Women Pilots Who Died in WWII by William M. Miller (CreateSpace, 2016).

PART IX
The Soviet Union

IN THE EARLY hours of June 22, 1941, Germany invaded the Soviet Union. For weeks, intelligence reports had revealed an enormous number of German troops and tanks massing on the border. But Joseph Stalin, dictator of the Soviet Union, refused to mobilize the Red Army, largely because he wanted to preserve the neutrality pact his government had signed on August 23, 1939, for as long as possible. He had deliberately kept his army from preparing for war so as not to offend Hitler, his ally in the destruction of Poland.

The army of the Soviet Union had been called the Red Army from the time of the Russian Civil War, to distinguish these Bolshevik (later Communist) forces from Russia's so-called White Army, which had been composed of multiple anti-Bolshevik forces.

When the Red Army defeated the White Army in 1921, a new country was formed. It was called the Soviet Union, and Vladimir

Lenin was its first leader. When Lenin died in 1924, he was succeeded by Joseph Stalin, even though Lenin had written a testament, to be read at the time of his death, warning of Stalin's dangerous lust for power.

When he was firmly in control, Stalin became a ruthless dictator, rigidly controlling every aspect of his people's lives and brutally punishing all dissenters. During the Great Purge of 1936–38, he ordered the murder of approximately 700,000 Soviet citizens and sent more than one million into Glavnoye Upravleniye Lagere, or gulags, a vast series of brutal labor camps.

Many Red Army officers had been imprisoned or murdered during the Great Purge, so when Germany invaded the Soviet Union on June 22, 1941, in what was called Operation Barbarossa, most surviving Russian officers were more fearful of Stalin than they were of the Germans. No one wanted to be the first to tell him that Hitler had broken the German-Soviet Nonaggression Pact.

Hitler had never meant to maintain this pact. He only wanted to keep Stalin from interfering with the German invasion of Poland in September 1939. Flush with his sweeping success there, followed by the rest of western Europe in the spring of 1940, Hitler was confident that he could conquer the Soviet Union within months, seizing its vast farmlands for his own people while killing or enslaving the Soviets.

The generals of the German army, the Wehrmacht, had warned their leader that a quick victory would be highly unlikely, despite the fact that the Red Army had very little modern military equipment. They knew that the Soviet Union was vast and its population enormous, two factors that would make a German victory difficult, no matter how old the Red Army's few tanks and planes were. However, by August, the Wehrmacht had seized hundreds of miles of land and imprisoned one million Red Army soldiers while killing or wounding 700,000 more. Even the most doubtful German officers now began to share Hitler's belief in his own invincibility.

But the Germans hadn't counted on one thing: the Red Army's fierceness. When cornered, it fought furiously. Not only had Hitler ordered the execution of all captured Red Army officers, but if any Soviet POW happened to escape German captivity, he would most likely have been shot as a traitor by his superior officer, just for having been caught. Families of captured POWs were punished by losing their precious food rations, or worse; when Stalin's own son was captured, Stalin had his daughter-in-law thrown in jail, accusing them both of a treasonous plot.

Furthermore, Hitler had decreed that no Wehrmacht soldiers who mistreated or killed Soviet civilians would be prosecuted. Widespread German atrocities against Soviet civilians caused outrage among the Red Army soldiers and surviving civilians, firing up a fierce desire to fight the invaders.

These civilians had been confused when Stalin agreed to the nonaggression pact. After all, while forcing a government-controlled economy on the nation, he had constantly railed against Fascism, claiming that it was the mortal enemy of Communism. When Germany invaded, in some ways it clarified this confusion and lifted a national depression caused by Stalin's heavy-handed control of his people. And when Stalin gave a speech on July 3, 1941, urging his people to fight the Germans, it stirred up their age-old mystical love of country and fueled their determination to withstand the invasion in what they referred to as the Great Patriotic War.

Soviet citizens would sorely need that determination. During the first months of the war, the Germans laid siege to several major cities, causing massive death by starvation without having to expend much ammunition. It worked: enormous numbers of Soviets starved or froze to death, especially as winter set in.

But the Russian winter would also, in a way, prove to be a valuable ally to the Soviets. The Red Army soldiers were intimately acquainted with its frigid temperatures, whereas the invading

German forces hadn't even been provided with winter uniforms. As temperatures fell, countless German soldiers suffered frostbite, or simply froze to death, and the battle came to a standstill in most areas.

As the Soviet Union prepared for spring, Soviet women were mobilized for the war effort on a large scale. Although many had volunteered immediately after the initial invasion, most had been turned down for military roles because they were women. Now it was clear that they were needed, so gender issues were pushed aside as women were trained as snipers, pilots, partisans, tank drivers, and machine gunners, as well as communications officers and medics.

The United States and Great Britain had, by this point, become allies of the Soviet Union. Although both were uncomfortable being allied with a Communist dictator, they saw Stalin's battle

Soviet partisans.
Wikimedia Commons

with Germany as a way to help Great Britain, especially, win its war against Hitler.

Stalin repeatedly asked his new allies to open a second front; that is, to invade German-occupied Europe and fight Hitler's troops from the west, while he battled them in the east. The Ango-American allies did open some fronts in North Africa in November 1942, and then Italy in the summer of 1943, but neither took much pressure off Soviet troops battling the Germans.

And as the Germans prepared for new offensives in the spring of 1942, it caused disaster for the Soviets in many places. When some military advisers suggested the Soviets pull back farther east, Stalin responded with Order 227, a command distributed throughout the military that became known as the "not one step back" order. In other words, retreating was absolutely forbidden.

Perhaps Order 227 was at least partly responsible for what happened that summer: When the Germans reached Stalingrad, the Red Army defended the city ferociously in what became house-to-house combat. The battle was a disaster for the Germans, and the German commanding officer's eventual surrender at Stalingrad on February 2, 1943, marked a major turning point of the war.

The promised second front finally began on June 6, 1944, when troops from the United States, Great Britain, and other Allied nations landed on the shores of Normandy and began gradually pushing the Germans west, out of occupied France, while the Soviets pushed them east out of the Soviet Union. On April 25, 1945, Soviet and American forces met in Torgau, Germany, and less than two weeks later, Germany surrendered.

As a reward for fighting the Germans alone in the east—a major reason for the success of the D-day landings since the Eastern Front had gutted the German Wehrmacht—Stalin demanded from his allies control of Eastern European nations. At the Potsdam Conference, held in the summer of 1945, President Truman agreed, publicly claiming that Stalin had promised to allow democratic elections in those nations. It wasn't true, and the elections, of course, never took place.

Winston Churchill would later lament that an Iron Curtain had fallen over Eastern Europe. The western democracies and the Soviet Union now entered what was called the Cold War, an enormously tense situation fueled by fears of nuclear war, which would last nearly five decades.

Zoya Kosmodemyanskaya

PARTISAN HERO

ZOYA KOSMODEMYANSKAYA was born on September 13, 1923, in the Tambov region of Soviet Russia, about 300 miles southeast of Moscow. When she was six years old, collectivization came to Tambov. All farmers had to give up their land and its profits to the government.

After Zoya's father dared to criticize this government takeover, the family—Zoya; her younger brother, Alexander (called Shura); and her mother, Lyubov—were punished by being sent to Siberia with other dissenting families.

They lived there for one year before moving to Moscow with the help of some family members. There Zoya excelled in school,

Zoya's Komsomol card.
The Story of Zoya and Shura

especially in literature; she often copied favorite passages into her notebook.

Her family's previous dissent was apparently forgiven after the death of her father, and when Zoya was 15 she became a member of the Soviet Komsomol, the youth branch of the Communist Party. When she came home from school that day, she told Lyubov that she felt different now, that becoming a Komsomol had altered her in some significant way. She also dwelled on one particular point. When asked what was the most important thing for a Komsomol to remember, Zoya had given the correct answer: "A Komsomol member must be ready to give all his strength to his Country and, if necessary, his life."

On June 22, 1941, when Lyubov came home from work, her children greeted her with dreadful news they had just heard on the radio: the Soviet Union was at war! Zoya was furious. "Germany has attacked us!" she cried. "They just crossed the border and opened fire!"

After a short silence, she continued, "Life will be quite different now."

Shura spun around. "Don't tell me *you* are thinking of going to the front?"

"I mean to do just that," said Zoya.

Shura, only 15, was the first to leave for the front with other Moscow boys on a work detail for Moscow's defense.

Shortly afterward, on July 3, 1941, Zoya and Lyubov heard Joseph Stalin address the nation on the radio.

Zoya was transfixed. When it was over, Lyubov said, "I wonder if Shura heard him."

"Everyone heard him," said Zoya, "all over the country." Then, in almost a whisper, she repeated, "My words are addressed to you, dear friends."

Shura came home in July, and that fall, when Zoya was 18, all the students in her grade were sent to pick potatoes on a collective

★★★ STALIN'S SPEECH OF JULY 3, 1941 ★★★

Most of Stalin's prewar radio speeches had been addressed to loyal Communist Party members. But now he reached out to a larger audience and gave one of the best speeches of his life. Not surprisingly, it had a galvanizing effect on most Soviets who heard it.

> Comrades, citizens, brothers and sisters, men of our Army and Navy!
>
> My words are addressed to you, dear friends!
>
> The perfidious military attack by Hitlerite Germany on our Fatherland, begun on June 22, is continuing. In spite of the heroic resistance of the Red Army, and although the enemy's finest divisions and finest air force units have already been smashed and have met their doom on the field of battle, the enemy continues to push forward, hurling fresh forces to the front. . . .
>
> The issue is one of life and death for the Soviet State, of life and death for the peoples of the USSR. The issue is whether the peoples of the Soviet Union shall be free or fall into slavery. The Soviet people must realize this and abandon all complacency. They must mobilize themselves and reorganize all their work on a new, wartime footing, where there can be no mercy to the enemy.

farm. Some of the teens reached their quota of 100 kilograms quickly, making speedy progress across the farm, whereas Zoya was remaining in one spot much longer. She didn't understand why she was taking longer than the others, so to solve the mystery Zoya broke off from the others and worked alone for a while.

The others accused Zoya of being an "individualist," a dangerous accusation in the Soviet Union's collective society.

"Perhaps I am an individualist," Zoya replied fearlessly, "but you don't work fair." She had realized that the others were moving quicker across the farm because they were only taking the potatoes close to the surface. Zoya, on the other hand, was digging deeper for the bigger potatoes.

One day, after she was back in Moscow, Zoya and Lyubov passed a house with a placard in its window showing the face of a stern soldier. Underneath were the words WHAT HAVE YOU DONE FOR THE FRONT?

"I can't pass that placard calmly," Zoya said to her mother, who replied that she had just completed difficult national work.

"Not enough," said Zoya.

Shortly after this incident, Zoya rushed into the house one day, telling her mother that she had signed up for a secret mission behind enemy lines.

"Why must it be you?" Lyubov cried.

"Listen, Mama," Zoya replied, "I'm certain that if you were well you would do the same as I. I cannot stay here. I can't! You told me yourself that one must be honest and brave in life. What else could I do now that the enemy is so close? If they came here I could not live. . . . You know me. There is no other way for me."

Moscow, the capital of the Soviet Union, was now under attack, and volunteers were being trained as partisans—members of an unofficial guerrilla army. Zoya had been accepted into a partisan group. She was given training and the code name Tanya.

The partisan base was in the woods west of Moscow. On November 4, 1941, Zoya left to spy out enemy-controlled territory with a young woman code-named Klava. Almost as soon as the two women set foot out of the camp, two German motorcycles flew past them, almost near enough to touch. Zoya and Klava quickly realized they had to be more careful, and so they crawled the rest of the way to the highway. The young women reported back that the area was clear of Germans. They all returned, and the young men then laid mines while four young women, including Zoya and Klava, kept watch.

The young men had just finished their work when the team heard a roar of motors approaching. They all sprinted for the woods; then they heard the sound of explosions, followed by a deafening silence, then shouts. Their mission had been a success.

A few days later Zoya and Klava laid spikes along a highway to destroy the tires of any German trucks passing by. Klava would later say that being with Zoya gave her courage: "She would do everything very neatly, coolly, and confidently."

Later that month, Zoya's group was sent to the outskirts of Petrishchevo, an occupied village near Moscow where there were 10 to 15 German soldiers staying in every village home.

The night before the operation, after cutting communication lines, the young people gathered around a campfire of fir, a type of wood that doesn't make smoke when burned. As they shared the last of their rations, one of the young women suddenly said, "How I want to live!"

Zoya responded by reciting the poetry of Vladimir Mayakovsky, a popular Soviet Russian writer. The lines she spoke described the severe economic difficulty experienced under Stalin, but the poem's final words ended with hope:

> I know there'll be a town,
> I know its garden will be grand
> While there are such people
> In the Soviet Land!

When she finished, the young people asked Zoya to recite all the other Mayakovsky poems she had memorized. After she'd finally finished, Boris, the team leader, prepared to send the young men out into the village to burn down the houses where the Germans were staying. Zoya wanted to go too.

"Only boys will be sent out on missions," Boris said.

Zoya protested. "Difficulties should be shared equally. Please!"

Klava, who overheard this conversation, thought that Zoya's "Please!" sounded like a demand, not a request. Boris agreed, and Zoya set fire to two structures in the village, hoping she had killed some Germans in the process.

Zoya seemed transformed upon her return and said to Klava, "You feel quite different when you're doing a real job!"

"Have you been doing nothing up till now?" Klava asked. "You go on reconnaissance and cut communications . . ."

"That's not the same!" Zoya interrupted. "That's not enough!"

Zoya returned to Petrishchevo, where she and two young men—Kraynev and Klubkov—were to set fire to the German-occupied houses and barns. But now the village, and the Germans in it, were on high alert. The three partisans were to meet up outside the village. Kraynev left the meeting place without waiting for the others. Klubkov was captured by the Germans. Zoya, upon coming to the rendezvous point and finding no one there, decided to enter Petrishchevo alone.

The Germans caught her as she attempted to set fire to a stable she mistook for a storehouse. She was interrogated in the house of a couple named Voronins.

"Who are you?" demanded the German lieutenant colonel.

"I won't tell you," answered Zoya.

Why, he asked, was she attempting to burn down the stable?

"To destroy you," she said.

"When did you cross the front line?"

"On Friday."

"You got here too soon for that."

"Why should I waste time?"

Zoya being led to her execution.
The Story of Zoya and Shura

Then they asked her to tell them where the other partisans were. She refused.

The couple, forced to remain in a different room, could hear Zoya being beaten. She was asked again to tell the location of her fellow partisans. Her voice grew fainter with each blow, but it remained clear enough to hear her words: "I won't tell."

After more beatings, one of the officers forced Zoya to march through the snow in her bare feet, only returning when he himself became cold.

In the morning, Zoya was led away to be hanged on a gallows the Germans had erected in the center of the village. They put a sign around her neck with the words I BURNED A STABLE. The villagers were ordered to attend the hanging. Moments before her death, Zoya cried, "Comrades! Why are you looking so downcast?"

A German tried to silence her, but she continued: "I am not afraid of dying, Comrades! It is a great thing to die for one's people!" Then she turned to the Germans. "You'll hang me now, but I am not alone. There are two hundred million of us, and you can't hang us all. My death will be avenged. Men, surrender while there is still time. Victory is sure to be ours!"

Moments later, Zoya was dead.

In January 1942, Petrishchevo was liberated from the Germans by the Red Army. Shortly afterward, a Soviet journalist named Pyotr Lidov came to Petrishchevo to discover what had happened there during the occupation. The villagers told him the story of "Tanya," the young partisan woman. Lidov interviewed all the eyewitnesses he could find, plus members of Zoya's partisan band. His research was published in *Pravda*, a major Soviet magazine.

On January 27, 1942, Lyubov was on her way home from work when she overheard multiple conversations about a courageous Soviet girl in a *Pravda* article.

When she got home, she asked Shura about it. Had he read it?

He had. "A young partisan girl called Tanya," Shura said, in a flat voice. "She was hanged by the Germans."

Lyubov suddenly felt cold inside. She switched on the radio. The announcer was also talking about Tanya. Shura asked her to shut it off.

The following day Lyubov went to the Komsomol District Committee, asking for news of Zoya, since she hadn't heard from her in months. They had nothing to share.

But when she came home, two strangers were there with Shura. No one said anything for several long minutes. Then one of the men spoke. "Lyubov Timofeyevna . . . the girl Tanya in *Pravda* . . . that was your Zoya."

When Lyubov and Shura were alone, Shura told his mother that he knew it was Zoya from his very first reading of the article.

There had been a photograph of the dead girl. He didn't want to show it to his mother, but she insisted on seeing it now. She knew then that Tanya was indeed Zoya.

When Stalin read the article, he bestowed on Zoya the Hero of the Soviet Union award. She was the first woman to receive this honor during the war, and her courage inspired the entire nation. In October 1943, Red Army troops came near the German division that included the officers who had tortured and killed Zoya. Before they went into battle against these Germans, the Soviet troops were given leaflets that read, "When you go into attack, remember Tanya! Smash the enemy for Tanya! Go into battle as avengers of Tanya!"

The Red Army won the battle. Five photographs of Zoya's execution were found on the body of a dead German officer.

Zoya's reputation as a national hero remained steady until the 1980s when the perestroika—a political movement calling for reform of the Communist Party in the Soviet Union—began. This government reform was accompanied by glasnost—"openness"—and during this time, the truth came out about many things that had been hidden during the brutal repression of the decades-long Communist regime. Rumors then swirled around Zoya's story: she had been a schizophrenic, not a hero; she had engaged in arson for reasons other than to fight the Germans.

But most Russians have since concluded that Zoya was indeed a hero who had endured torture and death rather than betray her fellow partisans. She has been memorialized in countless ways all over Russia.

★★★ LEARN MORE ★★★

Heroines of the Soviet Union 1941–45 by Henry Sakaida (Osprey, 2003).

Russia's Heroes by Albert Axell (Constable, 2001).

"Zoya Kosmodemyanskaya: The Execution of a Teenage Heroine" by Rupert Colley. www.historyinanhour.com/2011/11/29 /zoya-kosmodemyanskaya-summary.

Anna Yegorova

SOVIET PILOT

ANNA YEGOROVA WAS a teenager helping to dig Moscow's first subway when she learned that the government was recruiting young people to learn how to fly airplanes for the military. In response, the air club nearby had purchased four U-2 planes and three gliders. Anna had always wanted to fly. She applied, but when she told her subway brigade foreman he was less than enthusiastic. "What do you want to do that for, Yegorova?" he asked. "Let the men do the flying."

She ignored his advice, and by the summer of 1941 Anna not only had her pilot's license but also had become a flying instructor,

Anna Yegorova.
Red Sky Black Death: A Soviet Woman Pilot's Memoir of the Eastern Front

working at the flying club in Kalinin, 100 miles northwest of Moscow. Most of her students were young men.

On June 22, 1941, Anna was relaxing with three girlfriends in some woods near Kalinin. A man approached them. "Girls," he said, "It's war! I just heard it on the radio in the village." Nazi Germany had invaded the Soviet Union!

When Anna learned that the Kalinin flying club would be moving to the rear of the fighting, she took a train to Moscow. There, she asked the colonel in charge if she might go to the front.

The harried colonel replied, "Everybody's asking me the same thing over and over. 'To the front! To the front!'" He continued, "And who is going to *train* the pilots for the front? No, dear. Go back to Kalinin and do your job. Who's next?"

Anna wouldn't take no for an answer.

He finally relented, but when Anna arrived at the Moscow aeroclub it had evacuated. While wondering what to do next, Anna met a lieutenant from the 130th Air Liaison Squadron, an all-male unit that was headed to the front lines of fighting in the southern section of the war. Anna asked to join.

"But we don't draft females for front-line combat," he replied.

"Do you really need to be drafted to fight for your country?" she asked.

He apparently saw her point, and on the following day, after her papers and flying skills were checked, Anna was accepted into the 130th. Two days later she received her U-2, a biplane made of wood and cloth. The U-2s were slow and highly flammable, but they could land in small areas and were easy to maneuver out of danger.

Anna's job was reconnaissance and communications. The Red Army was suffering from lack of coordinated efforts, and so she was often part of the effort to improve communication between different fighting units.

One day Anna was ordered to fly to the First Calvary Corps—they needed a radio. But when she landed in the designated village, she didn't see them anywhere. Leaving the plane running, she ran to a nearby hut, tapping on the window to ask for information. An old man opened the door.

"Grandfather," Anna asked, politely, "have our troops been through here?"

"Run away from here, Sonny," urged the old man, mistaking Anna for a man. "The Germans are here! They got here late last night!"

Anna turned around. There were Germans standing near the next hut, their backs to her. But she couldn't seem to move her legs. The old man gave her a push, which did the trick. Anna ran to her plane and took off. Below her, she heard the crackle of machine gunfire. She looked down. The old man was lying facedown in the snow. And the Germans were now taking aim at her.

Bullets shattered the plane's dashboard mirror. But Anna escaped, and that evening she located the cavalrymen and delivered the radio.

In April 1942, she was nominated for adult membership in the Communist Party and was also awarded with the Order of the Red Banner for her work. But there was much more work to be done. On May 20, Anna was ordered to deliver a top-secret package to the headquarters of the Ninth Air Army. As she flew in her U-2 she could see the "frantic movements" of the Soviet troops below her as they retreated from the advancing Germans.

Stalin had refused to listen to his military advisors and had ordered an attack on this German-occupied territory to liberate it. The Soviets were badly outnumbered, and fires were breaking out everywhere from the battle; from Anna's airborne perspective it seemed that all of the Soviet Union was on fire.

Her attention was suddenly moved to the skies above her where two Soviet planes were battling six German Messerschmitt fighter planes. As Anna watched she saw one of the German planes break away and come after her!

Anna tried to fly out of his range, but the German pilot took aim and his machine gun bullets hit Anna's plane, setting it on fire. Anna landed the burning plane and jumped out, trying to put out the fire on her uniform as she ran for some nearby woods, the Messerschmitt pilot in hot pursuit, strafing her with his machine gun. Sometimes she would fall down, pretending to be hit, then get up again.

The Messerschmitt pilot eventually gave up—Anna thought he must have run out of ammunition—and she caught a ride to the Ninth Army headquarters, where she delivered the package and received medical attention for her burns. When she was returned to her base, her squadron welcomed her home "like a long-lost brother." She was upset about losing her plane, but one of the men tried to encourage her. "Don't fret about the airplane, Yegorova," he said. "The main thing is that you're alive," he said, "and that the package is delivered. An airplane isn't a living thing."

That fall the Germans continued to push the Red Army back in many places. Anna's squadron was doing reconnaissance missions in the Alagir region while being pursued by some Messerschmitts. Anna, trying to avoid being hit, accidentally crashed the right wing of her plane into a tree. She survived, but her plane didn't.

Anna knew that she was in trouble. There was no evidence amid the wreckage that the Germans had hit the plane. This was her fault.

"I crashed my aircraft," she said to the squadron commander, after locating her base, "and I am prepared to take full responsibility in accordance with wartime regulations."

The commander knew she was offering to be transferred to a so-called "penalty battalion" where offending fliers—or gulag prisoners—were punished by being forced on suicide missions. Instead, he transferred Anna to a different regiment where she asked to be trained to fly a Shturmovik plane.

"Do you have any idea what a hellish job that is?" asked the regimental commander. "Trust me, even well-trained male pilots have a hard time with the thing. You think you can keep the 'flying tank' under control while simultaneously dropping bombs, firing your cannons and machine guns, releasing your rockets, sending and receiving radio transmissions, all the while at treetop level in assault formation with the battle raging all around you? Think long and hard about it!"

"I've already thought about it," Anna replied.

"Good God, you're a stubborn one," the officer replied. "All right, then. Be my guest!"

In early 1943, the commanding officer of the 230th Attack Aviation Division came to inspect the training camp, looking for recruits. Anna told him she wanted to join. Impressed with her history, he took her on.

On midday, August 20, 1944, the 230th was ready to help the Red Army, which was pushing the Germans westward. Anna, now squadron commander, was waiting for the green flare, signaling their takeoff. She saw it, pulled on her parachute, jumped into the cockpit of her plane, cranked her engine, and tested the radio. Everything was working. She took off. Fifteen Shturmoviks followed her in formation.

The Vistula River soon came into view. To the right lay Warsaw, only Anna couldn't see it because it was covered in smoke.

Anna, 1943, after a mission.
Red Sky Black Death: A Soviet Woman Pilot's Memoir of the Eastern Front

Her navigator spotted German fighter planes and sent out a warning flare. Long-range antiaircraft guns fired at the Soviet planes, shells exploding close to her plane. Anna was in particular danger because the enemy always targeted the lead plane. She needed to get out of the range of antiaircraft guns before unloading her bombs on the German tanks below. Then, as she dropped the bombs, her plane jerked upward, as if someone had pushed it.

Anna felt two more such pushes. The plane was becoming difficult to maneuver. She heard someone say, over her radio, "Try to make it to our side!" The control stick wouldn't work. The canopy was stuck. And so was she! Flames and smoke filled the cockpit. The plane exploded. Anna was blown out of it and lost consciousness. When she came to, she was falling through the air. She pulled her parachute ring, but it had burned and opened only partially. She hit the ground hard.

When she opened her eyes, Anna was in terrible pain. She couldn't move. But worse than all of that was who she saw standing over her, his boot on her chest: a soldier in a gray-green uniform. "A Fascist!" she thought. "I'm in the hands of Fascists!"

Two Polish medics ordered about by the Germans put her on a stretcher. The Germans seemed very nervous, and Anna soon realized why: Soviet airplanes were still flying overhead.

A Soviet medic named Yulia Krashchenko stayed by her side, nursing her burns as best she could, even when they were both put on a cargo train for a five-day trip, which Anna described as "utter hell."

When she was unloaded from the train, German soldiers swarmed around her stretcher, trying to get a glimpse of the captured female pilot. Anna had just arrived at the Küstrin prisoner-of-war camp, called Stalag III-C, filled with male Allied POWs. As she was carried on a stretcher, Anna felt something light flying in her direction: the POWs were throwing her bits of food through the barbed wire fence.

Anna and Yulia were placed in a concrete cell with iron bars. The Germans didn't torture Anna. They were just going to let her die, slowly and painfully, of her wounds. The crash had injured her spine, head, arms, leg, and ribs, and had burned the skin on her legs and feet.

But there was a skilled surgeon in the camp, a Soviet prisoner named Georgi Fyodorovich Sinyakov. He demanded to treat Anna. Because Dr. Sinyakov had once healed the son of a Gestapo officer, he was granted his wish. The prisoners in the camp were rallying for Anna, and many gave the doctor their Red Cross packets for her and made her little gifts.

Dr. Sinyakov saved Anna's life. Then, without warning, he was replaced by a German medic who changed Anna's dressings in cold silence. Yulia was shot for arguing with an SS officer who tried to tempt Anna into turning against the Soviets. Anna was all alone.

On January 31, 1945, when the Red Army defeated the Germans at the Battle of Küstrin, the POW camp was liberated. All former camp prisoners were ordered to the town of Landsberg.

Although she had by this time flown over 270 missions and should have been considered a hero, Anna was placed in a prison with German POWs run by the SMERSH (an abbreviation of the Russian for "death to spies") counterintelligence agency. Why? All Soviet POWs were considered traitors just for having been caught. The commandant of this branch of SMERSH kept Anna up all night, accusing her of being a spy. Whatever she said, he would counter with, "You're lying, you German dog!"

On the 11th day of this, Anna gathered what little strength she had, ran up the stairs to the commandant's quarters, and cried, "When are you going to stop tormenting me? Kill me if you like, but I won't let you torment me anymore."

Anna fell unconscious. When she came to, she was told that the doctors from the Küstrin POW camp had approached the commandant of SMERSH on her behalf, vouching for her. Anna was free from false accusations. Did she want to stay with SMERSH and work with them, they asked?

"No, no," she responded quickly. "I want to find my regiment. They're fighting somewhere nearby." She found them, and they had a joyful reunion, although she was disappointed to be declared by the Soviet military doctors to be physically unable to fly.

When the war finally ended, Anna returned home to learn that her mother had held a memorial service for her. She had been told her daughter had been killed in action!

Anna married and, against all medical advice, gave birth to two sons. Then she turned her attention to something that had bothered her since the end of the war: the termination of her membership in the Communist Party because, she had been told, she had failed to pay her dues during the war.

After mailing multiple request letters, she was finally told that her membership card was in a warehouse in Moscow manned by

an army garrison. She went there, wearing her uniform and medals, walking with a cane, as she now did.

The friendly officer at the warehouse asked Anna what hospital she had been treated in.

Anna in the 1960s. Her Hero of the Soviet Union award can be seen on the top right. *Red Sky Black Death: A Soviet Woman Pilot's Memoir of the Eastern Front*

"I was a prisoner-of-war," she replied.

"We're not giving you your card," cried the officer. "We have no prisoners-of-war. We have traitors. That's what Comrade Stalin said. Leave the premises at once."

But after further efforts on Anna's part, her membership was finally reinstated. In 1965, Anna was honored for her wartime work with the Hero of the Soviet Union gold medal. The honor had been granted to her "posthumously" in 1944, but when it was discovered that she had survived the crash and had been taken prisoner, it had been revoked.

Anna died in 2009.

★★★ LEARN MORE ★★★

A Dance with Death: Soviet Airwomen in World War II by Anna Noggle (Texas A&M University Press, 1994).

Night Witches: The Amazing Story of Russia's Women Pilots in World War II by Bruce Miles (Academy Chicago, 1990).

Red Sky, Black Death: A Soviet Woman Pilot's Memoir of the Eastern Front by Anna Timofeyeva-Yegorova (Slavica, 2009).

Acknowledgments

BACK IN THE spring of 2008, I had a serendipitous encounter with a wonderful individual named Lisa Reardon, who happened to be an editor for Chicago Review Press. Our conversation that day led to the first edition of *Women Heroes of World War II* and four subsequent books. Lisa, I can't begin to thank you for opening the door to all of this. It's been a wonderful decade, and each of my books is better for having passed through your skillful hands. Thanks to everyone else from Chicago Review Press, past and present, who had a hand in the success of both editions of this book and all the others: editors Michelle Williams, Lindsey Schauer, Jerome Pohlen, and Ellen Hornor and book promotors Mary Kravenas, Meghan Miller, Olivia Aguilar, and Emily Lewis.

However excellent a book's editors and publicists, no second edition would be possible without an enthusiastic readership, so

I'm grateful to each of you who saw what I hoped you'd see in the stories of these courageous women. May their examples continue to inspire all of us as own destinies unfold.

I was thrilled when I discovered Muriel Engelman's beautifully written memoir, *Mission Accomplished: Stop the Clock*, because it meant I could include the story of an American military nurse in my book. I had no idea back then that I was also making a friend. Muriel, thank you for sharing your story with me so long ago, for giving all my books your enthusiastic thumbs-up, for writing the foreword to this second edition, and for being such a fabulous representative of the Greatest Generation.

Dr. Meredith Veldman of Louisiana State University, a high school friend turned professor of 20th-century history, was responsible for keeping some embarrassing errors out of the first edition's introductory material. Meri, you fully deserved that history award when we were students at TCHS, and you have my gratitude now. Your brilliant suggestions, corrections, and detailed answers to all my questions back in 2009 helped give the book its solid foundation and became something akin to a mentorship, which served me well as I launched into my subsequent research and writing. Thank you also for reviewing the Melitta von Stauffenberg chapter in this edition and for your most encouraging assessment.

Dr. Robert Messer, professor emeritus of 20th-century history at the University of Illinois at Chicago, who reviewed my books on the Pacific Theater and the Vietnam War, was kind enough to review the Soviet section of this book. Thank you so much, Dr. Bob, for everything. I've thoroughly enjoyed our communications and have learned so much from you.

While working on the first edition, I had some electrifying communications with history makers, their friends, family, and biographers. I had a similar experience with this edition, and my gratitude is due to the following people who reviewed the new chapters or provided additional material: Gerhard Bracke, Marthe

Cohn, Rupert Colley, Megan Haase of Texas Women's University, William M. Miller, Clare Mulley, Eitan Senesh, and Sig Unander.

Every writer should have at least one feline friend. Yes, this is the part where I thank some animals. The late, great, and nearly feral Lu was a constant presence while I wrote the first edition, purring on my lap while I waded through source material and waiting patiently while I worked at my desk. Allie, the surviving feline, isn't quite as devoted to me, but her occasional intense fondness for sharing my lap with my laptop might be illustrative of an intermittent interest in women's history or an appreciation of human- and machine-generated heat. While the latter scenario seems far more likely I'm not completely ruling out the former as her presence really does help me write better.

Writing my books has led to numerous speaking engagements at such distinguished institutions as the First Division Museum at Cantigny Park and the Atlanta History Center. But I've also been gratified by multiple invitations to speak at two local book shops that have done me the honor of stocking all my books: Centuries & Sleuths in Forest Park, Illinois, and the Looking Glass in Oak Park, Illinois. Thank you so much, Augie, Tracy, John, Steve, and Pattie. Your shops are fabulous.

I've also had the pleasure of speaking at dozens of public libraries and historical societies, and I'd like to thank the following hosts who extended multiple invitations: Kristen Edson of the Harold Washington Public Library in Chicago; Karen Hall of the Glen Ellyn Historical Society; Alicia Hammond Hoff and Skye Lavin of the Forest Park Public Library; Olivia Hoge of the Cleveland Public Library; Deborah Preiser of the Oak Park Public Library; and Rich Roche, formerly of the Thomas Ford Memorial Library in Western Springs.

Thanks to all the encouraging friends and family who have read my books, talked them up on social media, and/or filled a seat at one of my presentations: Aaron Atwood, Abby Atwood,

Darrel Atwood, Jeremy Atwood, Shirley Atwood, Herb Buetow, Bob and Teresa Blomquist, Carol and Steve Brown, Muriel Clark, Steve Coppola, Cynthia D'Acosta, Eleanor Deblecourt, Andrea and Joe Denner, Gail Friesema, Stefanie Glover, Geri Grant, Jan Haan, Ella Haas, Donna and Jim Hanert, Linda Hansen, Lila Harris, Karen Hermansen, Pat Hoekstra, Daniel Hoenisch, Rachel Hoenisch, Wanetta Hoenisch, Deborah and Marcus Hostetler, Margaret Jager, Marty Jayne, Carolyn Kelly, Timothy King, Karen Knapp, Chris and Melanie Kulig, Noreen Lake, Paul Martin, Pat and Wayne Matthews, Christiane Metzner, Nancy Newswander, Cynthia and Tim Nordberg, Maryann Nosek, Mary Beth Ossowski, Dan Perkins, Barbara and Sam Reed, Genefir Reisinger, Sonia Reppe, Jerry and Laura Skwerski, Suzanne Stanits, Sarah Stewman, Joan Stob, Annika Teune, Diane and Tom Teune, Ed Teune, Mariel and Gary Teune Jr., Hannah Williams, Tammy Williams, Corie Zylstra, and Nancy Zylstra. Thanks also to my nephew, Jim Haan, for asking when I was going to write *Women Heroes of the War of 1812*. Probably never, Jim, but I thoroughly enjoyed the question.

Special gratitude is due my sister, Helen Van Essendelft; brother, Gary Teune; and sister-in-law, Carol Teune, three of my biggest fans, who from the first book onward insisted on buying their own copies, reading each one cover to cover, and praising them to anyone who would listen. Your enthusiasm has meant the world to me, and I love you all.

My husband has been, perhaps, my biggest fan. John, I'll never forget how happy you were for me when I broke the news that CRP had accepted my proposal for *Women Heroes of World War II*. Your enthusiasm for my work has never diminished, and for that—along with your invaluable French-to-English translation efforts on the Pearl Witherington chapter, your willingness to act as an occasional sounding board, and for moving the PowerPoint slides along at my book presentations, freeing me to talk with my hands—you have my gratitude and love.

Glossary

Allied powers: The Allies were a union of countries who were military opponents to the Axis powers during World War II; usually refers to Great Britain, France, the United States, and the Soviet Union, but the Allies technically included all countries threatened or invaded by the Axis countries.

anti-Semitism: Hostility toward or discrimination against Jewish people.

armistice: A cease-fire during a war until formal negotiations can be arranged.

Aryan: A term originally identifying a large group of races but used by Hitler to refer to a race of people supposedly superior to all others: those of western European countries whose general populations possessed Germanic features.

Axis powers: The Axis was a union of countries who were military opponents to the Allied Powers during World War II; Germany, Japan, and Italy were the major Axis nations.

Battle of the Bulge: Also called the Ardennes Offensive, this was the last major offensive (rather than defensive) attack initiated by Nazi Germany during the war. It was a surprise attack against U.S. troops, begun on December 16, 1944, in the Ardennes Forest of Belgium. The Germans pushed the U.S. troops back far enough to form a bulge in their line, but the Germans were pushed back by the end of January 1945.

black market: An "underground economy," so named because its transactions are conducted outside the "light" of the law. During World War II, food was often bought and sold on the black market, without the use of Nazi-issued ration cards.

blitzkrieg: A mode of warfare whereby the simultaneous use of tanks, planes, and troops coordinated by radio, moving at top speed, and not confined to regular roads, creates a surprise attack.

buzz bombs: Also called V-1 bombs, robot bombs, or doodlebugs; a *Vergeltungswaffe* ("vengeance weapon") of Nazi Germany, buzz bombs were self-propelled, contained nearly 2,000 pounds of explosives, could travel at speeds of up to 350 mph, and could cover a distance of 250 kilometers before landing and destroying everything within a few hundred feet.

concentration camps: Located primarily in Poland and Germany, the hundreds of concentration camps run by the Nazi regime were designed to punish and kill large groups of people deemed undesirable by the Nazis.

D-day: The day that a certain military operation will begin. The term has become permanently associated with the Allied invasion of Nazi-occupied Europe initiated on the beaches of Normandy, France, on June 6, 1944.

Drôle de Guerre ("Silly War"): Called "the Phony War" in English, this period was the peaceful but tense eight-month period between September 3, 1939, when Great Britain and France declared war on Germany, and May 10, 1940, when Germany simultaneously invaded France and several other countries.

espionage: The practice of spying to secretly obtain important information about the plans and activities of a foreign government.

Fascism: A political ideology that promotes a centralized and authoritarian one-party system.

Germanisation (or Germanization): The process by which Nazis forced Aryan-appearing peoples to forsake their own culture and become German.

Gestapo: *Geheime Staatspolize,* "secret state police," established by Hitler in 1933 to locate and punish his political enemies, the Gestapo was later made to join forces with the intelligence brance of the SS, the Sicherheitsdienst or SD.

Holocaust: Greek for "a sacrifice completely consumed by fire"; in terms of World War II history, it means the murder of approximately six million Jews by Nazi Germany.

intelligence: Important information regarding an enemy power gathered from espionage (spying).

Judenfrei: "Jew-free." During Word War II it meant ridding certain areas of Jewish people.

Judenrein: "Jew-pure" or "Jew-clean," often also translated as "Jew-free." The concept went beyond *Judenfrei*, implying that Europe needed to be racially cleansed of the Jews by destroying them, not just moving them out.

Komosol: An abbreviation for the Russian term meaning "Communist Union of Youth," the Komosol was an organization run by the Soviet Union designed to indoctrinate teenagers 14 years and up with Communist ideology.

Kristallnacht: "Crystal Night" or "Night of the Broken Glass." The widespread, destructive attack against the Jews in Germany and Austria, coordinated by the Nazis on the night of November 9, 1938, and resulting in the destruction of thousands of Jewish businesses, homes, and synagogues and the arrest and deportment to concentration camps of thousands of Jewish men.

Luftwaffe: "Air weapon"; refers to the German air force.

maquis: A type of wild French plant. During the Nazi occupation of France the term referred to French men who banded together in rural areas to avoid forced labor in German munitions factories and to fight the Germans.

Morse code: A system of communication developed by American Samuel Morse in which a series of dots and dashes—long and short measures of light or sound—represent letters and numbers. World War II radio operators sent and received messages by Morse code.

Nazi: Short for Nationalsozialistische Deutsche Arbeiterpartei (National Socialist German Workers' Party, or NSDAP), the fascist political party led by Adolf Hitler that grew out of the tiny German Worker's Party and ruled Germany from 1933 to 1945.

NSB (Nationaal-Socialistische Beweging): The Dutch Nazi party whose members openly collaborated with the Nazi occupiers.

Office of Strategic Services (OSS): The U.S. wartime intelligence-gathering agency.

onderduiker: "Under-diver"; during the Nazi occupation of the Netherlands, this referred to individuals hiding either themselves or their real identities (by the use of a false ID cards) from the Germans because they were under arrest for Resistance work or had been ordered to work in German munitions factories.

Palmach: Formed in 1941, the Palmach (Hebrew acronym for "striking force") was the elite fighting force of the Haganah (Hebrew for "the Defense"), the secret Jewish military first created in British-controlled Palestine to protect Israeli settlers from Arab attacks.

propaganda: Communications presented as complete truth but instead using only certain facts, often appealing to the emotions (rather than to rational thinking), to purposely influence public opinion in a certain way. During the German occupation of Europe, propaganda was used constantly to promote Nazi ideology and support the occupation.

Red Army: Formed immediately after the Russian Revolution in 1917 to battle the so-called White Army during the Russian Civil War, the Red Army was the name of the Soviet Union's army and air force from 1922 to 1946.

Resistance: Sometimes also referred to as the Underground, this was the term given to the efforts of people in Nazi-occupied areas to fight the Germans in any way they could.

resister: A person involved with the Resistance.

Royal Air Force (RAF): The air force of Great Britain.

sabotage: Destructive action, usually involving explosives, meant to hinder an enemy's war effort, such as destroying the enemy's means of transportation and communication, military equipment, and munitions factories.

Special Operations Executive (SOE): A British Resistance organization formed in 1940 to conduct clandestine (secret) warfare in Nazi-occupied countries.

SS: Schutzstaffel, "Protection Squadron"; the Nazi unit primarily responsible for implementing Hitler's racial policies, including hunting down and imprisoning Jews and running the concentration and death camps. The SS had its own armed forces, the Waffen SS, which was distinct from the German Wehrmacht.

Third Reich: A term created by Hitler to refer to Nazi Germany.

underground newspaper: During World War II, these were newspapers secretly printed and distributed by Resistance workers in Nazi-occupied countries in order to encourage and inform occupied peoples and to counteract Nazi propaganda.

Vergeltungswaffen: "vengeance weapons"; See buzz bombs. The V-1 buzz bomb and the V-2 rocket used by Nazi Germany against the Allies.

Versailles Treaty: An agreement signed on June 28, 1919, between Germany and the countries it had been fighting against, principally France and Great Britain, seven months after World War I ended. The treaty was extremely punitive toward Germany and created vast economic problems and resentment there.

WASP: The acronym for Women Airforce Service Pilots, an American organization created to support the war effort by training civilian women pilots to train other pilots, test repaired planes, transport equipment, and fly military planes from factory assembly lines to U.S. Army Air Force bases.

Wehrmacht: The name for the German armed forces; it often refers to the regular German army as opposed to the Waffen SS, the armed service branch of the SS.

work camps: Camps where occupied peoples were forced to live while providing labor in Nazi munitions factories or agricultural areas run by Germans.

World War I: Referred to as the Great War before the outbreak of World War II, World War I was the destructive global conflict that took place between 1914 and 1918.

Yad Vashem: The world center for documentation, research, education, and commemoration of the Holocaust, located in Jerusalem, Israel, and the organization that grants the award of Righteous Among the Nations to non-Jews who assisted Jews during the Nazi occupation of Europe.

Notes

SOPHIE SCHOLL: THE WHITE ROSE

The indictment against the Scholls and Christopher Probst is contained in Appendix 3 of *Sophie Scholl and the White Rose* by Annette Dumbach and Jud Newborn (Oxford: Oneworld, 2007), pages 207–13.

"Somebody had to make a start!": Dumbach and Newborn, *Sophie Scholl*, 157.

"Who among us": First White Rose leaflet.

"If a state prevents": First White Rose leaflet.

"these days it is better": Charles Whiting, *The Home Front: Germany* (Alexandria, VA: Time-Life Books, 1982, 1990), 108.

The reasons for sending the leaflets to German intellectuals are taken from Dr. George Wittenstein's *Memories of the White Rose.*

Sophie was its heart: Toby Axelrod, *Hans and Sophie Scholl: German Resisters of the White Rose* (New York: Rosen, 2001), 62.

"Scholl lives!": Dumbach and Newborn, *Sophie Scholl*, 163.

MARIA VON MALTZAN: THE COUNTESS WHO HID JEWS

"For God's sake, Marushka": Leonard Gross, *The Last Jews in Berlin* (New York: Carroll & Graff, 1992), 136–37.

"I love this country": Gross, *Last Jews*, 191.

"If you're sure": Gay Block and Malka Drucker, *Rescuers: Portraits of Moral Courage in the Holocaust* (Teaneck, NJ: Holmes & Meier, 1992), 156.

"You're to hide": Gross, *Last Jews*, 187–88.

MELITTA VON STAUFFENBERG: THE PLOT TO KILL HITLER

Excerpts from *The Women Who Flew for Hitler: A Story of Soaring Ambition and Searing Rivalry* by Clare Mulley used by permission of the author.

"tiny clique of ambitious": Clare Mulley, *The Women Who Flew for Hitler: A True Story of Soaring Ambition and Searing Rivalry* (New York: St. Martin's, 2017), 244.

"without reservation": Mulley, *Women Who Flew*, 234.

"thoroughly addicted": Mulley, *Women Who Flew*, 17.

"It will come to a": Mulley, *Women Who Flew*, 71.

"marry someone desirable": Mulley, *Women Who Flew*, 72.

"racial burden": Mulley, *Women Who Flew*, 123.

"equal to Aryan": Mulley, *Women Who Flew*, 135.

"It is time I saved": Mulley, *Women Who Flew*, 178.

"Early call": Mulley, *Women Who Flew*, 217.

"needed to disappear": Mulley, *Women Who Flew*, 228.

"what a pity": Mulley, *Women Who Flew*, 250.

IRENE GUT: "ONLY A YOUNG GIRL"

"Whoever helps a Jew": Irene Gut Opdyke with Jennifer Armstrong, *In My Hands: Memories of a Holocaust Rescuer* (New York: Alfred A. Knopf, 1999), 105.

"What can you do?": Opdyke with Armstrong, *In My Hands*, 121.

Definition of *Judenrein* from "Aryanization: Leibensraum, Germanization, Judenrein," www.shoaheducation.com/aryan.html.

"I trusted you!": Block and Drucker, *Rescuers*, 194.

"No!": Block and Drucker, *Rescuers*, 194.

IRENA SENDLER: LIFE IN A JAR

"Your name isn't Rachel": Marek Halter, *Stories of Deliverance: Speaking with Men and Women Who Rescued Jews from the Holocaust*, trans. Michael Bernard (Peru, IL: Carus, 1998), 10.

Where did the friend hide the lists during Irena's arrest? In *Stories of Deliverance*, page 10, it says that the friend hid the lists in the sleeves of her robe. But later, Irena told the "Life in a Jar" girls that the friend hid the lists in her bra.

Irena actually saw posters: The Irena Sendler Project (www.IrenaSendler.org).

STEFANIA PODGORSKA: THE TEEN WHO HID THIRTEEN

Conscience and Courage, page 88, says that Stefania was "almost 13" years old when she moved to Przemysl, but in her interview included in *Rescuers*, page 207, she claims that she was 14 at the time.

"I can't leave my children!": Eva Fogelman, *Conscience and Courage: Rescuers of Jews During the Holocaust* (New York: Anchor Books, 1994), 90.

"It's Joseph": Fogelman, *Conscience and Courage*, 92.

"Maybe someone will be": Fogelman, *Conscience and Courage*, 95.

"So you're protecting us": Fogelman, *Conscience and Courage*, 95.

"That is my new boyfriend": Block and Drucker, *Rescuers*, 184.

"she was too nice": Fogelman, *Conscience and Courage*, 102.

MARIE-MADELEINE FOURCADE: "ONLY A WOMAN"

"I'm only a woman! . . . I'd rather serve": Marie-Madeleine Fourcade, *Noah's Ark* (New York: E. P. Dutton, 1974), 26.

The information regarding the map Alliance provided the Allies is taken from page 138 of *Women in the Resistance and in the Holocaust: The Voices of Eyewitnesses* edited by Vera Laska (Westport, CT: Greenwood, 1983).

ANDRÉE VIROT: AGENT ROSE

"This upsets you": Andrée Virot Peel, *Miracles Do Happen!*, trans. Evelyn Scott Brown (Ettington, UK: Loebertas, 1999), 11.

"This last mission": Peel, *Miracles*, 35.

"Take that woman's number": Peel, *Miracles*, 73.

"Take courage": Peel, *Miracles*, 81.

"The Americans are at the gates": Peel, *Miracles*, 86.

JOSEPHINE BAKER: SPY SINGER

"France has made me": Lynn Haney, *Naked at the Feast: The Biography of Josephine Baker* (London: Robson Books, 1995), 217.

"We are informed": Ean Wood, *The Josephine Baker Story* (London: Sanctuary, 2000), 222.

"I think that monsieur": Wood, *Josephine Baker Story*, 222.

"Often I knew": Haney, *Naked at the Feast*, 233.

MAGDA TROCMÉ: WIFE, MOTHER, TEACHER, RESCUER

"Well, come in!": Telephone conversation with Nelly Trocmé Hewett, April 25, 2009.

"I never close my door": Philip P. Hallie, *Lest Innocent Blood Be Shed: The Story of Le Chambon and How Goodness Happened There* (New York: Harper & Row, 1979), 153.

"We don't know Jews": Telephone conversation with Nelly Trocmé Hewett, April 25, 2009.

"We always said": Carol Rittner, R.S.M., and Sondra Myers, *The Courage to Care: Rescuers of Jews During the Holocaust* (New York: New York University Press, 1986), 104.

"The duty of Christians": Patrick Henry, *We Only Know Men: The Rescue of Jews in France During the Holocaust* (Washington, DC: Catholic University Press, 2007), xix.

"Why me?": Trocmé family documents, letter to Yad Vashem.

MARTHE HOFFNUNG: "DO I LOOK LIKE A SPY?"

Excerpts from *Behind Enemy Lines: The True Story of a French Jewish Spy in Nazi Germany* by Marthe Cohn with Wendy Holden used by permission of Marthe Cohn.

"Which one is Stephanie? . . . You're under arrest": Marthe Cohn with Wendy Holden, *Behind Enemy Lines: The True Story of a French Jewish Spy in Nazi Germany* (New York: Three Rivers, 2002), 60.

"What about you and me? . . . treated this way": Cohn, *Behind Enemy Lines*, 69.

"There will be times": Cohn, *Behind Enemy Lines*, 168.

"Heil Hitler!": Cohn, *Behind Enemy Lines*, 169.

"Look at me": Cohn, *Behind Enemy Lines*, 174.

"Spread out like a vast": Cohn, *Behind Enemy Lines*, 187.

"There's a little surprise . . . I like surprises": Cohn, *Behind Enemy Lines*, 197.

"I dutifully joined in": Cohn, *Behind Enemy Lines*, 212.

"strange groups of people": Cohn, *Behind Enemy Lines*, 213.

DIET EMAN: COURIER FOR THE DUTCH RESISTANCE

"If it is at all possible": Diet Eman with James Schaap, *Things We Couldn't Say* (Grand Rapids, MI: William B. Eerdmans, 1994), 186.

"storm the gates of heaven": Eman with Schaap, *Things We Couldn't Say*, 268.

"I have done nothing else": Eman with Schaap, *Things We Couldn't Say*, 279.

HANNIE SCHAFT: THE SYMBOL OF THE RESISTANCE

"Now!": Truss Menger, *Not Then, Not Now, Not Ever*, trans. Rita Gircour (Amsterdam: Nederland Tolerant – Max Drukker Stichting, 1998), 89.

"*We are no*": Menger, *Not Then*, 178.

"*I messed up*": Menger, *Not Then*, 102.

"*Oh Jan, Jan*": Menger, *Not Then*, 103.

"*I am a much better*": Menger, *Not Then*, 184.

JOHTJE VOS: A GROUP EFFORT

"*I'm burying a dead rabbit*": *Living Histories* video interview.

"*That's quite an honorable*": Johanna K. Vos, *The End of the Tunnel* (Mansfield, OH: Book Masters, 1999), 80.

"*If you only trust me*": Vos, *End of the Tunnel*, 83.

"*Patriots, you are free!*": *Living Histories* video interview.

CORRIE TEN BOOM: WATCHMAKER, RESCUER, RECONCILER

"*It is wrong to give people hope*": Corrie ten Boom with John Sherrill and Elizabeth Sherrill, *The Hiding Place* (Uhrichsville, OH: Barbour, 1971), 64.

Haarlem's Grand Old Man: ten Boom with Sherrill and Sherrill, *The Hiding Place*, 10.

"*Father! Those poor people*": ten Boom with Sherrill and Sherrill, *The Hiding Place*, 71.

"*What?*" . . . "*Your name!*": ten Boom with Sherrill and Sherrill, *The Hiding Place*, 127.

"*Tell me now*": ten Boom with Sherrill and Sherrill, *The Hiding Place*, 127.

"*If there's a secret room*": ten Boom with Sherrill and Sherrill, *The Hiding Place*, 131.

"*All the watches*": ten Boom with Sherrill and Sherrill, *The Hiding Place*, 152.

"*one normal person*": ten Boom with Sherrill and Sherrill, *The Hiding Place*, 157.

"*than a watchmaker*": ten Boom with Sherrill and Sherrill, *The Hiding Place*, 157.

ANDRÉE DE JONGH: THE COMET LINE

The story of the initial run through the Somme River comes from Airey Neave, *Little Cyclone* (London: Hodder and Stoughton, 1954), 19–20.

Regarding the number of people on the trial run of the Comet Line, page 119 of *Silent Heroes* by Sherri Greene Ottis mentions that the group comprised 13 men, while page 19 of Neave's *Little Cyclone* mentions that the group was made up of 10 Belgian men and 1 woman.

You'll see what we'll do: "Airmen Remember Comet Line to Freedom," BBC News, October 24, 2000, http://news.bbc.co.uk/2/hi/europe/988881.stm.

I am a Belgian: Neave, *Little Cyclone*, 13–15.

The number of Allied servicemen rescued on the Comet Line: Donald Miller, *Masters of the Air: America's Bomber Boys Who Fought the Air War Against Nazi Germany* (New York: Simon and Schuster, 2007), 101; Sherri Greene Ottis, *Silent Heroes: Downed Airmen and the French Underground* (Lexington: University Press of Kentucky, 2001), 145.

HORTENSE DAMAN: PARTISAN COURIER

"I'll give you one last chance": Mark Bles, *Child at War: The True Story of a Young Belgian Resistance Fighter* (San Francisco: Mercury House, 1989), 188–89.

"It's vital that you": Bles, *Child at War*, 113–14.

"My word, that is": Bles, *Child at War*, 117–20.

FERNANDE KEUFGENS: THE TEEN WITH THE BOLD VOICE

All excerpts from *Girl in the Belgian Resistance* reprinted by permission of Fernande K. Davis and Beach Lloyd Publishers, LLC, P.O. Box 2183, Southeastern, PA 19399-2183.

"Oui, c'est ca": Fernande K. Davis, *Girl in the Belgian Resistance: A Wakeful Eye in the Underground* (Chesterbrook, PA: Beach Lloyd, 2008), 68.

"Halt!": Davis, *Girl in the Belgian Resistance*, 68.

"Never show fear": Davis, *Girl in the Belgian Resistance*, 68.

"Can you not read": Davis, *Girl in the Belgian Resistance*, 68.

"Rause!": Davis, *Girl in the Belgian Resistance*, 69.

"You can't hold up": Davis, *Girl in the Belgian Resistance*, 74.

"No time, but": Davis, *Girl in the Belgian Resistance*, 74.

PART VI: DENMARK

Numerical breakdown of Denmark's Jews from Ellen Levine, *Darkness over Denmark: The Danish Resistance and the Rescue of the Jews* (New York: Holiday House, 2000), 20–21.

MONICA WICHFELD: IRISH HEROINE OF THE DANISH RESISTANCE

"As I have joined the struggle": Christine Sutherland, *Monica: Heroine of the Danish Resistance* (New York: Farrar, Straus and Giroux, 1990), 159.

"You are obviously pro-Allies?": Sutherland, *Monica*, 161.

"Two of my brothers": Sutherland, *Monica*, 161.

EBBA LUND: THE GIRL WITH THE RED CAP

"We've been occupied!": Levine, *Darkness over Denmark*, 7.

Numbers regarding *Frit danmark*: Levine, *Darkness over Denmark*, 36–37.

320 NOTES

Nazi edict of August 28, 1943: Jørgen Kieler, *Resistance Fighter: A Personal History of the Danish Resistance Movement, 1940–1945,* trans. Eric Dickens (Jerusalem: Gefen, 2007), 64–65.

Account of German soldiers hesitant to impede rescue operations is found on pages 102–3 of *Resistance Fighter* and page 85 of *Darkness over Denmark.*

"For me it was not a Jewish problem": Donald H. Harrison, "'Girl in Red Cap' Saved Hundreds of Jews," *San Diego Jewish Press-Heritage,* January 14, 1994, www.jewishsightseeing.com/denmark/copenhagen/1994-01-14_red_cap_girl.htm.

NANCY WAKE: THE WHITE MOUSE

"I resolved there and then": Nancy Wake, *The Autobiography of the Woman the Gestapo Called the White Mouse* (Sydney: Sun Books, 1985), 4.

"Do you want to search moi*?":* Peter Fitzsimons, *Nancy Wake: The Inspiring Story of One of the War's Greatest Heroines* (Sydney, Australia: HarperCollins, 2001), 239.

"No, mademoiselle": Fitzsimons, *Nancy Wake,* 239.

On page 135 of Nancy Wake's memoir, *The Autobiography of the Woman the Gestapo Called the White Mouse,* Nancy notes that the 500-kilometer bike ride was the accomplishment that gave her the most pride. The reason for the discrepancy (sometimes it's noted as 400 and sometimes 500) is that Nancy's original destination was 200 kilometers away, and if she had returned directly, the entire trip would have indeed been 400 kilometers. But her return route was not direct, and the resultant trip was 500 kilometers as notated in her memoir.

PEARL WITHERINGTON: THE COURIER WHO BECAME A LEADER

"If I had not": Pearl Cornioley with Hervé Larroque, *Pauline Parachutée en 1943, la vie d'une agent du SOE,* 3rd ed. (Clermont-Ferrand, FR: Editions par exemple, 2008), 58 (from an English translation being prepared).

HANNAH SENESH: BRITISH PARATROOPER

"Only now": Hannah Senesh, *Hannah Senesh: Her Life and Diary* (Woodstock, VT: Jewish Lights, 2004), 26.

"I've become a Zionist": Senesh, *Life and Diary,* 67.

"Our people are working": Senesh, *Life and Diary,* 298.

"In my heart": Blessed Is the Match: The Life and Death of Hannah Senesh, directed by Roberta Grossman (Katahdin Films, 2008), DVD.

"totally unconcerned": Anthony Masters, *The Summer That Bled: The Biography of Hannah Senesh* (New York: St. Martin's, 1972), 151.

"*exuded happiness and excitement*": Senesh, *Life and Diary*, 226.

"*wreathed in a smile*": Senesh, *Life and Diary*, 226.

"*We are late*": Blessed Is the Match.

"*What will happen*": Senesh, *Life and Diary*, 227.

"*a special mysterious quality*": Senesh, *Life and Diary*, 227.

"*Blessed is the match*": Senesh, *Life and Diary*, 306.

"*One—two—three*": Senesh, *Life and Diary*, 306.

"*Mother!*" . . . "*Speak to her*": Senesh, *Life and Diary*, 258.

"*branded*": Blessed Is the Match.

"*Don't worry*": Senesh, *Life and Diary*, 247.

VIRGINIA HALL: THE MOST DANGEROUS ALLIED AGENT

"*The woman who limps*": "We Must Find and Destroy Her," *US News and World Report*, January 27, 2003, www.usnews.com/usnews/culture/articles/030127/27heyday.hall.htm.

MURIEL PHILLIPS: U.S. ARMY NURSE

Muriel's letter describing buzz bombs is taken from *Mission Accomplished: Stop the Clock* by Muriel P. Engelman, World War II Army Nurse, retired RN (New York: iUniverse, 2008), 96. Used by permission of Muriel P. Engelman.

MARLENE DIETRICH: "THE ONLY IMPORTANT THING"

"*queen of German film*": Marlene Dietrich, *Marlene*, trans. Salvator Attanasio (New York: Grove, 1987), 90.

"*Do I rightly understand*": Dietrich, *Marlene*, 91.

Not just "*no,*" but "*never*": Steven Bach, *Marlene Dietrich: Life and Legend* (New York: William Morrow, 1992), 231.

"*Deserts Her Native Land*": Bach, *Life and Legend*, 231.

"*Shirt-sleeved judge administers oath*": Bach, *Life and Legend*, 232.

"*I was born a German*": Dietrich, *Marlene*, 216–17.

"*Lili Marlene*": Goebbels banned the song from civilian airwaves, but an attempt to keep it off German military radio failed. Field Marshal Rommel, the beloved German Wehrmacht leader stationed in North Africa, liked it so much he requested it be played via radio for his troops every night. It then became popular with the British soldiers in North Africa and was translated into English. It became an international hit song of the war.

"*Boys, don't sacrifice yourselves!*": Bach, *Life and Legend*, 292.

"*the only important thing*": Bach, *Life and Legend*, 287.

MARIA GULOVICH: SLOVAK FOR THE OSS

All excerpts from *Maria Gulovich* copyright 2009 Sonya N. Jason by permission of McFarland & Company, Inc., Box 611, Jefferson NC 28640.

"I want to tell you": Sonya N. Jason, *Maria Gulovich, OSS Heroine of World War II: The Schoolteacher Who Saved American Lives in Slovakia* (Jefferson, NC: McFarland, 2009), 128.

"You Americans are the brave ones": Jason, *Maria Gulovich*, 128.

"You stay with the Americans": Jason, *Maria Gulovich*, 75.

"The dangers you courageously": Jason, *Maria Gulovich*, 244–45.

MARTHA GELLHORN: WAR CORRESPONDENT

Excerpts from *The Face of War* by Martha Gellhorn, copyright 1936, 1988 by Martha Gellhorn. Used by permission of Grove/Atlantic, Inc.

"If you must be a writer": Caroline Moorehead, *Gellhorn: A Twentieth-Century Life* (New York: Henry Holt, 2003), 20.

"Red swine dogs": Moorehead, *Gellhorn*, 99, 106.

"People will be writing": Martha Gellhorn, *The Face of War* (New York: Atlantic Monthly Press, 1988), 110–11.

"If anyone had come": Gellhorn, *Face of War*, 119.

"What had been a man": Gellhorn, *Face of War*, 184.

"We sat in that room": Gellhorn, *Face of War*, 185.

HAZEL YING LEE: AMERICAN FLYGIRL

"Perhaps when I go up": Webster A. Jones, "Chinese Girl Flyer Hopes to Aid Women of Orient," *Oregonian* (Portland, OR), February 12, 1933.

"women are erratic in combat": *A Brief Flight: Hazel Ying Lee and the Women Who Flew Pursuit*, directed by Alan H. Rosenberg (LAWAS Productions, 2002), DVD.

"If everybody else is afraid": *A Brief Flight*.

"America must stop": William M. Miller, *To Live and Die a WASP: 38 Women Pilots Who Died in WWII* (CreateSpace, 2016), 194.

"a wonderful, jolly, joyous": Kay Gott, *Hazel Ah Ying Lee, Women Airforce Service Pilot, World War II: A Portrait* (Eureka, CA: Veteran's Quality Printing, 1996), 21.

"a courageous, very wonderful": Gott, *Hazel Ah Ying Lee*, 40.

"I'm going to kill you": *A Brief Flight*.

"Women don't fly": *A Brief Flight*.

"The flying keeps me": Hazel Ying Lee to sister Frances, 22 April 1944, Hazel Ying Lee Collection, Museum of Chinese in America, New York, NY.

"determined to laugh": A Brief Flight.

"[Hazel] knew somebody": Gott, Hazel Ah Ying Lee, 17.

"Drink some more tea": Gott, Hazel Ah Ying Lee, 15.

"a great thrill": Miller, Live and Die a WASP, 197.

"war weary": A Brief Flight.

"this war is going on too long": A Brief Flight.

"We're going to have a reunion": Hazel Ying Lee to Inez Woodward, 27 October 1944, Texas Women's University Libraries' Woman's Collection, the Women's Collection Special Collections and University Archives WASP Archive and Rare Books.

"died in war for the United States": A Brief Flight.

ZOYA KOSMODEMYANSKAYA: PARTISAN HERO

"A Komsomol member must": L Kosmodemyanskaya, The Story of Zoya and Shura (Moscow: Foreign Languages Publishing House, 1953), 162.

"Germany has attacked" . . . *"I mean to do"*: Kosmodemyanskaya, Zoya and Shura, 194.

"I wonder if" . . . *"dear friends"*: Kosmodemyanskaya, Zoya and Shura, 202.

"Comrades, citizens": "WWII Eastern Front: Stalin Speaks to the People of the Soviet Union on German Invasion," July 3, 1941, Jewish Virtual Library, www.jewishvirtuallibrary.org/stalin-speaks-to-the-people-of-the-soviet -union-on-german-invasion-july-1941.

"individualist" . . . *"Perhaps I am"*: Kosmodemyanskaya, Zoya and Shura, 210.

WHAT HAVE YOU DONE . . . *"Not enough"*: Kosmodemyanskaya, Zoya and Shura, 211.

"Why must it be" . . . *"no other way for me"*: Kosmodemyanskaya, Zoya and Shura, 213.

"She would do everything": Kosmodemyanskaya, Zoya and Shura, 237.

"How I want to live": Kosmodemyanskaya, Zoya and Shura, 241.

"I know there'll be a town": Kosmodemyanskaya, Zoya and Shura, 242.

"Only boys" . . . *That's not the same"*: Kosmodemyanskaya, Zoya and Shura, 243–44.

"Who are you" . . . *"Why should I waste time?"*: Kosmodemyanskaya, Zoya and Shura, 229.

"I won't tell": Kosmodemyanskaya, Zoya and Shura, 230.

I BURNED A STABLE: Henry Sakaida, *Heroines of the Soviet Union 1941–45* (Oxford, UK: Osprey, 2003), 49.

"Comrades!" . . . *"victory is sure to be ours"*: Kosmodemyanskaya, *Zoya and Shura*, 233.

"A young partisan girl": Kosmodemyanskaya, *Zoya and Shura*, 224.

"Lyubov Timofeyevna": Kosmodemyanskaya, *Zoya and Shura*, 226.

"When you go": Albert Axell, *Russia's Heroes* (London: Constable, 2001), 89.

ANNA YEGOROVA: SOVIET PILOT

Excerpts from *Red Sky, Black Death: A Soviet Woman Pilot's Memoir of the Eastern Front* by Anna Timofeyeva-Yegorova and Kim Green (Bloomington, IN: Slavica, 2009) used by permission of the publishers.

"What do you want": Anna Timofeyeva-Yegorova and Kim Green, *Red Sky, Black Death: A Soviet Woman Pilot's Memoir of the Eastern Front* (Bloomington, IN: Slavica, 2009), 25–26.

"Girls . . . It's War!": Timofeyeva-Yegorova, *Red Sky*, 63.

"Everybody's asking me": Timofeyeva-Yegorova, *Red Sky*, 66.

"But we don't draft" . . . *"Do you really need"*: Timofeyeva-Yegorova, *Red Sky*, 70.

"Grandfather" . . . *"The Germans are here"*: Timofeyeva-Yegorova, *Red Sky*, 89.

"frantic movements": Timofeyeva-Yegorova, *Red Sky*, 101.

"like a long-lost brother" . . . *"a living thing"*: Timofeyeva-Yegorova, *Red Sky*, 104.

"I crashed my aircraft": Timofeyeva-Yegorova, *Red Sky*, 112.

"penalty battalion": Timofeyeva-Yegorova, *Red Sky*, 112.

"Do you have any idea" . . . *"Be my guest!"*: Timofeyeva-Yegorova, *Red Sky*, 111.

"Try to make it": Timofeyeva-Yegorova, *Red Sky*, 182.

"A Fascist!": Timofeyeva-Yegorova, *Red Sky*, 183.

"utter hell": Timofeyeva-Yegorova, *Red Sky*, 185.

"You're lying": Timofeyeva-Yegorova, *Red Sky*, 196.

"When are you going": Timofeyeva-Yegorova, *Red Sky*, 197.

"No, no, I want to find": Timofeyeva-Yegorova, *Red Sky*, 197.

"I was a prisoner" . . . *"We're not giving you"*: Timofeyeva-Yegorova, *Red Sky*, 206.

Bibliography

BOOKS

Those titles marked with an asterisk are particularly suited to younger readers.

Alexievich, Svetlana. *The Unwomanly Face of War: An Oral History of Women in World War II*. Translated by Richard Pevear and Larissa Volokhonsky. New York: Random House, 2018.

*Axelrod, Toby. *Hans and Sophie Scholl: German Resisters of the White Rose*. New York: Rosen, 2001.

Bach, Steven. *Marlene Dietrich: Life and Legend*. New York: William Morrow, 1992.

Bailey, Ronald H., and the Editors of Time-Life Books. *The Home Front: USA*. Alexandria, VA: Time-Life Books, 1978.

Basu, Shrabani. *Spy Princess: The Life of Noor Inayat Khan*. Stroud, UK: Sutton, 2006.

Bles, Mark. *Child at War: The True Story of a Young Belgian Resistance Fighter*. San Francisco: Mercury House, 1989.

Block, Gay, and Malka Drucker. *Rescuers: Portraits of Moral Courage in the Holocaust*. Teaneck, NJ: Holmes & Meier, 1992.

Boolen, J. J., and Dr. J. C. Van der Does. *Five Years of Occupation: The Resistance of the Dutch against Hitler-Terrorism and Nazi-Robbery.* Secret Press of D.A.V.I.D, 1945.

Cohn, Marthe, with Wendy Holden. *Behind Enemy Lines: The True Story of a French Jewish Spy in Nazi Germany.* New York: Three Rivers, 2002.

*Colman, Penny. *Rosie the Riveter: Women Working on the Home Front in WWII.* New York: Crown Books for Young Readers, 1998.

Cornioley, Pearl, with Hervé Larroque. *Pauline: Parachutée en 1943, la vie d'une agent du SOE.* 3rd ed. Clermont-Ferrand, FR: Editions par exemple, 2008.

Davis, Fernande K. *Girl in the Belgian Resistance: A Wakeful Eye in the Underground.* Chesterbrook, PA: Beach Lloyd, 2008.

Dietrich, Marlene. *Marlene.* Translated by Salvator Attanasio. New York: Grove, 1987 (English translation 1989).

Elson, Robert T., and the Editors of Time-Life Books. *Prelude to War.* Alexandria, VA: Time-Life Books, 1976, 1977.

Eman, Diet, with James Schaap. *Things We Couldn't Say.* Grand Rapids, MI: William B. Eerdmans, 1994.

Engelman, Muriel P., World War II Army Nurse, Retired RN. *Mission Accomplished: Stop the Clock.* New York: iUniverse, 2008.

Fitzsimons, Peter. *Nancy Wake: The Inspiring Story of One of the War's Greatest Heroines.* Sydney, Australia: HarperCollins, 2001.

Fogelman, Eva. *Conscience and Courage: Rescuers of Jews During the Holocaust.* New York: Anchor Books, 1994.

Fourcade, Marie-Madeleine. *Noah's Ark.* New York: E. P. Dutton, 1974.

*Fuykschot, Cornelia. *Hunger in Holland: Life During the Nazi Occupation.* Amherst, NY: Prometheus Books, 1995.

Gellhorn, Martha. *The Face of War.* New York: Atlantic Monthly Press, 1988.

Gilbert, Martin. *The Righteous: The Unsung Heroes of the Holocaust.* New York: Henry Holt, 2003.

Goldberger, Leo, ed. *The Rescue of the Danish Jews: Moral Courage under Stress.* New York: New York University Press, 1987.

Gott, Kay. *Hazel Ah Ying Lee, Women Airforce Service Pilot, World War II: A Portrait.* Eureka, CA: Veteran's Quality Printing, 1996.

*Gourley, Catherine. *War, Women, and the News: How Female Journalists Won the Battle to Cover WWII.* New York: Atheneum, 2007.

Gross, Leonard. *The Last Jews in Berlin.* New York: Carroll & Graf, 1992.

*Gut Opdyke, Irene, with Jennifer Armstrong. *In My Hands: Memories of a Holocaust Rescuer.* New York: Alfred A. Knopf, 1999.

Hallie, Philip P. *Lest Innocent Blood Be Shed: The Story of Le Chambon and How Goodness Happened There.* New York: Harper & Row, 1979.

Halter, Marek. *Stories of Deliverance: Speaking with Men and Women Who Rescued Jews from the Holocaust.* Translated by Michael Bernard. Peru, IL:

Carus, 1998. Originally published as *La Force du Bien*. Paris: Editions Robert Laffont, 1995.

Haney, Lynn. *Naked at the Feast: The Biography of Josephine Baker*. London: Robson Books, 1995.

Hay, Peter. *Ordinary Heroes: The Life and Death of Chana Szenes, Israel's National Heroine*. New York: Paragon House, 1986.

Henry, Patrick. *We Only Know Men: The Rescue of Jews in France During the Holocaust*. Washington, DC: Catholic University Press, 2007.

Jason, Sonya N. *Maria Gulovich, OSS Heroine of World War II: The Schoolteacher Who Saved American Lives in Slovakia*. Jefferson, NC: McFarland, 2009.

Jones, Nigel. *Countdown to Valkyrie: The July Plot to Assassinate Hitler*. Chicago: Frontline Books, 2009.

Kieler, Jørgen. *Resistance Fighter: A Personal History of the Danish Resistance Movement, 1940–1945*. Translated by Eric Dickens. Jerusalem: Gefen, 2007.

Koskodan, Kenneth K. *No Greater Ally: The Untold Story of Poland's Forces in World War II*. Oxford, UK: Osprey, 2009.

Kosmodemyanskaya, L. *The Story of Zoya and Shura*. Moscow: Foreign Languages Publishing House, 1953.

Kramer, Rita. *Flames in the Field: The Story of Four SOE Agents in Occupied France*. London: Michael Joseph, 1995.

Laska, Vera. *Women in the Resistance and in the Holocaust: The Voices of Eyewitnesses*. Westport, CT: Greenwood, 1983.

*Levine, Ellen. *Darkness over Denmark: The Danish Resistance and the Rescue of the Jews*. New York: Holiday House, 2000.

Lukas, Richard C. *Did the Children Cry? Hitler's War Against Jewish and Polish Children, 1939–1945*. New York: Hippocrene Books, 1994.

Lukas, Richard C., ed. *Forgotten Survivors: Polish Christians Remember the Nazi Occupation*. Lawrence: University Press of Kansas, 2004.

Masters, Anthony. *The Summer That Bled: The Biography of Hannah Senesh*. New York: St. Martin's, 1972.

McIntosh, Elizabeth P. *Sisterhood of Spies: The Women of the OSS*. Annapolis, MD: Naval Institute Press, 1998.

Menger, Truus. *Not Then, Not Now, Not Ever*. Translated by Rita Gircour. Amsterdam: Nederland Tolerant – Max Drukker Stichting, 1998. Originally published as *Toen niet, nu niet, nooit*. The Hague: Leopold Publishers, 1982.

Miller, Donald. *Masters of the Air: America's Bomber Boys Who Fought the Air War Against Nazi Germany*. New York: Simon and Schuster, 2007.

Miller, Russell, and the Editors of Time-Life Books. *The Resistance*. Alexandria, VA: Time-Life Books, 1979.

Miller, William M. *To Live and Die a WASP: 38 Women Pilots Who Died in WWII*. CreateSpace, 2016.

Moorehead, Caroline. *Gellhorn: A Twentieth-Century Life*. New York: Henry Holt, 2003.

Motz, Roger. *Belgium Unvanquished*. London: Stephen Austin and Sons, 1942.

Mulley, Clare. *The Women Who Flew for Hitler: A True Story of Soaring Ambition and Searing Rivalry*. New York: St. Martin's, 2017.

*Nathan, Amy. *Yankee Doodle Gals: Women Pilots of WWII*. Washington, DC: National Geographic Children's Books, 2001.

Naudet, Jean-Jacques, and Maria Riva. *Marlene Dietrich: Photographs and Memories*. New York: Alfred A. Knopf, 2001.

Neave, Airey. *Little Cyclone*. London: Hodder and Stoughton, 1954.

Noggle, Anna. *A Dance with Death: Soviet Airwoman in World War II*. College Station: Texas A&M University Press, 1994.

O'Donnell, Patrick K. *Operatives, Spies, and Saboteurs: The Unknown Story of the Men and Women of WWII's OSS*. New York: Free Press, 2004.

Ottis, Sherri Greene. *Silent Heroes: Downed Airmen and the French Underground*. Lexington: University Press of Kentucky, 2001.

Pearson, Judith L. *The Wolves at the Door: The True Story of America's Greatest Female Spy*. Guilford, CT: Lyons, 2005.

*Peel, Andrée Virot. *Miracles Do Happen!* Translated by Evelyn Scott Brown. Ettington, UK: Loebertas, 1999.

Read, Anthony, and David Fisher. *The Fall of Berlin*. New York: W. W. Norton, 1992.

Rittner, Carol, R.S.M., and Sondra Myers. *The Courage to Care: Rescuers of Jews During the Holocaust*. New York: New York University Press, 1986.

Rossiter, Margaret L. *Women in the Resistance*. New York: Praeger, 1986.

Sakaida, Henry. *Heroines of the Soviet Union 1941–45*. Oxford, UK: Osprey, 2003.

Senesh, Hannah. *Hannah Senesh: Her Life and Diary*. Woodstock, VT: Jewish Lights, 2004.

Shirer, William L. *The Rise and Fall of the Third Reich: A History of Nazi Germany*. New York: Exeter Books, 1987.

Sutherland, Christine. *Monica: Heroine of the Danish Resistance*. New York: Farrar, Straus and Giroux, 1990.

Synnestvedt, Alice Resch. *Over the Highest Mountains: A Memoir of Unexpected Heroism in France During World War II*. Pasadena, CA: Intentional Productions, 2005.

*ten Boom, Corrie, with John Sherrill and Elizabeth Sherrill. *The Hiding Place*. Uhrichsville, OH: Barbour, 1971.

Timofeyeva-Yegorova, Anna. *Red Sky, Black Death: A Soviet Woman Pilot's Memoir of the Eastern Front*. Bloomington, IN: Slavica, 2009.

Tomaszewski, Irene, and Tecia Werbowski. *Zegota: The Rescue of Jews in Wartime Poland*. Montreal: Price-Patterson, 1994.

Ure, James W. *Seized by the Sun: The Life and Disappearance of World War II Pilot Gertrude Tompkins*. Chicago: Chicago Review Press, 2017.

Vos, Johanna K. *The End of the Tunnel*. Mansfield, OH: Book Masters, 1999.

Vromen, Suzanne. *Hidden Children of the Holocaust: Belgian Nuns and Their Daring Rescue of Young Jews from the Nazis*. New York: Oxford University Press, 2008.

Wake, Nancy. *The Autobiography of the Woman the Gestapo Called the White Mouse*. Sydney: Sun Books, 1985.

Weitz, Margaret Collins. *Sisters in the Resistance: How Women Fought to Free France, 1940–1945*. New York: John Wiley & Sons, 1995.

Wernick, Robert, and the Editors of Time-Life Books. *Blitzkreig*. Alexandria, VA: Time-Life Books, 1977.

Whiting, Charles, and the Editors of Time-Life Books. *The Home Front: Germany*. Alexandria, VA: Time-Life Books, 1982, 1990.

Wood, Ean. *The Josephine Baker Story*. London: Sanctuary, 2000.

Woolfitt, Susan. *Idle Women*. London: M&M Baldwin, 1986.

Yenne, Bill. *The American Aircraft Factory in WWII*. Minneapolis: Zenith, 2006.

WEBSITE ARTICLES

"Bombing, States and Peoples in Western Europe 1940–1945: The Bombing of Germany 1940–1945." Centre for the Study of War, State, and Society, University of Exeter. https://humanities.exeter.ac.uk/history/research/centres/warstateandsociety/projects/bombing/germany.

Colley, Rupert. "Zoya Kosmodemyanskaya—A Brief Biography." Rupert Colley's personal blog. November 25, 2014. http://rupertcolley.com/2014/11/25/zoya-kosmodemyanskaya-a-brief-biography.

Levitt, Aimee. "'This Is Not a Holocaust Story, This Is a War Story': The Life of Hannah Senesh." *Chicago Reader*, May 21, 2013. www.chicagoreader.com/Bleader/archives/2013/05/21/this-is-not-a-holocaust-story-this-is-a-war-story-the-life-of-hannah-senesh.

"Prominent Russians: Zoya Kosmodemyanskaya." Russiapedia. https://russiapedia.rt.com/prominent-russians/history-and-mythology/zoya-kosmodemyanskaya.

"WWII Eastern Front: Stalin Speaks to the People of the Soviet Union on German Invasion." July 3, 1941. Jewish Virtual Library. www.jewishvirtuallibrary.org/stalin-speaks-to-the-people-of-the-soviet-union-on-german-invasion-july-1941.

Sudakov, Dmitry. "USSR's Iconic Partisan Zoya Kosmodemyanskaya Made Her Death Her Biggest Accomplishment." *Pravda*, September 14, 2009. www.pravdareport.com/history/14-09-2009/109252-zoya_kosmodemyanskaya-0/#.

Suskind, Alex. "The 4'11" Jewish Woman Who Entered the Lion's Den to Spy on Nazi Germany." *Times of Israel*, September 17, 2017. www.timesofisrael.com/the-411-jewish-woman-who-entered-the-lions-den-to-spy-on-nazi-germany.

DOCUMENTARIES

Blessed Is the Match: The Life and Death of Hannah Senesh. Directed by Roberta Grossman. Katahdin Films, 2008. DVD.
A Brief Flight: Hazel Ying Lee and the Women Who Flew Pursuit. Directed by Alan H. Rosenberg. LAWAS Productions, 2002. DVD.

Index